"Katie Quinn takes the reader on a delicious meditation on cheese, wine, and bread, the fermented foods that are among the cornerstones of human culture. An erudite and enthusiastic look at the science, the creators, the issues, and the flavors that inform these daily staples."

—FUCHSIA DUNLOP, author of The Food of Sichuan

"Get ready to join my friend Katie on a wild trip through Europe as she dives headfirst into the world of fermentation. With her characteristic enthusiasm and wit, she introduces us to some of mankind's oldest and smallest allies—the microbial partners we rely on to transform milk into cheese, grapes into wine, and grain into bread."

—J. KENJI LÓPEZ-ALT, author of The Food Lab

"Katie's writing is unique and immediately inviting, blending memoir with travel documentary with food-science study to illuminate the people and processes behind some of our favorite foods. Cheese, Wine, and Bread should be on any reading list for people who love food and travel, or who just want to know what makes the best mac and cheese tick."

—KRISTEN MIGLORE, author of Genius Recipes

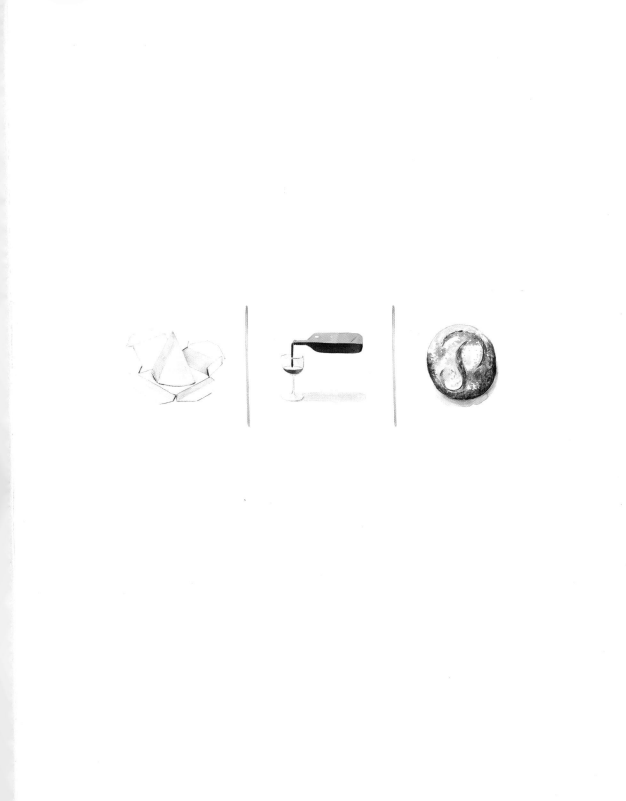

WILLIAM MORROW
An Imprint of HarperCollins*Publishers*

CHEESE, WINE, AND BREAD

DISCOVERING THE MAGIC OF FERMENTATION IN ENGLAND, ITALY, AND FRANCE

KATIE QUINN

FOR CONNOR

CONTENTS

A NOTE TO THE READER

Cheese, wine, and bread, I think you'll agree, are three of life's most delightful things. They can be found worldwide, each place informing them with its own unique history and stories that extend far beyond the delicious dance on the plate.

I can't possibly encompass all the locations, people, and cultural implications in this book, nor can I touch upon all 1,400 cheese varieties in the world today, nor the more than 350 varieties of indigenous grapevines in Italy alone! This is not an encyclopedia. Far from it. The fact that I adventured through England, Italy, and France to better know these foodstuffs—and myself—was the result of circumstance as much as research and strategy. I jumped into opportunities as they arose. The interviews I conducted and books I devoured went only as far as informing the experiences I lived. While everything I write about happened, and I am as faithful to my memory as possible, I have taken small liberties in terms of chronology for the reader's ease.

These three locations and three fermented items could have been paired any number of ways. Cheese in Italy? Amazing! Bread in England? There's an outstanding bread scene in the UK, in fact. Wine in France? A no-brainer. And how about cheese in France? I'm sure some of you will be dismayed that these weren't the focus, but I'm sharing *my journey*, one of entanglements as much as connections and magic moments like fermentation itself.

INTRODUCTION

Fermentation comes from the Latin word *fermentare*, meaning "to leaven."

Leaven /'lɛv(ə)n/ *(noun): a pervasive influence that modifies something or transforms it for the better.*

I have no memory of the entire week following the accident. I don't even recall the moments before it, strangely—before my brain was hit the way a pneumatic ram strikes a wheel of cheddar cheese. I'll tell you what I do remember, and what I've been told happened in those days.

It was my first ski run of the morning on one of the towering peaks at Utah's Canyons ski resort, and I was still getting my legs under me when an unruly snowboarder crossed my path, a narrow miss, and I lost control. I gained speed until I went headfirst—*sans helmet*—into a block of ice and tumbled like a rag doll into a nearby ditch. My then boyfriend watched it all happen (which is the only way I have this information, and it feels foreign—like it didn't happen to me). He ran to the crevice and found me facedown in the snow. When he rolled my body over, I was unresponsive and brown liquid was seeping from my nose. *Cerebral fluid.* He'd taken various backcountry first-aid courses and learned about those indicators. I was unconscious for about eight minutes—enough time for the medics to caution, "She may be paralyzed."

On the way to the hospital, as the EMTs whisked me down the slope, I regained consciousness and illogically fought to escape the bindings—*phew, she's not paralyzed*—that secured me on the bodyboard. My mom and dad flew from Ohio to Utah the next day and walked into my hospital room to find their twenty-seven-year-old daughter intubated and unresponsive, in a medically induced coma. By day three, I was awake and could respond but I couldn't remember things as basic as my birthday; my traumatic brain injury prevented much, if any, recollection. You know that crisp autumn apple that goes perfectly with a wedge of Brie? Grab a bat and swing it at the apple; now picture my brain as that apple. I was in bad shape.

1

FIVE DAYS AFTER THE ACCIDENT, I WAS discharged from the hospital, but I was far from my normal self. The doctor's notes indicated there was a blood clot on my thalamus (the part of the brain that relays motor and sensory signals to the cerebral cortex) and an abnormality in the midbrain extending to the pons (part of the brain stem). I vaguely remember moments starting a few days after the crash, like snapshots from a movie I might have seen under the influence of heavy cold medication. It's a highlight reel of being pushed through the airport in a wheelchair, sitting next to my mom on the flight to Ohio.

During my first week at my parents' house, I began to comprehend what had happened to me—why I couldn't stand on my own, why I couldn't walk without assistance. My mom supported the weight of my naked body to maneuver me in and out of the bathtub. I began to appreciate the erasure of my memory as a blessing.

LIFE HAD BEEN ROLLING ALONG splendidly before that. In the six years I'd lived in New York City after college graduation, I had worked my way up from the NBC Page Program—the highly competitive internship-like job made famous by Tina Fey's television series *30 Rock*—to get a job on the *Today* show, becoming chummy with the hosts, who greeted millions of Americans bright and early every morning. From there I landed my dream job as an on-camera host at *NowThis News*, a video news start-up. Always chasing the next big opportunity, I was looking forward to an upcoming several-months-long trip to Brazil for a video series about the food of the World Cup. I was dating a man I adored (but mind you, I fully intended on going to Brazil a single lady . . .), and my career was on the rise. Needless to say, I had a sizable ego.

Everything was perfect, or close to it, until everything came to a complete halt. The ensuing three months at home were composed of frequent physical therapy sessions and lots of chocolate ice cream. I attribute my recovery to both. The head injury most aggressively affected my vestibular system, the body's balance center—it's why humans can stand on two feet without falling over. (I fell a lot in those months.) Our brains, I learned, are miraculous little self-healing balls; they're elastic—like a rubber band—and can learn, recover, and adjust accordingly.

Slowly, I pieced myself back together, and as I began to feel like myself, the first thing I reached for was my DSLR camera.

I started to make videos using skills from my career—which felt like a parallel life somewhere in the stars—to investigate the things on my mind: love, loyalty, hunger. (Hunger both metaphorically and literally—I voraciously consumed food during my recovery. My brain was working hard to heal and needed every calorie it could get.) I was a foodie before the accident, and my curiosity about the role food plays in our identity, our interactions, and our traditions was piqued. I turned on the camera and started recording as I explored these interests. Those videos were the blueprints of what would become my YouTube channel, and eventually my new career.

The months in Ohio were my cocoon months, and I returned to New York a butterfly. The next couple of years were exciting: tens of thousands of online followers, flights to Australia and Thailand and Indonesia for video projects, and returning to 30 Rock and the *Today* show studio, this time as a guest rather than a script runner behind the scenes. If I thought my dreams were coming true

before that trip to Utah, after the jolt to my brain I found a stratosphere that had felt completely unattainable.

The man I was falling for at the time of the ski outing, Connor—the guy I was definitely going to break up with before an exciting few months in South America—stayed by my side throughout it all and, a few years later, stood by my side at the altar as we exchanged vows. When Connor's job offered us the opportunity to move to London, we strapped on our metaphorical skis and threw ourselves down the hill. Ready or not, we packed our bags and moved to England.

MY FINGERNAIL TRACED THE GRAIN LINES of the wooden table . . . back and forth. I sat alone in my London kitchen, lost in thought, the glow of a single lamp illuminating the darkness of a winter evening. I'd just finished a shift as a cheesemonger at England's preeminent cheese shop, Neal's Yard Dairy, and, having put my staff discount to use, I had swaddled a chunk of Montgomery's Cheddar before journeying to my

3

apartment in East London, stopping to pick up a deep brown loaf of bread along the way.

I now lifted my index finger from its fiddling, cut a thick slice of the cheese, and hugged it up against the pocketed sourdough crumb of a torn-off portion of the bread. I reoriented my body in my chair like it was a school desk and I an eager student. I leaned over the table and bit into the bread and cheese. An almost brothy savoriness from the cheddar, a sweetness from the caramelized bread crust, and a yeasty aroma hit my senses. I reached for my red wine, a ruby ambrosia I swirled in its glass before I brought it to my lips. I sipped, swallowed, and exhaled.

My husband, Connor, was elsewhere that evening. After a day standing on my feet interacting with customers and spreading the word about British farmhouse cheeses, I contentedly withdrew into an introverted cocoon and opened the book I was reading, *An Everlasting Meal* by Tamar Adler. I sat cross-legged on the chair and delightedly flipped the pages to a section about cheese (in which Adler accurately writes, "Cheesemongers are categorically zealous. Their counters are their pulpits, and they live to share their gospel." *This woman knows what she's talking about*). I couldn't help but notice how the title of the chapter, "How to Have Balance," accentuated a woeful lack of balance in my own life.

I cycled through my cheese-and-bread-layering routine as I read, and subconsciously rubbed the narrow stem of the wineglass as though I were polishing it.

I looked through Adler's recipe for savory baked ricotta, the last line of which reads, "Put bread and cheese, and whatever condiments you've chosen, on the table. Serve them, a salad, and not much else." *Well, I've got the bread and cheese here. Don't have a salad, but I've got wine—the three are all I need.*

The next sentence hit me like an emphatic revelation: "Wine and beer are the third member of this holy trinity of fermented things."

Whack.

I looked at the spread on my table and blinked as I reached for an uncapped pen that sat on the countertop. I drew a diagram in the margin of the book: a triangle pointing down. I labeled each corner according to what I saw in front of me: cheese in one, wine in another, and bread on the apex, facing where I sat. Cheese, wine, and bread. *That's it.*

I'M NOT A HIGHLY CURATED, PICTURE-perfect human. I'm a quirky, line-drawing-scribbles person. Also, I would operate at lightning speed if I could. Thankfully,

I've found an antidote to this haste: fermentation. When things aren't moving fast enough for me, fermentation reminds me of the value of waiting. Feeding my sourdough starter every morning, brewing a new batch of kombucha weekly—at the risk of sounding like an unhinged hipster, these are the routines that ground me. The practice of fermentation is as old as civilization itself, but the splendor of it found me in my early thirties as I was settling into my new home.

Bread and beer, kimchi and sauerkraut, wine and cheese: all are examples of fermented products; many of our most common kitchen items are. Fermentation is right under our noses, but is only now entering most people's awareness.

Fermentation is the process by which a substance breaks down into a simpler substance, altering food with microbes rather than by cooking it with fire. If this produces the most essential, delicious foods on earth, what can the same process do for us, as humans? Our lives ferment—we all have awkward, smelly phases along with delicious, robust ones—and mine certainly did, as I made discoveries about myself while exploring cheese, wine, and bread in England, Italy, and France.

The draw of these foods is that they take time to be transformed almost magically by the microbes within, which is a comforting prospect and a necessary antidote to our live-tweeting culture. For instance, when you post a photo on Instagram or Facebook, do you automatically refresh the page as the likes pop up? Imagine if you had to wait two weeks, or two months, before you could see the responses, but when you received them, those responses, although not instantaneous, were somehow able to endure, like a lingering hug or a letter that's traversed an ocean to land in your mailbox. Rather than the quick high of a digital fist bump, you receive a warm embrace. To me, that's akin to the satisfaction fermentation offers.

It's what makes a bread of rich flavors that meld beautifully, presented as a pillowy braid or boule with a perfume of yeast, and is similar to how my brain's neurons relearned how to fire together after my skiing accident (not an exact scientific parallel, but you get the idea). Both are time and conditioning working in tandem to create something altogether different and wholly incredible.

The crisis that accompanied moving abroad broke me out of my comfort zone to seek unfamiliar trades, poke my curiosity, and learn new languages to strengthen my connection with the people I encountered. Circumstance and intention can give birth to something wonderful, just like cheese, wine, and bread.

This book is my exploration of those three things. To me, this trio is life's essence, a microcosm representative of its nourishment and joy. I began studying fermentation in order to dive even deeper into the things that fed my body—literally and figuratively. It's with this realization that my story begins.

...CHEESE,
MILK'S LEAP
TOWARD
IMMORTALITY.

—CLIFTON FADIMAN

PART ONE

CHEESE // ENGLAND

My first year as a cheesemonger; ready to offer cheese—"Try this!"—to passersby

When I worked on a goat farm in rural England, the milk came pouring in via a pipe every morning at seven, fresh from the goats' teats. In the evenings, more fresh milk was poured by hand into a large stainless-steel tank, where we fetched it the following morning. It was often my job to move the evening's supply from the tank into one of the vats in the cheese room, handheld bucket by handheld bucket. A spout released the contents, and the milk was sometimes under such strong pressure from its own weight, it shot out like water from a fire hydrant across the length of the room. If I wasn't quick with the lever, the milk sprayed upward and outward and splotched my face and glasses like a Jackson Pollock painting. That happened more than once.

Cheesemaking is a wet endeavor: you are constantly surrounded not just by milk, but subsequently by whey—the liquid by-product of coagulation—and then by water to wash the whole mess away. (Wellies and waterproof aprons are essential wardrobe items in the cheese room.)

As I sloshed milk from one basin to the next, I couldn't have told you about the amino acid filaments ricocheting off each other inside the buckets as I jostled them around. Even as I dove my hands into vats of curds daily, I didn't know the science behind what I was doing. *A micelle, huh? A kappa-casein . . . is that a fraternity?* It was only after I knew how to make cheese that I learned why it was all possible.

Everything else will make sense once you understand the basics, so I'll start here, with milk. Jenn Kast, the resident science buff at Neal's Yard Dairy—the London cheese shop I worked in—told me, "Milk defines cheesemaking—microbiologically and enzymatically." Science was never my strongest subject, and I didn't really understand the deluge of terms that subsequently poured out of Jenn, but after going through a cheesemaking boot camp with her, quizzing various cheesemakers, and spending many days with my nose in a book in the British Library, it clicked. *And it's awesome.* Let's dive in.

IT ALL BEGINS WITH MILK—THE SUBSTANCE of cheesemaking. The reason milk can be transformed is because it isn't technically, in the strictest sense of the word, a liquid. (Yeah, crazy, right?) It's a colloid, which means one substance is microscopically dispersed and suspended in another substance.

Think of milk like one big dance floor, where water, fat, lactose, minerals (like calcium phosphate), casein proteins (curds), and serum proteins (whey) are all boogieing to their own beat. We focus on the casein proteins to get the cheese party started.

On this dance floor, there's no Macarena or Cupid Shuffle—it's a party in which the casein proteins cluster together like the girls at a middle school dance. This group of girls is fairly diverse: a bunch of different caseins come together to form a micelle, a spherical arrangement of molecules. (In other words, a glob. It's a glob of proteins.) The micelle includes alpha-caseins, beta-caseins, and kappa-caseins (and a small number of other components, like the calcium phosphate I

mentioned, which helps the micelle keep its structure).

The caseins are hydro*phobic*—they don't like water (or boys, to continue the metaphor)—they cozy up together in the center of the micelle, with kappa-caseins all around the perimeter because they have a filament (like a tail—a peptide tail of amino acids) that is hydro*philic*—it *likes* water. In other words, the kappa-caseins, with their filaments, are the flirty girls standing on the outside of the group, the ones tossing their hair over their shoulders and eyeing the cute boys.

Since the filaments all around the edge have a negative charge, the micelles bounce off each other, ensuring that the particles stay suspended in the colloid, which is how milk can *be* a successful colloid. *Until . . .* we start to make cheese.

To do so, we need to disperse the elements of the colloid—to separate the curds from the whey. This can happen naturally (it's the oldest method of cheesemaking known to humanity), because over time and with the application of heat, the harmless lactic acid bacteria that exist in milk—*Lactobacillus*, *Lactococcus*, *Leuconostoc*, and so on— proliferate and convert lactose into lactic acid. As the all-knowing DJs of this dance, cheesemakers do some things to speed that along.

A microbial starter, or *starter culture*, is often added to introduce the specific bacteria used to initiate the transformation of milk to cheese, and it can have a big impact on the final taste of the cheese. It can be introduced in

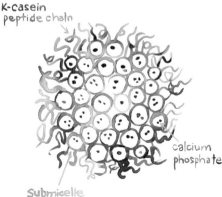

K-casein
peptide chain

calcium
phosphate

Submicelle

powder form, although some cheesemakers rely on the lactic acid bacteria (LAB) in the whey from the prior day's batch and add some to the milk to jump-start fermentation, a technique known by the oh-so-sexy term *backslopping*. The LAB breaks down the micelle by consuming lactose (a milk sugar) and creating lactic acid, slowly denaturing the protein (this is what happens when milk turns sour). Picture the dancers gradually dispersing.

The other way to coagulate milk is to use rennet—a complex set of enzymes. There are a few different kinds of rennet: the most traditional form is animal rennet (a substance found in the stomach lining of ruminant animals, such as calves, lambs, and goats), but there is also microbial (vegetarian) rennet, and some plant sources found in nature (like thistles, which were used to coagulate one of the varieties of goat cheese I made at the farmhouse where I worked).

Chymosin is the main enzyme in animal rennet, and when rennet is added to milk, the chymosin clips off the kappa-casein filaments . . . which was the only thing preventing the micelles from joining together. Without those tails, the micelles attach to one another like sticky balls, and that is *the* magic moment in cheesemaking; the transformation has begun. Those balls are the curds, and this is called "setting the curd."

Steps of Cheesemaking

1. INTRODUCING CULTURES TO MILK.

2. COAGULATION. ADD RENNET OR RELY ON NATURALLY OCCURRING LACTIC ACID BACTERIA.

3. LADLE OR CUT THE CURD.

4. DRAIN CURD FROM WHEY, MOLD & SALT.

5. AGING, MATURING, RIPENING, AFFINAGE.

Lactic acid coagulation and rennet coagulation can occur simultaneously, with emphasis on one or the other, depending on the character of cheese the cheesemaker aims to produce. Lactic acid–coagulated cheeses are more fragile, with higher hydration—think of cheeses that are softer, less pliable, and prone to break into little pieces; rennet-coagulated cheeses are sturdy, drier wheels that are easier to transport (although they become more brittle as they age)—think of hard, rubbery wedges of cheese.

In physics, there's a term from chaos theory that describes a furtive force that makes a pattern within a chaotic system: *strange attractor*. To me, rennet (or another coagulant) is the strange attractor in milk. It organizes everyone on the dance floor to clap and pivot together, doing the Macarena of milk.

Once the curd has set—you'll know because it solidifies into a thick, custardy substance—it's time to put it on its path to becoming the cheese it's destined to become. In some cases, the curds are ladled into a cheese mold; for other varieties, the cheesemaker will break the curds apart—using their hands, a cutting tool, or machinery—to give them more surface area and therefore release more whey, tightening the curds. Sometimes the gelatinous curds are "cooked" by heating the whey to harden them and increase enzymatic activity. However it happens, the curds are removed from the whey and placed in molds, where they continue to expel liquid through the holes in the molds. Sometimes salt is rubbed on the outside; sometimes the wheel is placed in a brine bath. (Salt is used for flavor and to slow down fermentation by decelerating bacterial growth.) It then goes into a drying room for one to three days, and from there into an aging room, where it stays for anywhere from a couple of weeks (for a soft goat's-milk cheese) to a couple of years (for a hard cow's-milk cheese like Parmigiano Reggiano).

Not only does milk have unique properties that scientifically *allow* for cheesemaking, it also brings flavor components to the cheese. There's a simple rule: the better the milk, the better the cheese. Many cheesemakers I've talked and worked with prefer using raw milk over pasteurized, because it better reflects the animal and its environment. If you know how to decode milk, you can understand the origins of your cheese.

Before the process begins, a cheesemaker is faced with innumerable decisions, each of which affects the end result. Which animal? Raw milk or pasteurized? Set the curd with rennet, or rely on lactic acid bacteria, or both? Use starter cultures? Once the curds and whey have separated, what temperature should they be heated to, and how much whey drained? How small should the curds be broken? Is the cheese washed in brine? Rubbed with salt? Eaten fresh or aged? If aged, for how long?

With countless choices, a certain mental ambidexterity is needed. "Cheesemaking is inherently interdisciplinary: it is equal parts art, science, and intuition," explain Bronwen and Francis Percival in their book, *Reinventing the Wheel: Milk, Microbes, and the Fight for Real Cheese.* One artisan I made cheese with, Joe Schneider of Stichelton Dairy, told me he loves the multifaceted craftsmanship aspect of shaping a product; he takes pride in being a steward of microbes. "We're bacteria farmers!" he gushed.

All cheeses experience transformation, whether it's from the lactic acid bacteria in the milk or the further microbial activity in a maturing wheel. The artisans at the helm—the "bacteria farmers"—need to keep the microbes happy: dividing and thriving. Ask anyone interested in zymology (the study of fermentation) and they'll tell you that preserving foods in

1%
other (camel,
donkey, yak, horse,
and reindeer)

1%
sheep

2%
goat

14%
buffalo

82%
cow

SOURCE: Food and Agriculture Organization of
the United Nations

this way goes back to the beginning of civilization, long before humans knew the science behind the process. They put together the puzzle blindfolded.

The first cheeses predate recorded history. Legend has it that cheese was discovered about nine thousand years ago, somewhere in what we now call the Middle East, when a nomad transported milk in the stomach of a ruminant (*what a thermos!*), which is where animal rennet is found. Obscure myths aside, lactic coagulation is likely the oldest method of milk coagulation—and therefore cheesemaking—known to humanity, since it takes place naturally. (This would suggest that the earliest cheeses were fresh cheeses, eaten shortly after the curds formed.)

It was the recognition of the role of microorganisms that informed the procedures and allowed the making of cheese to become a measured activity with predictable results. There's archaeological evidence of cheesemaking in ancient Egypt (3100 BCE), and *The Oxford Companion to Food* notes that cave paintings in the Libyan Sahara dating to 5000 BCE depict milking and what may also be cheesemaking. The earliest direct evidence of it, according to the scientific journal *Nature*, was found near what is now Poland, and dates to the sixth millennium BCE. Ancient Roman author and philosopher Pliny the Elder described cheesemaking as a sophisticated pursuit, and the ancient Greeks dubbed Apollo's son Aristaeus the god of cheesemaking (and beekeeping!). This is all to say: cheese is one of civilization's oldest and most prized accomplishments.

Now that you're a microbe pro, I'll rewind to where my transformation began, and how I fell into this vat of curds in the first place.

I woke up bleary-eyed. *Where am I?* I tumbled out of the unfamiliar bed like a Slinky and my feet met the ground with a thud. *Oh, right, London. We live here.* Connor and I were shacking up in a pint-size flat in Central London until we found a long-term lease, and I was alarmingly disoriented. *Okay, Connor's in the bed. I'm supposed to be here.* I slowly recalled the night before; we had the best Indian food of our lives in a humming, colorful restaurant, and the Chicken Ruby seemed to jingle in tandem with the vintage Bollywood music as it lit up my mouth.

It was the taste I had yearned for: something new, something different. We could have been in Bombay, until we emerged onto a calm street not far from Trafalgar Square just before midnight and saw one lone black cab roll by. We drifted in lockstep along the vacant path of the Thames River, amazed that London seemed to shut down at night in a way New York City never did. As we approached Big Ben, sturdy and significant, we felt like we had the city all to ourselves. Necks craned, looking up, Connor gave my hand two gentle squeezes, like a heartbeat—*We're here.*

I gulped.

Didn't I want this?

Living overseas had always been a dream of mine, but after we landed I had a visceral fear that my career was slipping away—or worse, that it had straight up evacuated the plane, parachuting into the Atlantic Ocean as we flew over. I had made the mistake of checking my email as we disembarked at Heathrow and saw a note from a producer at the *Today* show, asking if I was available Thursday to demo a recipe. *Well, crap.* This might be a tougher relocation than I had anticipated. It was Connor's job that had brought us to England, and I had followed my love, but I couldn't help wondering if that was a mistake.

Leading up to the move, I completely underestimated the changes that would take place in moving after a decade of living in New York City. *What'll be the big difference, anyway?* Such a typical New Yorker attitude—confident I could handle anything. At that point in my career, I was a professional YouTuber—I made money from views, brand partnerships, and various video gigs buoyed by the growing success of my channel. I produced, shot, edited, and hosted; our little Brooklyn kitchen transformed into my work studio during the day while Connor went to his office in Manhattan. My set was anywhere I propped up my tripod, and my audience was on the internet; to my mind, my exact geographical location was no concern. The year prior, I'd lived in Paris for three months while I went to culinary school at Le Cordon Bleu *and* kept a rigorous video production schedule, all without much issue. So, I reasoned, the transition to England would be seamless. Sure, there would be some fine-tuning, but most everything would continue uninterrupted . . . *right?*

Wrong. But this assumption remained unchallenged, largely because the months leading up to the move were consumed by wedding planning, and I was too stressed out by that to identify other areas of stress. We moved to London at the end of March and our wedding was in New York at the end of June, three months to the day after we moved to England.

During those pre-wedding months in our temporary flat in Central London, I'd uncork a bottle of wine right around five o'clock, before Connor got home. I'd finish emails and video edits while sipping on the sweet nectar of a Chianti or Sancerre, and by the time he walked through the door, I was on glass number two. When dinner rolled around, I mean, it was *only normal* to have some wine with my meal.

I would offer to pour one for Connor and he'd curtly decline; in the tension of the transition, it felt like another little thing piled on top of the baggage we were about to carry with us down the nuptial aisle. Connor doesn't love wine—he'll drink it, but he's pretty *meh* about it all. I *love* wine. On the list of my joys that Connor did not share, it was scribbled under number one: cooking (but above number three: baths). This weighed heavily on me as I fretted about a lifetime commitment. *How can the things I'm obsessed with, the things I believe link us all as humans and are the lifeblood of connection and upon which I have built my entire career, be so unimportant to my person? I'm about to marry a man who would rather have cereal five nights a week than dirty multiple dishes! But I'm in love with him! Gah, life!*

There are moments in cheesemaking when one of the main components goes rogue. It's a domino effect, each problem creating others in a tumbling cascade. Take heating the curds and whey: a few degrees too high or too low can ruin everything. That temperature variation could be caused by a distracted cheesemaker, environmental changes, or any number of reasons. High risk, high reward, right? Therein lies the challenge of cheesemaking. It's a fine line.

Fine, and sharp as a knife.

There are moments when an element in life goes rogue, too. It must've been the first week after we landed (I was still getting my sea legs) when I went on a lunch date with a cousin of a friend. Ten to fifteen years older than me, she was casually coiffed and beautiful. She and her husband, both Americans, had moved to London years ago, and she'd be helping me feel at home. That was the idea, anyway.

I followed her lead and we both ordered Earl Grey tea (*so British!*) and the roasted tomato and goat cheese quiche as she told me she had left her successful career (in what? I don't remember) to follow her husband's job opportunity in Hong Kong, then again when his promotion took them to London. *Um, will that be me and Connor? His job was the impetus for uprooting our lives* . . . "But it worked out wonderfully!" she said.

Even as I chewed, my sense of taste diminished. She continued, offering tales of adjusting to life in London, which she had now contentedly called home for close to a decade. A wonderful place to raise kids, she said. She was highly involved in a women's group, coordinated her family vacations and children's extracurricular activities, organized events for her Pilates class, delegated all home-related tasks to helpers; her calendar was always full, but she was happy to squeeze in time to have lunch with me.

Holy crap, is she a lady who lunches? I set my fork down. *Are we ladies who lunch?*

At one point, she sweetly reached across the table to place her hand on mine as she said the words that would ring in my head, ricocheting around my skull, for months (nay, years) to come: "But such is the life of a trailing spouse, right?"

Trailing spouse.

There's a fine line between allowing a person's categorization of you to sink in and letting it bounce off you. A fine line, yet sharp as a knife. I was the milk, and she was the cold front that stopped the cheese from reaching its necessary temperature. In this metaphor, I was also the cheesemaker who didn't check the temperature before moving to the next step. I nodded and urged the conversation forward without letting on how affected I was by her pronouncement that I was "trailing."

In cheesemaking, the maker might not know a step went awry until much later in the process. Some cheeses are gooey, some are squeaky. Some are covered in mold and others have mold throughout their interior. With holes or without. Each of these characteristics is coveted only when it is the desired outcome. If a cheesemaker expects to produce a cheddar but ends up with a blue cheese that melts at room temperature, things went wrong somewhere.

After my lunch meeting, I was melting at room temperature. Anxiety compounded anxiety, like a fuzzy mucor growth (the unintended kind of mold) spreading to all the cheeses in the maturation room. That evening, Connor and I sat down for dinner, and as I fumed silently and reached for a bottle of wine, he stepped up like a good assistant cheesemaker and checked my pressure valves. He held up a mirror: this was more drinking than was typical for me. I love my husband for his ability to gently keep me in check. We had lived together in Brooklyn for two years and he knew my Happy Katie consumption habits. Wine had become my transition vice, and once this became clear to me, I didn't buy a bottle for months; I was mortified at slipping into a problem that needn't be one. (When I returned to my relationship with wine months later, it was a healthy and happy reunion.)

WE EVENTUALLY STARTED TO SETTLE IN; we took to including the words *pram*, *mate*, *quid*, and *queue* in our lexicons. We lived in a *flat* and went shopping for *jumpers* and *trousers*. (In the UK, if you ask for *pants*, they'll think you want underwear.) We took the *lift*, not the elevator.

Fake it till you make it, they say, and sure enough, before long things began to click for me professionally, too. A few months after our move, I was offered the project that altered the course of my experience in Europe: a contract to make a series of videos *all about cheese*.

Comté Cheese Association—the organization behind one of France's most beloved cheeses—hired me to create a series of videos about the long tradition of Comté: how it's made and why it is special. I spent an immersive week in the Jura and Doubs regions of eastern France, across the border from Switzerland. I walked the fields at the foothills of the French Alps with the farmers whose cows produce the milk that becomes Comté. I stirred curds in the *fromageries* (also called *fruitières*—

the cheesemaking space), where milk becomes cheese, and tasted the results of maturation in the affinage cellars, where thousands of two-foot-wide wheels of Comté lined the walls of long rooms, aging on spruce shelves. I ate breakfast, lunch, and dinner with these new friends, exercising my conversational French skills to their limit and receiving heaps of cultural insights and cheese doctrine in return. Oh, and I ate a whole lot of cheese—from fondue for dinner with a dairy farmer and his family to slices with my coffee for breakfast to *more* fondue for lunch at an inn nestled in the mountains. (What can I say? They love their fondue— and you can't blame them.)

After my Comté immersion, I hopped on the Eurostar train and made my way home to London, exhausted yet undeniably inspired. London Katie had at last found her creative happy place. After those rough few months, I was desperate to continue moving forward; slipping into a depressed state was to be avoided, and I wanted to see where the cheese trail led.

A newfound ally from the Comté project, Jean-Louis Carbonnier, sent an email introducing me to Bronwen Percival, author of the previously mentioned *Reinventing the Wheel*, a buyer at Neal's Yard Dairy, London's preeminent cheese shop. Like a dairy godmother, she revealed an entire world of artisan cheese to me and urged me to try helping at the shop as a cheesemonger. I didn't need much convincing.

Fondue is a favorite vehicle for the consumption of cheeses the world over, but this classic Alps preparation only became popular on a larger scale thanks to a real-life cheese cartel. *Yup.*

Prior to World War I, the Swiss made a fortune exporting cheese; this played a major role in the country's economy. After the war, almost all the European countries importing cheese were too broke to continue buying, and that's when the Swiss government formed the Swiss Cheese Union (Schweizerische Käseunion), which has been nicknamed the "cheese mafia." It worked like a cartel; they forced every dairy farmer and cheesemaker to have fixed prices, told them how much cheese to make, and ran quality-control measures. They also mandated that the innumerable variety of cheeses made in Switzerland be whittled down to only three: Gruyère, Emmental (what we think of as "Swiss cheese"), and Sbrinz.

The Swiss Cheese Union played puppet master for the domestic and global marketing efforts of these cheeses and pushed for their ideal usages: in fondue and raclette (a dish of melted cheese over new potatoes, with a few cornichons to crunch on the side). Both of these became Swiss national dishes, again thanks to the union's lobbying efforts. The campaigns worked, and the Swiss Cheese Union controlled the supply for decades. It kept prices high and competition low. The cartel paused operations during World War II, but shortly thereafter resumed the work of increasing Swiss cheese sales at home and abroad. By the 1970s, they had the genius idea of promoting fondue in America—a huge market for cheese. It was a major success. Fondue became as popular as bell-bottoms and shag carpets.

Sure, the Swiss Cheese Union protected Switzerland's cheese industry during uncertain economic times, but it also homogenized (and arguably downgraded) cheese production in an otherwise richly diverse cheese land. Like most cartels, the Swiss Cheese Union was eventually revealed to be corrupt, and for some of its officials, accepting bribes and breaking international trade laws led to jail time. In 1999, the Swiss Cheese Union was officially dismantled. The cheese scandal of the century!

Happily, cheese innovation in Switzerland has resumed, and there are now around 450 unique types of cheese made in the country. In honor of the magnificent varieties that exist and are indeed delicious in fondue, I hope you'll make some fondue tonight (recipe opposite).

British Cheese Fondue

I can thank my friends at Neal's Yard Dairy for this combination, which uses Lincolnshire Poacher (it tastes like a mix between a mild cheddar and a Comté, smooth on the tongue, a bit sweet, and slightly nutty; it melts beautifully) as the base cheese and then adds crumbly, buttery Lancashire (a British territorial cheese, the lingo used for traditional cheeses produced in a certain part of the country and that exhibit defining characteristics in production, texture, and flavor), Ogleshield (a British raclette cheese), and Rollright (a soft cow's-milk cheese not unlike Camembert). For a fun color pop and a flavor-forward fondue, swap the Lancashire for burnt-orange Red Leicester; crumbly and savory, it makes for an atypical pot of fondue. Or if you're a die-hard blue cheese fan, you won't regret subbing in some Stilton. Hat-tip to the shop's Fondue Nights, an event open to the public, which is essentially a fondue feast, complete with wine pairings and a variety of fun dipping items and side bites like baked new potatoes, cornichons, and balsamic-glazed pearl onions—all of which I'd certainly recommend as additions for your at-home fondue meal.

1 garlic clove, peeled

6 ounces (170 grams) base cheese, such as Lincolnshire Poacher (or Comté or Gouda), cut into small cubes

4 ounces (115 grams) Lancashire cheese (or any British territorial cheese, like Wensleydale or Cheshire), crumbled into chunks

4 ounces (115 grams) Ogleshield cheese (or other suitable raclette cheese, like Gruyère), cut into cubes

4 ounces (115 grams) Rollright cheese (or other soft, Camembert-esque cheese that you can scoop into the fondue pot)

¾ cup (175 milliliters) dry white wine (use an acidic white wine, like a sauvignon blanc, rather than a fruity one)

3 tablespoons (50 milliliters) kirsch (a clear cherry brandy; or use more white wine)

Bread (stale bread works best), cut into cubes, for dipping

Rub the garlic clove over the inside of the fondue pot, then discard the garlic. Add the base cheese to the pot and set over medium heat. Add the other cheeses, including the edible rinds. Add the wine, which helps slacken the cheeses and prevents them from setting together, and the kirsch, which has a similar textural effect and balances the richness of the cheese. Stir until the cheeses are well melted and the fondue is smooth, with the same consistency throughout. Serve with cubed bread for dipping.

NOTES

- If the fondue is too thick, stir in more wine or a bit of crème fraîche.
- If the fondue is too runny or has begun to split, mix 1 to 2 teaspoons cornstarch with 1 tablespoon water, add the mixture to the pot, and stir quickly to incorporate.

Fondue party! The pot on the left contains traditional French cheeses (like Comté and Gruyère), and to the right is British Cheese Fondue (recipe on previous page). Fondon't you want some?

FONDUE ETIQUETTE

1. After dipping your bread, don't let your fondue fork go into your mouth—we're not at the dentist's office. Pull the dipped bread off the fondue fork with your teeth or move the bread to a plate with a table fork and use that fork to eat it.

2. The proper dipping method is to scrape the bread in a slow figure eight on the bottom of the pot, then lift it out and let the excess fondue drip off, then move it to your plate (or your mouth).

3. The film of hardened cheese on the bottom of the pot, which you'll discover once you've eaten most of the cheese, is known as *la courte* or *la religieuse*. It's considered a treat, so don't wash it away in the sink! Scrape it from the bottom and munch it; your fondue experience is complete.

THE CHEESE SHOP

It was spitting rain, as London does, when I emerged from the Tottenham Court Road tube station. Bundled up for the December chill and holding my rain jacket hood in place like a turtle in its shell, I scurried past the construction site near the majestic theater where *Harry Potter and the Cursed Child* was running, through the busy shopping streets of Covent Garden, to the quiet meandering cobbled paths of Seven Dials, a road junction designed in the 1690s where seven streets converge at a sundial column. I was on my way to another shift as a cheesemonger at Neal's Yard Dairy.

Tucked away on a narrow street, the storefront could be easy to miss, like the spine of a thin book amid a dozen others on a long shelf, but missing it would be a shame: the windows display stacked wheels of cheese, some cut into wedges and tilted at an angle, just so. To a cheese lover, the display is as tantalizing as a model playfully inching a dress up her thigh. This cheese is *sexy*, and if you thought the window display was a thing of beauty, the real eyeful lingers inside.

Up a step and into the shop is a cheese sanctuary. An intimate, tiny one at that. The walkway is barely wide enough for two humans, and it goes straight to the back, with cheeses piled high on either side. As you proceed forward, look to your right, and you'll find whole wheels of cheese maturing on wooden shelves beside various chutneys, crackers, and loaves of bread from local purveyors. To your left is the cheese slate, a counter with opened wheels. The space behind the slate is even more confined than where you stand, and that's where eager cheesemongers launch into action, offering samples and explaining the flavors, textures, and origins of the cheeses.

I HAD ENTERED THE KINGDOM OF cheese. I hung up my rain jacket and donned a white coat, steel-toed white wellies (just like a butcher), and a navy blue cap (like a newspaper boy). It wasn't until I lifted the blue apron that read NEAL'S YARD DAIRY over my head and secured the string around my hips that the look came together: cheesemonger, ready to spread the gospel of good cheese.

Why did I want to work in a cheese shop? I would ask myself this question in my time at Neal's Yard Dairy (usually as I scrubbed and squeegeed the floors in the near-freezing storage room), but I never wavered in my curiosity to learn more about cheese and the industry around it. It gave me the creative and culinary outlet I sought. There was that intellectual pull, but the other impetus, honestly, was my yearning for community. I was a stranger in a strange land, and this was an attempt to find my place. Where better to do that than one of the most revered cheese shops in the world?

A month prior, when general manager David Lockwood first welcomed me to his office—in a different location, tucked beneath the railway arches of South London—he waited for me just inside the entrance. David is immediately likable; he's got a gentle authenticity and an endearing, dutiful passion for cheese. He walked me through the packing room and the maturation room, then up the stairs to a conference room, where we talked about how I could help out at the shop and absorb as much cheese knowledge as possible in the month I'd be working there. His main advice was to taste constantly. "It's the only way to learn."

If you say so.

Neal's Yard Dairy sells cheeses exclusively from Britain and Ireland (with a few exceptions, like Parmigiano

Reggiano). "We want to improve British cheese. We want to change the world," said David, providing me with the manifesto of the movement I was joining. *Change the world? With cheese?* Artisan cheeses, aka farmhouse cheeses, were the priority. They're the kind in which even subtle changes in a cow's diet (or a goat's diet, or a sheep's . . .) cause a change in the flavor of the cheese. It's the opposite of factory farming and industrial-scale food production in which those differences are eradicated in the production process to create a product that is consistent and replicable en masse.

One thing that surprised me about David was his upstate New York–cum–Midwest accent. *An American is one of the head honchos at England's most celebrated cheese shop?* David fell in love with British cheese from afar while working at Zingerman's, the specialty food shop with an ardent following based in Ann Arbor, Michigan, where he imported cheeses from Neal's Yard Dairy (NYD) for Americans to enjoy. He became such a fan of the shop's cheeses and ethos that he moved to England almost thirty years ago to dedicate his life to the pursuit of keeping British farmhouse cheeses alive.

The best way to do this? Get other people—as many humans as possible—to adore these cheeses, too, and to understand the difference between something like Montgomery's Cheddar, in its clothbound wheel the size of an adult's abdomen, and Kraft singles. David explained, "We help people appreciate what they put in their mouths." Of course,

the first step is to *get something* into their mouths.

One thing I noticed about Londoners—at least those who frequented NYD—was that they rarely asked for samples. Even when a person was dying to try some Tymsboro (having heard about the rolling, fertile Somerset countryside on which the farms' goats dine), etiquette prevented them from asking for a taste before one was offered. To cut through this formality, the cheesemongers at NYD deliberately welcome customers by urging them to sample—or rather, by proclaiming, "Try this," one outstretched arm holding a dull knife with a sliver of cheese hanging off its end.

Humans learn about food by tasting it. At culinary school, I was taught to taste everything at each stage of the cooking process. It was hammered into my head so hard, I can't believe there was ever a time I plated what I cooked without tasting it first. Nibbling in the cheese shop offered a different tasting experience: discerning subtle flavor distinctions between cheeses, rather than judging if, or how, to adjust flavors.

One time when I was working in the shop, I overheard a bespectacled customer note, "Wow, these taste different to the cheeses at Tesco!" (Tesco is a middle-of-the-road grocery store chain in the UK.) The monger in front of him, Sebastian, noted, "You're not in a supermarket anymore. You're in the cathedral of cheese."

Cathedral of cheese! That's the best description I've heard yet. Without a moment's delay, Sebastian extended his arm, holding out a sample of Berkswell—a hard sheep's-milk cheese similar to Manchego—for the man. "Here, try this."

"Mm, hm. It's good." His face looked perplexed as he nibbled. "I'm not sure if I've tried anything like it before . . . mm . . . Interesting . . ."

"Yeah," acknowledged Sebastian. "It's funny how supermarkets dictate our tastes."

The man raised his eyebrows as though enlightened, then narrowed his gaze in contemplation as he went in for another nibble.

"But to only taste what the supermarkets sell," Sebastian continued, "is to not see the whole story."

Sebastian was as tall and lean as a basketball player, with surfer-dude blond hair pulled up in a bun and a hipster mustache to match. He smiled easily and charmingly and was passionate about artisan cheese and all things fermented. Many young women left the store with a crush and more cheese than they had intended to buy. Once, when a customer exclaimed to Sebastian that he preferred a type of cheese from Lidl (another grocery chain), Sebastian could hardly contain his befuddlement. After the man left, Sebastian, still flummoxed, continued his conversation with the departed customer, mumbling to himself, "You *do* know that taste you like is manufactured in tubes, right?"

I shifted my attention to the cheeses. We had more than forty varieties out on display, ready to be tasted and discussed.

The shop's cheesemongers needed to know all of them by sight, and it helped when I began the day by sketching a quick mental diagram of the groupings, which changed depending on which monger arranged them. *Goat cheeses here, semi-soft cow's-milk cheeses next to those, hard cow's-milk cheeses piled over here . . .* As I reviewed the day's layout, I cut a sliver of the addicting washed-rind sheep's-milk St James. The practiced among us could call to mind a cheese's place of origin, whether it was produced from pasteurized or raw milk, and whether it was made with vegetarian rennet versus animal rennet, and could even recall anecdotes about specific cheesemakers. It was a lot to remember, and a lot to taste. On this particular day, my retention was spot-on and I felt proud of myself; if there were a Standardized Aptitude Test for cheese (the Chee-SATs?), I would've aced it. I began my shift in a cheerful and social mood. Which, of course, couldn't last forever.

By early evening, as the sun set, my brain began to turn to mush. At the tail end of the day, in my eighth hour on my feet, I helped a reserved, posh-looking gentleman determine which blue cheese he wanted for a pre-Christmas party. Together, we tasted and discussed the options. "This one is slightly creamier," I noted as he tried the Stichelton, and "Here we've got a bolder flavor," as he ate the Colston Bassett Stilton. Within a few minutes we had developed a nice rapport; his demeanor had loosened, and we were enjoying our chat. He decided on the Stichelton, a raw cow's-milk version of the better-known Stilton, and said he'd take an entire half wheel. That's approximately the size and weight of a baby, and it's not cheap, going for £76 (about a hundred US dollars) per half wheel. I rung up the order and handed my newfound pal his purchase as we bid each other a pleasant evening. I watched him bounce away, then looked down for the credit card receipt to nestle into the cash register. I couldn't find it. Brow furrowed, I scanned the floor and down the slate. I felt around the computer, probing the printer slot—"Did this thing run out of paper?" Another cheesemonger came to my aid, took one look at the credit card machine in my hands, and said, "Did you charge him?" I peered at the blue screen and saw the amount—*£76.00*—shining up at me, blinking and ready to accept payment. "Oh no," I exhaled, as I ran from behind the counter and out the front door to find him.

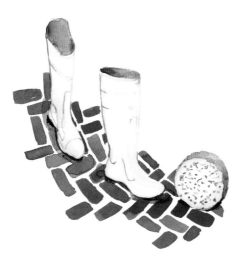

My wellies hit the uneven bricks with heavy thumps as I darted down the dark street, running toward the lights and hubbub at the end of the path, where hordes of Christmas browsers and tourists careened around the pedestrian-only holiday stalls with their mulled wine and bags of gifts. *Is that him? No. Wait, is that him?* On tiptoe, I strained to see as I picked up speed for brief moments, only to realize that my preened pal looked like every other dark-haired, black-overcoat-wearing shopper in sight. I didn't know which way to turn. My staccato heart rate accelerated as I frantically scanned the waves of humans pulsing through the market. I guessed a direction and ran into the crowd, tripping on a woman's crutch in my haste. "Hey, watch it!" she yelled, as I was swallowed into the beehive of activity. A few steps in, I did a 360-degree turn and prayed the man would appear. When he didn't,[*] I felt a numbness spread through my body, and I came to a full stop. Standing there, jostled by people passing all around me, my eyes welled up and it was all I could do not to cry. *What am I doing?* I was standing on a street in London, unsure where I was going—neither on that street nor in my life—and reeking of cheese. I still had so much to learn.

---

* I never found him.

Winter weather in London can be rough. Not that there are blizzards like those I experienced in New York, but the cold in England is the wet kind that sinks into your bones, settling in your marrow, and requires a scalding bath to shake.

To keep the cheeses at Neal's Yard Dairy in their optimal conditions for selling, the entire shop was refrigerated—a big igloo. Therefore, my primary concern that December was staying warm. I bought fleece booties and sheepskin insoles that fit inside my wellies, wore long johns under my clothes, wrapped a scarf around my neck, and even tucked hand warmers into

my backpack, just in case. Like an Arctic explorer, I entered the cheese arena for each shift hoping I'd still be able to feel my fingers by the end of it.

Although the cheese shop was chilly, working there thawed my unease at having been labeled a *trailing spouse*. I felt I had purpose beyond hustling for the next gig, beyond gaining social media followers. My objective was greater than selling cheese; it was to spread the word about real cheese, incredible cheesemakers, and quality food made locally.

One blessedly mild winter day, I arrived at the shop and underwent the hygienic routine I had been taught to complete before taking my place behind the slate—"scrubbing in," we called it. I washed my hands and stood behind the stacks of cheese on the slate. Without thinking, I readjusted my green glasses on my nose, then realized I had "contaminated" my newly washed hands and had to go wash them again. *Darn it, every time.* I walked back to the sink, dispensed the soap, and lathered up, as I imagined how chapped my knuckles would

TYMSBORO

Made by Mary Holbrook near
Timsbury, Somerset, England

Raw Goat's Milk
Animal Rennet

£ 5.40/Half

PERROCHE,
PLAIN

Made by Charlie Westhead & Team
near Dorstone, Herefordshire,
England

Pasteurised Goat's Milk
Animal Rennet

£ 6.70

NEAL'S YARD
Perroche
CREAMERY

Honing my cheesemonger chops during my first year at Neal's Yard Dairy be by the end of the day. I dried my hands, determined to keep them in contact with cheese only.

Just then, a customer walked through the doors. Like the cheese ninja I aspired to be, I withdrew my knife and deftly sliced a sample of creamy, lemony Innes Brick goat cheese. The customer was an older man with thin wire-rimmed glasses and styled hair. As he approached, I extended the sample to him and said, "Try this!"

I've mentioned the importance of getting customers to try the cheeses, but another key element was that we were honest about the fact that we sold a food that was never quite the same from one day to the next. Cheese is a fermented product, bound to change because of any number of circumstances, and that outcome was more likely with the cheeses we sold, since they were small-scale farmhouse cheeses, the opposite of standardized big-industry cheeses. If you had bought a wheel of Camembert-style Tunworth in the past, the current wheels might not taste exactly the same, which was why "Try this" was an important request.

"What's this?" the bespectacled man asked as he studied the cheese speared on my knife.

"This is Innes Brick, it's a raw goat's-milk cheese made in Staffordshire." I was proud my memory seemed to be processing at top speed. "It's my favorite goat cheese of the moment—almost the texture of mousse, pleasantly lactic." I offered another slice, pressing my elbow farther

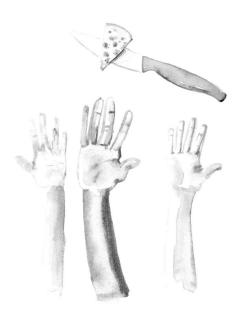

up to make my arm a straight line to the gentleman.

"Well, okay," he said, as he excitedly pinched the sample between his thumb and forefinger and slid it off the knife.

The goal was to welcome and disarm the customer simultaneously, and we were looking to start a conversation. By engaging in an exchange of opinions and information, the door opened to productive dialogue that was more than a typical commercial transaction. This strategy was rooted in Neal's Yard Dairy from its nascency and was central to the shop's evolution.

When NYD first opened on July 4, 1979, near a small alley in Covent Garden called Neal's Yard, they made Greek-style yogurts and fresh cheeses. Randolph Hodgson, founder of the dairy, admitted that he didn't know what he was doing, "so we gave the customers

Cut pieces of cheese should be kept in the refrigerator to slow the growth of mold on their exposed surfaces. The caveat here is that refrigerated cheeses are more likely to dry out (especially if they're not well wrapped). Your best course of action is to wrap the cheese well in its waxed paper and store it in a covered container in the fridge. The container will help to prevent the cheese from drying out and from absorbing off flavors and odors from other foods.

a taste of everything and asked them what they thought." An openness and desire to learn have been at the core of the business ever since. After a year, the dairy started to buy matured cheeses, too, and yet again, customer feedback was crucial because Randolph would report their opinions to the cheesemakers. It's a cool communication system; shops like Neal's Yard Dairy enable the farmhouse dairy industry—from small one-person operations to larger creameries—to collect feedback from customers about what it needs to improve.

A question I got asked frequently was "Can I eat the rind?" My answer depended on the cheese they were eating. For the majority of cheeses—all the goat's-milk cheeses, bloomy-rind (think: Brie, Camembert) and washed-rind (like a Taleggio) varieties, and many of the hard cheeses—I'd say, "Sure! Think of it like the crust on bread." Some people are quite particular and prefer not to eat it regardless—that's okay, too. It comes down to personal preference. The only rinds I'd

steer people away from eating are those made of wax or bark, and those that are distractingly thick and not pleasurable on the palate.

Of course, the beautiful thing about all this was how *I* got to taste so many cheeses! (Perhaps the most selfish statement in this book?) Tasting cheeses every day was the best way to become an expert. That's what David told me during my initial interview, and my time at the shop proved it to be true.

Let me answer the question you're probably asking: *No, I never got sick of eating cheese while I worked there.*

When I'd return to the shop for my next shift, the smell that hit my nose upon walking in—an undeniably yeasty scent of fermentation—became comforting, and I'd inhale deeply. It was like being in a playground of curds, and as I continued working, and eating, many favorites emerged—Spenwood, a hard sheep's-milk cheese made in Berkshire (using a vegetarian coagulant); Ogleshield, a raclette-style cheese made in Somerset that is delicious as is but heavenly when melted; Lincolnshire Poacher, a nutty cheddar-style cheese; St Cera, the closest thing we carried to the stinky Époisses de Bourgogne; and many more!

Knowing what I preferred—and why—came in handy in conversations with customers, although I was surprised when some people deferred to my opinions rather than standing by their own. Francis Percival, coauthor of *Reinventing the Wheel*, summed it up perfectly when he told me, "British people see cheese boards as a social minefield." The number of questions I fielded about cheese boards was remarkable. Miranda, one of my managers that first year at the Covent Garden shop, gave me the refrain I still use: "The first rule is that there are no rules." And it's true. I've eaten an all-blue cheese board before, and it was awesome! If you're going for a typical spread, most cheese boards aim to offer a variety: a hard cheese like cheddar; a soft option, such as a goat cheese or perhaps a Brie-style cheese; and a blue.

If you're navigating the cheese board at a party, it's routine to start with the least strong option and work your way up to the strong and stinky ones or those with added ingredients—like truffled cheeses or those dotted with cranberries. But any party where you're chastised for starting with the blue cheese and then reaching for the Brie sounds like a judgmental gathering, and I suggest you find new friends.

I occasionally brought home favorites for Connor and myself, even though I was eating cheese all day long, nearly every day.

The difference between cheese at home and cheese in the shop was that after weeks of nibbling morsels, it felt like a true luxury to slam a piece of cheese three times the size of my thumb onto a cracker, smear chutney on top, and take multiple bites to finish it off. I have a memory of blue cheese crumbs and cracker shreds raining down as I gluttonously ate huge, satisfying chunks of funky Sparkenhoe Blue in my kitchen. In those moments, I understood why a cheese bank[*] exists. Cheese is worthy of being its own form of currency.

If I wanted to understand *why* cheese could be extraordinary, though—why age-old tales like Little Miss Muffet invoke this food, why my greedy Cookie Monster–inspired shoveling of it onto a biscuit and into my mouth was so satisfying—there was something I still needed to do: get my hands dirty by plunging them into a vat of curds. I needed to apprentice at a cheesemaking operation—so I put feelers out with Bronwen Percival. As a buyer for NYD, she was constantly on the road visiting cheesemakers. That set the wheels in motion . . . but first, we had to get through Christmas.

---

* *The Italian bank Credit Emiliano (in the Emilia-Romagna region) has accepted wheels of Parmigiano Reggiano cheese as collateral for small-business loans since 1953. It takes young cheese, valuing it at the current market price of mature cheese. The bank then matures the cheese in its own maturation rooms. If producers default on their loans, the bank sells the cheese upon maturation (on the short side, 18 months; on the aged side, 36 months). The longer it ages, the more unctuous and valuable it becomes.*

Going into the Christmas crunch, I had to get my cheesemonger game face on like a competitor. Working behind the slate would be an endurance test, and I needed to prepare.

Luckily, I was in good company. My fellow cheesemongers showed up to work ready and raring to go. It was in the break room, where we refueled and removed our aprons and caps, that we had the chance to get to know one another beyond the slate. Of course, conversation usually continued to revolve around cheese, including sharing recipes for favorite ways to enjoy cheeses from the shop. From a bitter greens salad with Stichelton, to my vegetarian Scotch Eggs with Cheddar,

I received plenty of kitchen inspiration in these chats. (It also prompted a quick getting-up-to-speed on the distinctions between the American English and British English lexicons, food words and otherwise. Here are just a few examples.)

AMERICAN ENGLISH	BRITISH ENGLISH
arugula	rocket
bok choi	pak choi
cilantro	coriander
eggplant	aubergine
zucchini	courgette

Scotch Egg with Potato and Cheese

MAKES 4 SERVINGS AS A STARTER, 8 AS AN HORS D'OEUVRE

Despite its name, a Scotch egg isn't Scottish, and there are a few competing stories about where it *does* originate. One is that it was the perfect portable snack for the upper class of London to enjoy while they traveled to their country homes. Another legend suggests they were made for the working-class Brits in northern England's Yorkshire region as a compact, handheld treat that could be taken along to work. Still other stories note that the Scotch egg might be rooted in the cuisine of India from its days as a British colony, a version of *nargisi kofta* or *dimer chop*. Any of these, or a combination of them, could be true.

Scotch eggs don't traditionally include cheese, but I like my version better than the meaty ones, to be honest. I wrap a layer of cheesy potatoes around a peeled hard-boiled egg, then bread it and fry it. I make it with my favorite English cheddar, Montgomery's (Monty's for short); the color of the cheese is roughly the same as the potato. (Bright orange is not cheddar's natural color; it's often the result of coloring with annatto seed and is not typical in cheddars from England.) It may be visually subtle, but it's big in flavor.

2 to 4 russet potatoes (approximately 1½ pounds/650 grams total), unpeeled

2 tablespoons fine sea salt, plus ½ teaspoon and more as needed

5 large eggs

1 tablespoon neutral oil (such as sunflower oil, peanut oil, or canola oil), plus more for deep-frying (around ½ liter)

1 white onion, finely chopped

½ teaspoon freshly ground black pepper, plus more as needed

2 garlic cloves, minced

1 cup (3½ ounces/100 grams) shredded cheddar cheese

1½ cups (150 grams) fine bread crumbs (I prefer homemade, see page 319) or panko bread crumbs

Piccalilli, for serving (optional)

1. Fill a large pot with water to a couple of inches below the rim. Bring the water to a boil over high heat. Add the potatoes and the 2 tablespoons of salt. Boil for 20 to 30 minutes, until a fork or knife easily pierces the center of each potato, then drain and set aside to cool.

2. Meanwhile, fill a medium saucepan with enough water to cover the eggs. Carefully place 4 eggs in the water (set the fifth egg aside) and set the pan over high heat. When the water begins to boil, immediately cover the pot, turn off the heat, and let sit for 6 minutes. (Now is a good time to prepare an ice bath for the eggs by filling a medium bowl with ice and then cold water.) Using a slotted spoon, transfer the eggs to the ice bath and let them cool until you can comfortably handle them. Gently crack the shells with a light but sturdy tap on the counter and peel the eggs under cool running water, placing them on a plate as you go. Set the soft-boiled eggs to the side.

(recipe continues)

33

3. When the boiled potatoes are cool enough to handle, peel them (either with pressure from your fingers—the skin should slide off fairly easily, though you may need to scrape at it with your fingernail every now and again—or using a vegetable peeler) and return them to the pot. With a potato masher, squash the naked potatoes into a rough, chunky mash.

4. Heat the 1 tablespoon oil in a medium skillet over medium heat. Add the onion, ½ teaspoon salt, and pepper and stir to combine well. Spread the onion evenly over the bottom of the pan and cook until it begins to soften, 1 to 2 minutes. Add the garlic and cook for 1 minute, until fragrant, then add the potatoes and mix until well incorporated. Taste and determine if you'd like to add more salt. Transfer the mixture to a medium bowl and let cool.

5. Stir the shredded cheese into the cooled potato mixture. Divide the mixture into 4 equal portions (you'll use one portion to cover each egg). Take a handful of the potato mixture (roughly a heaping ½ cup/80 grams) from one portion and flatten it on your palm. Place one of the soft-boiled eggs in the center of it, then with your free hand, grab another handful of the potatoes and use the potatoes to cover the other side. Cupping your palms, press the potatoes all around the egg, distributing them evenly. If one part feels bulky, pinch off some potatoes; if a section seems thin, add more. Rotate the potato-covered egg continuously in your hands as you compress the potatoes with your palms. This is the key to a smooth, rounded shape. You'll know it's ready to set aside when the potato forms a compact layer without any cracks (which would indicate that the potatoes might crumble off the egg during

frying). Set aside on a plate. Repeat to coat the remaining eggs with the potato mixture.

6. Crack the remaining egg into a wide, shallow bowl. Add a pinch of salt and beat until smooth. Place the bread crumbs in a separate wide, shallow bowl.

7. Dip a potato-coated egg into the beaten egg, rolling it around to coat completely and letting any excess drip off. Then dip it into the bowl of bread crumbs, turning it until it's thoroughly coated. Finally, dip it into the beaten egg again, then into the bread crumbs. Place the breaded egg on a plate and repeat to bread the rest.

8. Pour a few cups (½ liter) of oil into a deep, heavy pot, such as a wok or Dutch oven. The eggs won't need to be fully immersed in the oil (you will rotate them as they fry), but they should be largely covered. Heat the oil over high heat to 375°F (190°C; if you don't have a thermometer, drop a small bit of bread into the oil; if it begins to sizzle immediately, it's ready). Line a plate with paper towels or a dish cloth (it will be soaked with oil shortly).

9. Gently lower one egg into the hot oil, adding a second one if there is room in your chosen pot (I fry two at a time in my 12½-inch/32-centimeter wok). Fry, turning the egg(s) gently a few times, until cooked to an even golden brown on all sides, 3 to 4 minutes. Use a slotted spoon to transfer the egg(s) to the lined plate to drain excess oil and immediately sprinkle with a few pinches of salt. Adjust the heat to medium-high so the oil doesn't get too hot, and cook the remaining eggs the same way.

10. Let the Scotch eggs cool for about 5 minutes before serving. If you want to serve them as an hors d'oeuvre rather than a starter, cut them lengthwise into halves.

Neal's Yard Dairy

Christmas cheese in England is a *thing*. A *fifth* of the shop's yearly sales happened in December, and sales of blue cheeses associated with Christmas doubled in this month alone. Londoners need their Christmas cheese!

Stilton, a blue cheese, is a celebrated staple of the festive British table, as necessary and ubiquitous at holiday gatherings as mince pies and Christmas jumpers. If the cheeses at NYD competed—Olympics-style—for Christmas glory, the blue cheeses would top the podium: Colston Bassett Stilton, the pasteurized cow's-milk blue that represents Brits the world over, would take the gold medal, and Stichelton, its raw-milk counterpart, would take silver. The bronze would go to one of the other non-blue favorites, like Montgomery's Cheddar, Brie-style Baron Bigod, or a goat cheese like Dorstone. (And for you Wallace & Gromit fans, I'll put Wensleydale on the podium, too.)

The holiday offers both a benefit and a burden for the cheese industry. The benefit is obvious: there's so much money to be made. NYD had a transparency policy that was effective in getting everyone involved in the financial goals of the company, which is how I know the whopping number of pounds of cheese expected to be sold the Friday before Christmas; when that goal was met in the early evening, a coded announcement was made and all

the cheesemongers let out a cheer before getting back to business. *That* kind of profit—more than the annual salary of many Londoners I know—for *this* kind of cheese (made by farmers rather than corporations) is quite a feat! Christmas props up the farmhouse cheese industry for the rest of the year, not only financially, but in terms of exposure and winning lots of small battles in the fight for real cheese. In other words, a successful December means cheesemakers will be able to continue their worthwhile craft and farmhouse cheese in the UK won't go extinct.

The burden of Christmas also comes with opportunity: it puts both makers and mongers under legitimate pressure. In my small role, I experienced the extremely busy days as though I were sprinting a marathon. When I say it was busy, I mean it was completely *bonkers*. I honestly didn't think it was possible for so many human bodies to fit inside the small space of that shop. There could be a queue stretching several storefronts down the block with a wait time of about 45 minutes (for cheese!). Even when customers got through the doors, it felt like a crowded elevator inside the shop.

A similar crush happened behind the counter. Sometimes there would be a dozen of us behind the 20-foot slate; I was elbow to elbow with my coworkers. At the height of the day, my co-mongers and I would weave under each other's arms to use the wire cutter or reach over one another's heads to grab a wedge of cheese. It's incredible how few accidents occurred,

how few snippy comments were made. Amid this pandemonium, my coworker Eleanor poetically noted under her breath, "We're like fish, swimming around each other in the pond." Behind the slate we were either fluid and nimble, like dancers delivering cheese, or halting and prone to collisions, like bumper cars. It depended on the day, the moment, and the monger.

DURING THE HEIGHT OF THIS MAYHEM, the shop's managers—Gareth and Miranda—directed the staff like choreographers. Walkie earpieces in, they coordinated with the person controlling the floodgates at the entrance to the shop, who would shout, *"Any mongers free?"* to keep the line moving. Gareth and Miranda had eyes like hawks, and they were quick to offer backup when a particularly challenging customer or request came in. I felt lucky to have them as my guardian cheese angels. It would have been all too easy to turn into a dictator when so much was at stake.

Gareth was about my age, with a big beard and kind eyes. He was a man of few words, but he knew the shop's cheeses like a jockey knows his horse. One of my fellow mongers told me, "Gareth likes cheese more than he likes people." I chuckled because it rang true. On my first day, Gareth thoroughly trained me on cheese handling, cutting, and wrapping. "We cut soft cheeses, like goat cheeses and soft-rind cow's-milk cheeses, with a blunted paring knife," he explained, "and hard wedges with the cheese wire off the center of the point, or 'nose,' all the way to the rind, to ensure each slice has the full range of flavors." (A different wire was reserved for blue cheeses, which have a tendency to imbue anything they touch with a distinct taste and aroma.)

Wrapping the cheeses was like a form of origami. Depending on the size, shape, and texture of the wedge, different techniques were employed. We used a special waxed cheese paper to achieve the best possible balance between maintaining humidity around the cheese and allowing it to breathe. (If you wrap cheese in plastic wrap, it can sweat, which will negatively affect cheese's flavor. So avoid plastic wrap.)

I like to think of Miranda, the other manager, as part glamour queen, part samurai; she handled whatever was thrown at her, by customer or by employee, with grace. She had an acuity for the nuances of the industry. For example, when the misunderstood (and sometimes contentious) topic of vegetarian cheese arose with customers, Miranda would point them to the cheeses that used a vegetarian coagulant rather than animal-derived rennet.

However, Miranda, a vegetarian of many years herself, chose to eat cheeses that were made using animal rennet. I remember that on one of my first days at the shop, she explained the philosophy behind her decision: vegetarian coagulants, which are typically made in the lab, are not traditional and don't support a holistic farming ecosystem, which clashed with her food values (the same values that had prompted her to stop eating meat). The more she learned about the small-scale artisans behind the farmhouse cheeses sold at NYD, and how extraordinarily well they treat their animals, the more certain she became that she'd rather eat cheese made with traditional animal rennet than cheese made with "fake, processed" coagulants.

Determining what to buy and what to put in our bodies is not always an easy decision, and I don't think it should be. We *should* question things as we determine our own personal food philosophy and broader values. Cognitive dissonance exists for a reason, so if something you've heard about the food you're eating gives you pause, investigate!

BEHIND THE SLATE DURING THE PRIME-time crush, little bits of cheese were constantly flying to the ground. With so many mongers sampling from the many cheeses, the floor was a vision of cheese confetti. At a certain point in service, we'd hear, *"Mongers back!"* Regardless of what we were in the middle of—talking with a customer, cutting, wrapping, or weighing—we had to step back as one of the "floater" mongers came through with a big scrub brush to pry away all the cheese stuck to the tiles, followed by another monger with a bucket of water and a squeegee. There were only a couple of feet in which to move backward or forward, so to get the entirety of the floor, they'd shout, *"Mongers up!"* to scrub the other half. We were like foosball players, synchronized in our steps.

My fellow mongers were mostly young,

obsessed with cheese, and exceptionally personable. Put through the wringer of Neal's Yard Dairy at Christmastime, we became mates pretty fast, and the vibe at end-of-day cleanup was almost celebratory, because we had completed another big day at the shop. Someone would play music through the speakers (the Allergies, Anderson .Paak, Motown classics) as we scrubbed the floors and wrapped the cheeses to be returned to the cold room overnight.

When I first got to London, I didn't know anyone. What I was learning was that a mutual delight in something (*ahem*, cheese) was enough to crumble walls among strangers.

I've come to see the Christmas rush as a unique opportunity to educate a large group of people about British cheese in a short period of time. When a customer asked for Brie, a French cheese, we offered "Baron Bigod, our Brie-style cheese" from Suffolk, England. If there was an inquiry

for raclette, a Swiss cheese, we gave them a taste of Ogleshield, from a farm in Somerset. There was palpable pride for local British cheeses among the NYD leadership, and an admiration for the farmers and cheesemakers with whom the company had built strong relationships.

British cheeses are generally solid and crumbly (as opposed to continental cheeses, many of which are firm in texture and less acidic in taste), which stems from the way, historically, the cheeses were made. The rural food production of Great Britain featured a farmhouse with two to five cows. A day's milk from that many cows is not enough to make cheese, so there were two main ways to handle this conundrum. Much of continental Europe (e.g., France, in the production of Comté) developed community cooperative systems in which all the neighboring farms pooled their milk at the end of each day, making a wheel of cheese and sharing the results. In the British Isles, the farmers didn't pool their milk; instead, individual farmers collected their own milk over several days before beginning production. As a result of resting for days at a time, the lactic acid bacteria in the milk increase and the milk becomes acidic. (British territorial cheeses are set by a mixture of lactic acid coagulation and rennet coagulation.)

Lactic acid coagulation makes the cheese more delicate because when curds are highly acidic, they don't knit together well. The finished cheese is therefore more sour and crumblier than a typical continental cheese. If you've ever had Lancashire, Stilton, Cheshire, Double

Gloucester, or Red Leicester, you'll understand what I mean.

There aren't many people who know British varieties more intimately than Bronwen Percival, my dairy godmother. When I spoke with her about the role consumers have in the industry, she shared her firm belief that "Cheese is our opportunity as consumers to actually taste a farming system. To taste all of the choices made by a farmer." When that bespectacled customer, talking with Sebastian in an earlier chapter, noted an elemental taste difference between NYD cheeses and those at the supermarket, he was likely tasting the terroir[*] of the land that cow ate from, but his taste buds were accustomed to standardized industrial cheeses; he didn't know what to make of those novel flavors. I'm not trying to demonize industrial cheeses—predictability has its place—but in terms of excellence and value, industrial cheese certainly shouldn't be our only understanding of cheese.

"We need to redefine quality," Bronwen continued. "If we understand what those flavors are, they are by definition better flavors than something that can be made with commodity milk that's intensively farmed or with flavors that come out of a packet. That is what we call the 'moral value' of flavor."

It's a bit like the adage "Give a man a fish, and you feed him for a day. Teach a man to fish, and you feed him for a lifetime." Give a man cheese, and he'll eat it. Teach a man how to taste cheese, and you enable him to eat with integrity for the rest of his life. This is what we cheesemongers tried to do during the height of the Christmas mayhem. This integrity was what attracted me to what NYD was doing in the food world.

Christmas Eve was my last scheduled day at the shop, and walking down that cobbled street on the twenty-fourth was a bittersweet farewell. I worked until the early afternoon close at two o'clock, and I was home by four with a veritable sleigh-load of goods: the obligatory blue (I opted for Stichelton); the traditional northern England variety Lancashire, with its buttery crumble; some sharp Montgomery's Cheddar, with crystals of maturity; a hefty wedge of melty Baron Bigod; a petite wheel of gooey Tunsworth; and stinky St Cera.

"Welcome home!" Connor called from across the flat when he heard the door open, his slippered feet pitter-pattering toward me. "How was the cheese shop?" he asked as he joined me in the kitchen. Jolly as ever, I made a show of letting the cheeses spill from my backpack onto our big wooden kitchen table. I smiled with the pride of a fisherman who's just made the year's most epic catch. "Happy Christmas!"

From now on, I'll forever associate the Christmas holiday with cheese: the ripe blues in which the mold pockets are beginning to ooze with maturity and the rind provides a biscuit-y balance; whole cheddar wheels, the size of a medium

---

* Yep, just like in wine! Terroir is all the local environmental factors that influence the product, from farming practices to climate.

tom drum, freshly broken open; and the beautiful spill of a meltingly soft cow's-milk cheese onto the slate. That formative Christmas, my first that didn't involve a pilgrimage to Ohio to spend the holiday with my parents and brother, was swept up in a whirlwind of cheese.

Just as a runaway pet dog doesn't realize the agony it put its human through while it was frolicking out of sight, I was so preoccupied with my adventures at the cheese shop that I didn't stop to consider that I had essentially abandoned Connor up until the last moments of the pre-Christmas excitement. It was my first Christmas stepping out of familial tradition, and it was his, too. I had been wrapped in a cloak of self-preservation, because our dynamic had somehow evolved into the falsity that he was doing fine—his job had brought us to London, after all—and I was the one who needed to "figure it out." I was still trying to brush away the tumult of our move, and in doing so, I failed to recognize his feelings.

We shared what we were each going through as we ate the Stichelton, the Baron Bigod, and the Lancashire straight from their wrappings. That Christmas, both of us started a new chapter that put the other squarely in front of moms and dads and siblings. I like to think the cheeses acted as a binding agent between us as he wrapped me in a big bear hug and said, "I'm excited to spend Christmas with you."

Cheese is milk that has grown up.
—EDWARD BUNYARD

Stilton, the "King of English Cheeses," is as festive as mulled wine; it's synonymous with Christmas, in a quintessentially English way.

Why Christmas is closely associated with Stilton is contested. One theory is that the first big supply of cow's milk was collected on farms in the spring, and the excess was turned into this blue cheese, which was at an exemplary stage of maturation as Christmas arrived. (Other historical sources, however, suggest the initial recipes called for a longer maturation, which would void that supposition.) No one knows where the significance got its foothold. However it began, it seems like it's here to stay.

I wanted to see how this cheese is made, so after the New Year, I took the train from London up to Nottinghamshire to visit Joe Schneider and his team at Stichelton Dairy. I had met Joe at Neal's Yard Dairy, and he'd impressed upon me the magic of his work, saying, "The cool thing about a blue is it's even more transformative [than other cheeses]. The mold breaks down the fat and protein; it's what gives you that lovely creamy, buttery texture." He was right: when I tasted the *young* wheels (still in the maturation cave, not yet on the shelves at NYD), in which the mold was just beginning to develop, they were chalky, crumbly, and completely unlike the aged version. Given time, the mold transforms the entire wheel into a product I never wanted to stop eating.

What, exactly, makes blue cheese blue? It begins with the same milk as any number of other cheeses. The difference is that blue varieties (which include Stilton, Gorgonzola, Roquefort, and others) contain streaks of a fungus called *Penicillium roqueforti*, which is added to the milk at the beginning of the cheesemaking process and encouraged to flourish as the cheese ages during a step called "piercing," in which little holes are poked throughout the wheel from the bottom and top, going about two-thirds of the way through, allowing air to flow into the cheese. As maturation continues, the mold grows where oxygen has reached, and it transforms the texture and flavor of the cheese with its particular enzymes. This gradual metamorphosis may not be as instant and dazzling as coagulation,

Stichelton cheese

but it is just as dramatic—and both events display the wonders of microbes in fermentation.

You know how Champagne can be labeled as such only if it was made in the Champagne region of France? Well, Stilton also has a protected designation of origin (PDO); by law, Stilton must be produced within the borders of one of three counties in England: Leicestershire, Nottinghamshire, or Derbyshire. That's not entirely atypical as far as PDO rules go—but the other box a cheese needs to check to win the Stilton title is that the product must be made with pasteurized milk rather than raw milk.

In the United States, the Food and Drug Administration (FDA) mandated in 1987 that all milk products (domestic and imported) for human consumption must be pasteurized—with the exception of raw-milk cheese, which the FDA ruled had to be aged a minimum of sixty days to ensure that any pathogens have died out. (Individual states, additionally, may have further laws on the sale and use of raw milk.) While the FDA's law about aging unpasteurized cheeses is no hurdle for a cheese like Parmigiano Reggiano, which, by Italian law, must be made from raw milk and aged for an average of two years, it makes it hard to get an ideal Camembert or Brie in the States, because they have a short shelf life and are meant to be consumed relatively young. In the 1990s, the FDA tried to ban all raw-milk cheeses, but groups like the Cheese of Choice Coalition (now known as the Oldways Cheese Coalition) successfully lobbied to prevent this ban. In 2014, the FDA tightened its rules regarding the maximum allowable bacteria level, so even small levels of harmless bacteria can prevent a cheese from being sold in the United States.

I tried hard to objectively comprehend what my European cheesemaking colleagues told me about raw milk and weigh it against what I had grown up understanding. Banning cheeses filled with bacteria was thought necessary to keep people safe . . . except that certain bacteria—the microbes that *are* cheese—are completely harmless.

As a cheesemonger, I learned about the nuances in this debate and became accustomed to rattling off how Stilton and Stichelton use the same recipe, the raw milk in Stichelton being the distinguishing factor between the two.

The man behind Stich (as Stichelton is affectionately called) is Joe Schneider, an American who started making cheese in the Netherlands (a Turk hired him to make Greek cheese there), and then moved to England to make cheddar in Sussex in the 1980s, when British farmhouse cheese was close to extinction, as Randolph Hodgson was kicking off a cheese renaissance with the founding of Neal's Yard Dairy. Joe told me he got his motivation to make exceptional cheese from the prospect of earning a spot at NYD.

He recollected the first time he went inside the Covent Garden shop and saw "a full-sized cheddar wrapped in a cloth! A Cheshire with that orange paste!" His eyes twinkled as he told me about it, as though he were reliving the moment: "Twenty-three years ago, when I was learning how to make cheese, no one was teaching how to make good, traditional cheese. There were maybe some industrial courses. It's the same with bread bakers now—you'll probably be steered down an industrial path; food students might not even know there's another option, that a fork exists."

NYD exposed Joe to an almost forgotten way of making cheeses, showcasing wheels that used a traditional recipe, made in a particular area, by an actual *person*. "The triumvirate!" Joe exclaimed. "I'd never seen that before. You had Montgomery's Cheddar, Mrs. Kirkham's Lancashire, Appleby's Cheshire. All the parts were connected."

He paired up with Randolph Hodgson to make a Stilton the way it would have been made—with raw (unpasteurized) milk. "We're trying to make something proper, but we're not even allowed to call it a Stilton." He gave his product the old Anglo-Saxon name for the town of Stilton: Stichelton. This cheese arguably has a more nuanced flavor, because the raw milk retains elements that affect taste, like the health of the cows and their diet. "The PDO laws exist to *protect* the heritage of this product, but perversely they end up *preventing* the way it was traditionally made," Joe said.

Wait a minute, aren't laws about pasteurization there for a reason?

Yes, but it's complicated.

One of the most famous zymologists (people who study the science of fermentation) was the French scientist

Joe Schneider, Stichelton Dairy

Louis Pasteur. He proved that the growth of microorganisms is responsible for spoiling fermented beverages like milk (and wine and beer), then invented a method to prevent this spoilage—a method that later became known as pasteurization. In pasteurization, the liquid is heated to a certain temperature. (To pasteurize milk, cheesemakers heat it to 162°F/72°C for 15 seconds.) This understanding of beverage contamination led Pasteur to the realization that microorganisms can infect animals and humans, causing disease—a breakthrough that led to the use of antiseptics becoming standard in surgery, saving countless lives.

It's worth considering: if producers of raw-milk cheese follow stringent food safety requirements (and are held accountable for doing so), why regulate against it? (For the purpose of this discussion, let's distinguish between raw-milk cheese and raw milk.) Makers, academics, and lab technicians offer evidence that raw-milk cheese is not nearly as dangerous as some regulations might have you think.

Dr. Catherine Donnelly, editor of *The Oxford Companion to Cheese*, noted that Europeans tend to believe the *only* way to make high-quality cheese is to start from high-quality raw milk handled hygienically. In fact, for many European cheese appellations, the law dictates that the cheese must be made from raw milk to earn the designation. (Favorites that require raw milk are Comté, Roquefort, and, as mentioned earlier, Parmigiano Reggiano.)

In the United States, on the other hand, milk is produced and intended for pasteurization from the get-go. But this assumption of pasteurization puts milk from factory farms on the same level as milk from well-treated animals with pasture to roam; it doesn't give farmers any incentive for treating their animals humanely, because once the milk is pasteurized, it's more or less rendered equal in value. There's also the taste argument—raw-milk cheeses have layers of flavor and reflect terroir in a way that pasteurized cheeses can't. In *Ending the War on Artisan Cheese,* Donnelly writes of the untrue myths related to raw-milk cheeses and, using the current scientific understanding of microbiology, creates a compelling argument that small-scale artisan producers (like Joe) are unjustly regulated. There is a direct correlation between cheese and agriculture, and artisans want to do everything they can to show that in the finished product.

In *The Great British Cheese Book*, author Patrick Rance says that with pasteurization, there's an "encouragement to use low-quality milk" (read: from factory farming), and there is a loss of character, too, by heating the milk to the point of pasteurization. "The best hope of salvation from [cheese] monotony in the future is that research will overcome the need to pasteurize milk," Rance says. It's no wonder artisans and cheesemongers across the globe prefer raw-milk cheese. He goes on, "It is not the nature of real cheese, however well made, to be uniform." If we're talking about making things on an industrial scale, of course flavor and texture uniformity are the goal, and pasteurized milk is a must. But it's clear that a greater understanding of safety and science is needed when it comes to regulations on farmhouse cheeses.

Raw-milk controversy aside, nothing can knock Stilton from its place as the top seller at Christmastime. Colston Bassett Stilton, made in a single-story red-brick building in Nottinghamshire, has been a staple at Neal's Yard Dairy since 1979. It is an awesome cheese; I love it, and I love Stich, too—same recipe, different canvas. You should do a taste-test![*] I think it proves what I've learned: both raw-milk cheese and pasteurized cheese can be completely safe and utterly delectable when done well.

---

[*] *Both of these cheeses are available in the United States via Zingerman's.*

Stilton Scones with Cranberries

MAKES 8 SCONES

Scones are as English as Stilton. If you're American, you probably pronounce it *scoan*, like "stone." In England, it's often pronounced *scon*, like "con" (though the pronunciation varies regionally). However you say it, scones are an essential part of the afternoon-tea tradition (and also wonderful any time of day, in my opinion).

Cranberries and blue cheese are a winning combination, and especially Christmasy. Another of my favorite variations is to swap out the cranberries for 2 tablespoons of coarsely chopped hazelnuts; if you do opt for the hazelnuts, try the scones with a smear of red onion and port marmalade or another fruity jam to bring the sweet kick.

6 tablespoons (¾ stick/90 grams) unsalted butter, at room temperature, plus more for greasing

2½ cups (300 grams) all-purpose flour

¼ cup (50 grams) sugar

4 teaspoons (15 grams) baking powder

½ teaspoon fine sea salt

⅔ cup (160 milliliters) whole milk

1 large egg

2 tablespoons (about 20 grams) dried cranberries

6 ounces (180 grams) Stilton blue cheese, broken into large chunks (about 1⅓ cups)

1. Position a rack in the middle of the oven and preheat the oven to 400°F (200°C). Grease a sheet pan with a little butter.

2. In a large bowl, whisk together the flour, sugar, baking powder, and salt until well combined and lump-free.

3. Add the butter and use your fingertips to rub it into the dry ingredients until the butter is fully incorporated. The mixture should have the consistency of coarse cornmeal. Add the milk, egg, and cranberries and mix with a wooden spoon or silicone spatula until the dough comes together. Gently fold in the blue cheese chunks until just incorporated (you want those chunks to remain intact, not break down into smaller crumbs). The dough will be fairly wet.

4. Using a tablespoon, take a heaping scoop of the dough (about 2 inches/5 centimeters in diameter, a bit smaller than a tennis ball but bigger than a golf ball) and place it on the prepared sheet pan. Repeat with the rest of the dough, spacing the scoops 1 inch (2.5 centimeters) apart. (The dough spreads as it bakes, so if your pan isn't big enough to space out the scones, you'll need to use two.)

5. Bake for 5 minutes, then rotate the pan and bake for 5 minutes more. They're done when they're golden, with some browned bumps on the uneven surface. Bake for 2 to 6 minutes more, as needed.

6. Remove the pan from the oven and transfer the scones to a wire rack. (Some of the melted cheese will have escaped and gotten crispy on your baking sheet—that's the cook's treat to nibble on!) Enjoy warm or at room temperature.

Storing cheese in the freezer is not ideal, because freezing changes the protein structures within the cheese, but it is possible to freeze cheese, thaw it, and enjoy it. Hard cheeses freeze better than soft cheeses.

You can freeze these baked scones to enjoy later, a good option if you know they won't all be consumed within two days. To reduce the effects of freezing on the cheese, let the frozen scones come to room temperature, then warm them briefly in the oven before serving to evoke a "just baked" quality.

Maturing wheels of Lynher Dairies' nettle-wrapped Cornish Yarg cheese

It was a mild summer day in Central London when the taxi dropped us off at the bustling curb in front of Paddington Station during rush hour. Connor and I were with my parents, who were visiting us. We were going to the far west side of England, beyond London's urban sprawl, where the cliffs of Cornwall peer into the Atlantic Ocean. With suitcases rolling alongside and bags strapped over shoulders, we entered the train station, the towering arched ceiling stretching far above our heads, its wrought-iron ribs pointing us inward. It felt like a step back in history, and I imagined the space as it was when it was first built in 1851. We maneuvered through the station, past a candy stall with little kids begging their parents in high-pitched whines—"Please, Mum! I really want one!"—and through a group of German tourists intently watching the departures board. My family and I hoisted ourselves and our belongings into the coach car and settled in for the six-hour train ride southwest, Cornwall-bound.

Internationally, Cornwall's food scene is marked by its most popular exported item: the Cornish pasty (pronounced *past-y*, not *paste-y*). This pocket food, enjoyed by coal miners in Cornwall and the Upper Peninsula of Michigan alike, usually consists of meat or cheese wrapped in dough (like an empanada, *salteña*, or calzone).

The food I was most excited to eat in Cornwall was Cornish Yarg—a succulent semi-hard cheese wrapped and aged in *stinging nettles*. Yes, the nettle that makes you feel like a thousand minuscule needles are pricking you. (Don't fear—freezing the nettles first disarms them, making them safe to eat.)

Yarg is best enjoyed on a cheese plate with sparse accompaniments: some crackers, olives, maybe a few walnuts. It has a delicate, milky taste that can easily be overwhelmed by other flavors. Its slightly crumbly texture (crumblier in the core than near the rind) might leave some runaway bits behind on your cheese board, but I'd put my money on them not going uneaten; either you or your guests are sure to hoover up any stray morsels. It's one of those cheeses that just disappears, its mild, lactic flavor always inviting just one more bite.

The trip promised to offer a refreshing escape from reality, as vacations often do, and Cornwall provides life evasion better than most places: it is fairly hard to reach. (From London, continental Europe is more accessible than Cornwall: Paris is a two-hour train ride, whereas Cornwall requires a slower sojourn through Somerset and Devon to reach Penzance, where a rental car is a necessity to complete the journey.) Once you've reached a town like St. Ives, where we stayed, the narrow stone walkways enfold you—an atmosphere ideal for hiding from your fears, be they haunting regrets or future uncertainties. The quaint little shops with chatty owners zap you to a time before smartphones, and the epic hiking paths on the coast fill your lungs with salty fresh air as gusts blow the worries right out of your mind.

We woke bright and early most mornings (the chatty seagulls made sure of that) and spent the days walking trails. The southwestern edge of England boasts lush green landscapes with rugged cliffs, accompanied by wild moorlands that stretch across the inland landscape. My brother, Brian, couldn't join us, so it was the four of us wandering, windswept. It was the first time my parents and my partner and I had spent so much time together, and despite any anxieties going into it, it was a perfect vacation.

On the only day we didn't hike, I arranged a visit to Lynher Dairies, the lone creamery that makes Cornish Yarg. My travel cohort insisted their legs were glad of a break, but I knew they were appeasing me and my obsession with British cheese. I was grateful the dairy welcomed my family on a tour of the facilities, since the creamery didn't typically give public tours.

Lynher Dairies is a specialist cheesemaking operation, and it has the task of producing Yarg, one of the most beloved British cheeses, using a recipe that dates to 1615, which was rediscovered in the 1980s by a man named Alan Gray (*Yarg* is Gray spelled backward). Lynher Dairies, at the time of our visit, was also the reigning champion of the World Cheese Awards—an annual global event organized by the Guild of Fine Food for the past three decades, which has the ability to springboard a cheesemaker to success and acclaim. However, Lynher's winning cheese was not Cornish Yarg; they won the 2017 supreme honor with their Cornish Kern (nutty, with sweet endnotes, it's a hard Alpine-style cheese inspired by a trip to the nearby Netherlands).

We were going to see where *the world's best cheese* was made! I was giddy with excitement. It was an hour's drive from where we were staying in St. Ives to Truro, the little town marked by farmland and this award-winning creamery. By that point, I'd been in a lot of creameries, and the process of slipping on booties to cover my shoes, buttoning a white lab coat over my clothes, and stretching on a hairnet was par for the course. My parents, on the other hand, were like kids who'd won Santa's lottery and were being welcomed into the elves' workshop. They love cheese but had never seen it made. If I thought I was giddy, I was put in my place—they totally out-giddied me.

The dairy director, Dane Hopkins, guided us from room to room. I jotted notes, Connor took pictures, and my mom and dad listened and asked questions like those students who perennially sit at the front of the class, curious as ever. (It's no wonder I turned out to be a journalist.) Seeing the process through their outsiders' eyes was a real treat—they expressed an appreciation of the craft and were almost surprised it wasn't an assembly-line production. "We stay true to the recipe and to traditions and methods," Dane explained. "We don't steer away from the way it was made fifty years ago." The only machines were big metal grates that cut the curds and a pasteurization machine that used steam to sterilize raw milk.

"The minute I walked through the door of cheesemaking, I was addicted," Dane said, as he recounted his career pivot from chef to cheesemaker. He quickly found himself in a position of significance, since Lynher Dairies is one of the most successful makers of artisan cheese in Britain. The dairy processes 2 million liters of milk, handpicks over 4,000 pounds of nettle and wild garlic leaves with which to wrap some of the wheels, and produces more than 400,000 pounds of cheese a year. They employ thirty people—from herdsmen to briners, nettlers to packers. By industry standards, that puts Lynher in the small-to-medium-scale dairy bracket, so even though they make one of their country's most lauded cheeses, they sometimes struggle to stay in business.

"Our cheese regulations do nothing to protect the Real Cheesemaker or customer," writes Patrick Rance in *The Great British Cheese Book*. Rance argues that fierce pride in a product by enough people (a "tipping point" of people) is the only thing to safeguard it from demise, since licensed cheesemaking laws restrict the growth of farmhouse cheese operations, creating nearly insurmountable obstacles to scaling up. "Public clamor is necessary to preserve any rich heritage which does not conform to the convenience of mass manufacturers and sellers," he says. Even the locals in Cornwall, outstandingly proud of Cornish Yarg, couldn't save it from obscurity. The success of Yarg under Alan Gray outgrew his resources, and if Lynher Dairies had not carried it on, it would have become an extinct cheese.

We helped wrap some Cornish Yarg wheels in their nettle coats and left Truro feeling grateful such a unique and unctuous cheese had survived.

I WAS BECOMING A PROPER cheese obsessive, so after my first stint as a cheesemonger at NYD, I was reeled into the Christmas crunch the following year—this time at the shop's Borough Market location. Just as quaint outside and dreamy inside as the Covent Garden shop (but significantly less cramped), this store had the benefit of being part of Borough Market, London's most historic and popular food center.

Estelle Reynolds, one of my managers at the Borough Market shop, is half French. I asked her how she felt about working for a company that puts British cheese on such a pedestal, given that many people assume France to be the reigning royalty of the cheese realm. "I have no issue with supporting how incredible British cheese is," she said. "I mean, I grew up eating Camembert, but I didn't even have Comté until I moved to London. It's a regional cheese in France, and we only ate the popular cheeses near Bordeaux."

Whoa! Not everyone in France eats all the French cheeses all the time?

On another occasion, I met up with Brenda, a British friend of mine, in East London's Victoria Park. A lifelong Londoner, Brenda was raised in a vibrant West African community not far from where we sat, sipping our teas on a park bench. I told her I was beginning to write about my experiences with cheese in England. "Cheese in England?" she pressed. *"Why? Do cheese in France!" My point exactly.*

There's something about being a foreigner that prompts you to study a place through a hyperaware lens, like something Inspector Gadget would whip out. From the moment I arrived in London, I was in awe of the pubs, their sidewalk real estate overflowing with people in their business casual on a sunny Tuesday afternoon—folks in office clothes who couldn't let their desk jobs get in the way of the rare dose of vitamin D—of how dogs were welcomed in those pubs, and of the polite speaker announcements to "Mind the gap" in the tube stations, the houseboats along the canal, and crisp mornings in green parks. My outsider's lens also helped me appreciate the history and craft of traditional British cheeses and the emerging contemporary cheese scene, which had gone undetected by my British friend. I grinned at the prospect of convincing her.

THAT CHRISTMAS, CONNOR AND I elected to stay in Europe over the holidays, just the two of us, for our second year as transplants. I worked a shift at the cheese shop up until the twenty-third of December, and on the twenty-fourth, we flew to the far northern part of Norway.

Ironically, right before we arrived, Norway won that year's top honors at the thirty-first annual World Cheese Awards. With that, Cornish Yarg passed the baton.

Norwegian cheeses took first *and* second place and made our trip to Norway feel serendipitous. On our layover in Oslo— before we took a hopper flight up to the far north of the long, slender country—I spotted the winning cheeses in an airport shop and purchased them. The supreme champ was a Gouda-style wheel, but I was most excited to try the traditional *brun geitost* (*brunost*) for its uniqueness: it's made of cream (goat's milk or cow's milk) that's added to fresh whey and brought to a boil as soon as it's drained from the curds. The result is a brown cheese that is not particularly appealing to the eye but is richly savory on the palate. Slices as thin as a book jacket are preferred for consumption. Like Marmite—the polarizing dark brown yeast extract spread popular in England—if you use it like peanut butter and take a huge bite, you'll think you don't like it, but if you eat a thin layer on buttered toast, the odds you'll enjoy it are much higher.

We rented a cabin on the Lofoten Islands, an archipelago on Norway's northwestern coast known for its breathtaking mountain peaks emerging next to vast expanses of open sea. Of course, in December, we had twenty-three hours of darkness, so catching the sights had to be strategically planned. The sun was in the sky for forty-five minutes each day, with around a half hour of dawn and dusk to cushion the overwhelming depth of nighttime. We were subjecting ourselves to this awkward nighttime living because we were hoping to see the aurora borealis, aka the northern lights.

We landed at the teeny remote airport in northern Norway around three thirty in the afternoon on Christmas Eve and set out in the eerie darkness that is December in the Arctic Circle. It was snowing heavily, so we upgraded to a four-wheel-drive car outfitted with weather-appropriate tires and drove into the night . . . *er* . . . afternoon. Within our first few minutes on the road, we saw a moose take slow, majestic steps through the powerful gusts of wind, a blanket of white flakes gathering on its fur. *Okay, this is going to be cool.* We drove another three hours, stopping at a grocery store to load up on provisions for the week, before arriving at our cabin. Once there, we cheers'd with a shot of Norwegian aquavit, lit a fire, and cuddled up to watch *Home Alone* before drifting off to sleep.

I woke up with no idea what time it was. It was dark outside. The clouds were dense and heavy—making the sky opaque in its blackness and blocking out any glow from the moon. The wall was to my right and Connor's slumbering body was to my left in the tiny double bed. I crawled over him, his warmth emanating from below the sheets, and stumbled into the kitchen, where I had left my phone. It was eight thirty on Christmas morning.

I flipped on a lamp in the corner of the room and put logs in the wood-burning stove. Trying to be quiet, I began building the fire: I crunched the newspaper and fumbled with the matches, inadvertently clanking around as I cautiously adjusted the logs, and blew to try to spread the flame. After maybe ten minutes of

attempting this, Connor emerged from the bedroom, sleepily grumpy for having been awoken prematurely. He silently took over the fire-making duties, lighting the stove rather immediately (surely because of all the work I had done up until that point . . .) and promptly returning to bed. No "Merry Christmas!" and no warm hugs. I thought of the sunlight that would greet our families on Christmas morning, and the hot chocolate my dad would be stirring on the stovetop, and the piano notes my brother would effortlessly draw from the baby grand in the living room, and the way my mom would make the whole house smell like heaven by baking a challah wreath, and how, if I were home, they would each greet me with a colossal hug. I started to cry.

Christmas rituals are a funny, personal thing; I doubt any two families celebrate the same way. In our house, the Christmas Eve movie viewing wasn't complete without Mom falling asleep

before the credits rolled; and on Christmas morning, the presents couldn't be opened before Brian played an original song on the piano, and breakfast wasn't right without Dad toasting way too much bread and slathering it with butter. That was our house, but traditions are as varied as flavors of ice cream. I had a new family in my chosen partner, and we hadn't formed any Christmas traditions of our own yet. I slinked into the kitchen and stood over the stove, stirring hot chocolate mix into warm milk in a pitiful re-creation of my Christmas morning tradition. I'd chosen a new, decisively different path—but I keenly missed the feel of home.

That Christmas morning, I sliced the brown goat's-milk whey cheese I'd bought in Oslo and nibbled it. The dirt-colored brunost filled my mouth with enough umami kick to help me feel *something* aside from bitter abandonment and jumbled regret; my tears added salt to the mix.

Connor heard my sniffles and came out, immediately concerned and caring. He brought out a surprise Christmas gift—a journal, "for the best writer in all of London," even though we told each other the trip to Norway was our gift to each other—and enveloped me in his arms. Both gestures of kindness only made me cry harder. Change is hard, even when it's a positive step at a fitting time.

The emotional turmoil of the first couple of days dissipated as we went on epic hikes during that narrow window of daylight, although the thick clouds continued to block any hope of seeing the northern lights. We fell into a routine with a pace slower than any vacation I've been on and had little contact with other humans (it was like early practice for the COVID-19 isolation we'd experience in a couple years' time). There was the friendly older Norwegian man who had built our cabin with his own hands and would stop by every few days to drop off firewood (although he didn't speak a word of English), and there was the lack of daylight hours, which was an adjustment.

We had given up on seeing the aurora borealis; the overcast cap of clouds would hint at the display behind them, giving the entire sky a softened green glow like Emerald City behind a diffuser screen.

On our last night in Norway, the day before New Year's Eve, I used the remaining wedge of the world's best cheese in a simple potato-and-cheese casserole for a late dinner. We ate it straight from the ceramic baking dish, soaking up the remaining cheesy bits and oils with chunks of potato. We were full; we were happy. At around ten o'clock, it was as if the clouds took a cue from our spirits—they lifted. Connor peeked outside and said, "I *see* them!"

We shoved on our boots and ran through the door of the cabin. We watched the fading brushstroke of green in the sky, and kept our eyes glued there, necks craned toward the vast expanse of stars. Then another aurora appeared, bright green and forming in real time, taking shape like a serpent unspooling from the heavens. It was something like fireworks, but serene and stunning; Mother Nature

showing off. For about twenty minutes straight, we watched with rapt attention. The clouds scurried back in, as if to say, All right, move along, there's nothing to see here; but we were on a total high. We turned to walk back to the cabin, wearing smiles that grew like the auroras when our eyes locked. What a way to kick off our Christmas tradition; I guess rites of passage have their perks.

Few things are more sensual than melted cheese. The science behind it is equally seductive, and I say that as someone who was not particularly interested in science class.

Cheese doesn't "melt," in the strictest sense of the word; melting occurs when a solid crystalline structure turns into a liquid (like ice to water). What happens when you heat cheese is that the solid milkfat begins to liquefy, the protein molecules unravel, and the cheese softens. Dan Souza, editor in chief of *Cooks Illustrated*, explains it well in a video on the *America's Test Kitchen* YouTube channel: "The proteins in cheese are not generally crystalline, but rather inflexible molecules that become flexible when heated, allowing cheese to flow in much the same way plastics do." Whether it's on your tongue or in the oven, the chemical bonds that hold the proteins together break, and when they do, the structured piece of cheese collapses into a thick (and oh-so-inviting) liquid.

Multiple factors affect meltability, and two of the big ones are correlated:

moisture and age. As a cheese ages, it loses moisture, and its protein matrix becomes concentrated. Young, moist cheeses, on the other hand, have proteins (casein molecules) that hold loosely together, with lots of water between them. This means the proteins in a young cheese more readily break and liquefy when warmed up. The melting point for a young, moist cheese is around 120°F (49°C), whereas a drier, older cheese like Parmigiano Reggiano will need to be heated closer to 180°F (82°C).

Take mozzarella, a fresh, wet cheese: the bonds of the casein molecules loosen easily, and as they loosen, they get tangled up together, which is why you get those long, stringy strands. I love the image chef and writer J. Kenji López-Alt came up with for this denaturing of the protein, which he describes in his book, *The Food Lab*. He compares the cheese proteins breaking down as heat increases to spools of wire that get tangled up with each other, "forming a stable matrix and giving the cheese structure." We can thank those warm, tangled "spools of wire" for the come-hither strands falling from your forkful of mac 'n' cheese. He also points out that some cheeses "have emulsifiers added to them to ensure they melt smoothly at low temperatures without breaking. (Here's looking at you, American cheese!)"

(A DIY hack is to add cream to shredded flavorful aged cheese as you melt it, since cream contains lipoproteins that act as an emulsifier and prevent the fat from separating.)

Consider (young) cheddar as another example: even though it's a hard cheese, it melts well, because the aging process breaks down its casein proteins; with the application of heat, the caseins are prone to rupture, and the cheese flows smoothly. The difference between melted cheddar and mozzarella is in *how* it runs: in cheddar, there aren't as many protein molecules to get caught on each other as they break down—the wire spools don't get as tangled—so you don't get lengthy strands as you do with melted mozzarella.

The more mature a cheese is, the more water will have evaporated, bringing up the relative fat content and destabilizing the emulsion; when you melt an aged (sharp) cheddar, you're likely to get pools of fat because the emulsion has broken, while a younger (or milder) cheddar will melt more smoothly.

There's an exception to the young-and-moist rule when it comes to meltability, and it has to do with protein structure: some fresh, wet cheeses like feta and halloumi have such tight protein structures that they don't melt well even at high temperatures. Same with goat cheese, which has snug and clingy caseins (caused by the cheese's high proportion of lactic acid bacteria). It's hard to break those bonds, so goat cheese won't melt well. I do love lightly warming goat cheese to use in salads or other dishes—but it gets creamy, not melty.

FOR YOUR CONSIDERATION WHEN CHOOSING A GOOD MELTING CHEESE

- American Cheese*
- Brie
- Cheddar (young)
- Colby
- Comté
- Emmental
- Fontina
- Gorgonzola
- Gouda (young)
- Gruyère
- Lancashire (young)
- Mozzarella
- Provolone
- Roquefort
- Taleggio

* Debatable whether or not this qualifies as cheese, but it does melt well

Pub Mac 'n' Cheese

MAKES 6 TO 8 SERVINGS

Here is a dish inspired by a British pub hang, complete with ale and spicy, crunchy chili-flavored rice crackers, a classic bar snack. For the recipe itself, I was inspired by my friend Teresa, who makes a killer mac 'n' cheese with béchamel sauce as a base, and my buddy Izy Hossack, who suggested I add mozzarella for its alluring stringy pull. Hat-tip to Teresa for her use of cavatappi as the pasta, rather than the staid elbow noodle. Trust me, once you go cavatappi, you won't return. Its hollow, vivacious curves are ideal for holding the gooiness, and its length inspires a slurp of the cheesy goodness. (Fun fact: *Cavatappi* is the Italian word for "corkscrew.")

You start with a roux, which will be your base for the béchamel sauce (a term used whenever dairy is added to a roux), and I go an unconventional step further by adding a hefty swig of ale. The last move is to transform the béchamel into what's called a Mornay sauce by mixing in shredded cheeses: Comté, a quality cheddar, beautiful burnt-orange Red Leicester (or Colby), and some mozzarella. The nutritional yeast adds a touch of umami.

3½ tablespoons (50 grams) salted butter

⅓ cup (40 grams) all-purpose flour

¾ cup (180 milliliters) ale or lager (my favorite is Camden Town Brewery's Hells Lager)

2½ cups (600 milliliters) whole milk

Coarse sea salt, for the pasta water (see Note)

16 ounces (400 grams) dried cavatappi pasta

1 teaspoon fine sea salt

1 teaspoon freshly ground black pepper

1 teaspoon paprika

2 cups (200 grams) shredded Comté cheese

2 cups (200 grams) shredded good-quality cheddar cheese

2 cups (200 grams) shredded Red Leicester cheese (or Colby or Prairie Sunset)

1½ cups (150 grams) shredded mozzarella cheese

¼ cup (15 grams) nutritional yeast or grated Parmigiano Reggiano cheese

Sweet chili rice crackers or chips/crisps, or other crunchy sweet chili–flavored items, for topping

1. Position a rack in the middle of the oven and preheat the oven to 350°F (175°C).
2. Melt the butter in a wide pan over medium heat. Whisk in the flour to form a paste and cook, stirring, for 1 minute as the paste begins to bubble. (This is called a white roux because it doesn't cook further and get brown and toasted.) Whisk in the ale, then, after about 30 seconds, add the milk. Bring to a simmer, stirring, then reduce the heat to low and cook, stirring occasionally to lift anything sticking to the bottom of the pan, for 15 minutes.
3. Meanwhile, fill a large pot three-quarters full of water and bring it to a boil over medium-high heat. Add a generous amount

(recipe continues)

of coarse sea salt (the adage "It should taste like the sea" is a good gauge of how much). Add the cavatappi and cook according to the package instructions until al dente (typically around 7 minutes). Drain the pasta in a colander and briefly rinse it under cold water to halt the cooking.

4. Add the fine sea salt, pepper, and paprika to the béchamel sauce and stir until well combined. Add the Comté, cheddar, Red Leicester, and mozzarella cheeses and the nutritional yeast. Stir until all the cheeses have melted and everything is well combined.

5. Add the cooked pasta to the sauce and stir to coat, then transfer the mixture to a 9 x 13-inch (23 x 33-centimeter) casserole dish. Bake for about 10 minutes; you'll know it's ready when the cheesy pasta has begun to get golden brown in some places and the sauce is bubbling. Remove from the oven and let sit for 5 minutes to cool slightly.

6. While the cheesy pasta cools, put a handful of rice crackers in a zip-top bag and smash them with a rolling pin to break them into small chunks. Sprinkle the crushed rice crackers evenly over the top of the cheesy pasta and tuck in!

Note: In the Wine section, I note that in Italy, cooks swear by using coarse sea salt to salt their pasta water. That's the direction I give for cooking all the pasta in the next section, so for consistency I have suggested using coarse sea salt here, too.

I rode the train to Bath, two hours southwest of London, then hailed a cab and rode twenty minutes into the countryside to a Somerset property called Sleight Farm. I rose out of the car to open the entrance gate, stepped over nettles as I walked from the gate to the side of the driveway, and peered at the gravel path leading up a green and rather daunting hill, then curving out of sight.

I motioned the cab through and walked the gate shut and latched it behind me. I pulled up my sunglasses and craned my neck to see the top of the hill. *Nothing.* A half dozen cows staring at me, their lower jaws working diligently on the grass they munched. (I could've sworn a few of them stopped chewing entirely and gawked at me with their jaws flopped open, like, *What's this city slicker doing out here?* But I may have been mistaken.) I returned the sunglasses to my nose and ducked back into the car, hiding from the curious bovines like a celebrity evading the paparazzi.

Half a mile up the hill, a stately old stone home came into view, perched regally atop the plateau. I couldn't take my eyes off this quintessentially English countryside abode, with its white trim and four powerful stone chimneys. As I stepped out of the car, I turned to take in the view *from* the home: we were in the clouds above Somerset. I could have leaned from a hot-air balloon and caught the same frame—the pastures, with animals leisurely wandering; the narrow road of the local high street; and the couplets of

Above: *My favorite morning walk from Sleight Farm; opposite: The side entrance to the farmhouse, often "guarded" by these two gregarious and affectionate barn cats*

trees that dotted the landscape. (Now *I* was the one standing slack-jawed. Sorry for picking on you, cows.)

As I turned and made my way to the house, I was confronted by my reason for being here: two young goats ran past me, then doubled around, ricocheting off the side of the barn next door as they frolicked about and caused a ruckus. (Teenagers are all the same, regardless of their species.) *Oh yeah . . . I'm here because of the goats!* I would stay in that regal stone house for the next couple of weeks, and I'd be in that barn every morning by seven moving buckets of goat's milk, to make goat's-milk cheese.

JUST INSIDE THE FRONT DOOR OF THE BIG stone farmhouse, through a little mudroom filled with sodden boots and mismatched slippers, was the kitchen.

Catherine Ochiltree ushered me in; she had recently taken over the farm from the late Mary Holbrook (the "reluctant guru of goat's cheese," per the *Guardian*), and was in touch with Bronwen Percival, who had called on me to help during the dairy's transition of ownership.

It was the midmorning tea break—a ritual I came to love. After the first of the morning's work was done, everyone gathered in the kitchen, and a flurry of activity and conversation ensued—arms reaching over each other for the butter, plates clattering as fresh toast was tossed onto them, hands fumbling with the Marmite lid. And at the center of the table: a big jug of fresh goat's milk that everyone added to their black tea.

My eye went straight to James, the groundskeeper and general handyperson, because he was wearing a bright yellow coat that you could see from outer space. He pulled out a wooden chair at the table for me—"Welcome to the 'ouse!" Across the table was Kay, who milked the goats and cared for the livestock on the farm—not just the goats, but pigs and cows, too. Ever understated, she nodded at me as a welcome. Beside her was Debbie, one of the cheesemakers, who also did the milking on weekends when Kay had off. Charley, Kay's fiancé who helped out on the farm as needed, said hello, then introduced me to Kay's daughter, Emily, who sat at the end of the table. Thirteen years old and seeming shy, she stirred another spoonful of sugar into her mug of instant coffee. "Hello," she said, barely glancing up.

"Katie will be helping us the next couple of weeks," Catherine said. "She's American but lives in London. She's been working with Neal's Yard Dairy! We love them, don't we?" She glanced around the room for consensus. "I don't know how we could've carried on after Mary without them."

"Did you just move from 'merica?" James asked.

"Actually, no." I shifted in my seat. "It's been two years! I've worked at Neal's Yard Dairy the past two Decembers. Kind of crazy how time flies."

"Oh, you've been here for yonks!" Charley exclaimed.

Yonks? Everyone at the table, aside from Catherine, was local and spoke in what's known as West Country English. (The West Country comprises the counties of Cornwall, Devonshire, Dorset, Gloucestershire, Hampshire, Somerset—where I was—and Wiltshire.) My London friends amicably picked on the dialect as though it were a linguistic dunce. It wasn't until I got to rural Somerset and heard sentences like "Ee bist gert!" (meaning, when spoken to a goat kid, "You're big!") and "I don' want to be fanny-assin' about" (in reference to doing unproductive work in the washing-up room) that I understood the depth of regional dialects. Sure, we all spoke English, but I practically needed flash cards for the new words I was learning: *yonks* = a long time; *gert* = big; *spuddling* = arguing; *Alright, me 'ansum?* = Hi, how are you?

Debbie Sullivan, cheesemaker

Every day the cast of characters rotated—James and Charley would pop in as needed, Kay was a weekday stalwart, Teresa came through twice a week, Millie and Leen tag-teamed cheesemaking duties with Debbie. Everyone had taken a different path to Sleight Farm. Teresa used to work in the corporate world but traded it in to join her husband's family's farm down the road, and Millie, who was my age, had left a marketing career in London and was newly smitten with the art of cheesemaking. Leen was another injection of youth, a Belgian woman in her thirties who had ascended to the role of head cheesemaker at Sleight Farm; my arrival overlapped with her departure, and the hope was that I could help until a new head cheesemaker stepped in.

There had been a lot of transition at the farm before my arrival. No one could fill the big shoes left by Mary Holbrook, a titan in England's farmhouse cheesemaking scene who had built a loyal following for her handmade goat's-milk cheeses. She had passed away rather suddenly a few months prior, in February, as the goats were swelling with life, about to give birth to the first kids of the year.

Everyone was trying desperately to occupy the gaping void. Each person on the team had deeply admired Mary, and everyone wanted to continue her legacy. She had been a one-woman operation, keeping her genius in her head and training her helpers only enough to get the job done, not teaching them her craft. This secrecy, whether purposeful or not, made continuing her work an uphill battle.

As the goats gave birth and started to lactate, Leen pored over Mary's daily cheese diary, trying to decode her scribbles and make a recipe of sorts from the notes. She had worked side by side with Mary, but that could only help so much. Miraculously, Sleight Farm made new batches of Mary's cheeses—without Mary—and by the time I arrived, the whole motley crew was determined to continue this cheesemaking operation.

There were about 130 goats on the farm (a mix of breeds—Alpines, Saanens, Boers, Nubians), which supplied all the milk used to make an assortment of raw-milk cheeses:

- TYMSBORO—a mold-covered pyramid shape about the size of a tumbler glass, and the lauded favorite
- OLD FORD—a hard, matured wheel, floral and silky when young, briny and crystalline when aged
- SLEIGHTLETT—a fresh cheese disc meant to be eaten within days of being made; brightly acidic and lightly tapped with salty charcoal
- CARDO—a semi-soft washed-rind wheel (inspired by the Portuguese Serra da Estrela) that uses cardoons (also known as artichoke thistle) for their enzymatic properties to coagulate the milk (the other cheeses use animal rennet); the savory rind gives way to a creamy interior with a chalky center

NYD sold them all, so I knew their goaty taste well, and I couldn't wait to be a part of creating them. I was to report for duty at seven the next morning.

MY BODY STIFFENED AS I LAY IN THE single bed, my long legs peeking over the end of the mattress, nudged out from under the sheets. *Did I hear something?* I blinked my eyes open to see the motion-sensor lights outside the window clicking on, clicking off, clicking on. *Who's there?* The lights clicked off. The moon was a thin sliver and I couldn't see anything outside; it felt like a heavy cloak had descended over the world—it was truly pitch black. I was in an old farmhouse at the top of a hill in the countryside, and in my paranoid state, I thought an intruder—twitching with psychotic energy and maybe dragging a bum leg behind him—may have stalked up the long driveway, knowing (perhaps having heard through the town grapevine?) that I was alone here with only one other woman, on the other side of the house.

Then I heard a *thump!* of metal hitting the pebbled walkway, and as my heart jumped out of my chest, I ran to the window to look, prepared to witness a burglar (who might resemble Joe Pesci in *Home Alone*) cursing after stubbing his toe. Instead, I saw one of the farm cats slinking around a pile of lawn equipment. *Not a countryside creep, Katie . . . just a cat.* Take a city girl to the country, and

illogical fears will quickly overrule her common sense.

My first week on the farm, I helped out in any way I could, tripping over myself to be of use. In my eagerness to help in *and* out of the cheese room, I was spending a fair amount of time with the goats. After my cheese shift ended, I'd ask Kay or Debbie, whoever was milking and caring for the goats that day, how I could help. It was early April and kids were being born daily, so the late afternoon usually involved a newborn kid pooping on me. *Ew.* I clenched my teeth and held back a gag reflex every time.

One day, after I had wiped the daily poop off my trousers with some hay, I asked Debbie how *else* I could help.

"Get that bucket there, the one with some water in it, empty it and fill it with water from the trough here," she directed over her shoulder, gesturing with one hand as she juggled milking gear in the other.

I grabbed the bucket. "This one?" I stammered, aware of my poop-stained fingers and being out of my comfort zone. I hoisted the bucket toward the trough and poured the dirty water into the pool of clean water.

Debbie looked back in time to witness my flustered faux pas. "No, you ninny!"

Welcome to farm life, city girl.

"That *was* the clean water," Debbie said, turning her back on me to finish whatever task she was doing. "Well, fill it up," she said resignedly, unable to expend another ounce of energy on my *helpfulness*. I was sure she'd never trust me to do anything right.

Debbie was a no-nonsense person. She didn't gossip, she never complained; she just did the work she loved. I've never seen anyone as happy at a job as Debbie was when she was making cheese. Once the morning's fresh milk came in and the curd was set, she would be giddy as a schoolgirl. "Ooh, I love making cheese!" she'd say to herself in a singsong tone, the last syllable a high note in her little celebration jingle. I came to look forward to our time together in the cheese room, just she and I. I wore her down; she came to trust me, even after the dirty water incident.

The other women—we were all female, a relative rarity in contemporary cheesemaking—were also lovely and kind and passionate about cheesemaking, but there had been a fair amount of confusion and overall dysfunction since Mary's passing, so the room could quickly be transformed into the Red Tent. The artisan cheesemaking process offers prime conditions for gossip, because certain

elements were downright monotonous: ladling scoop after scoop of curd into small containers, which slowly, continuously drain all day long, then ladling additional curd on top every few hours as the whey flows out and the curds compact. While we worked, we talked. Some of the women were justifiably concerned with the new direction of the farm, and let their opinions be known. I was immediately engulfed in the drama, wide-eyed, impressionable newbie that I was.

The cheese room was different when only Debbie and I worked in it. She regaled me with stories from her days as a chef in London and her stint as a veterinarian. "Whoa," I noted, "cheesemaking and caring for the goats is like the perfect combination of your past lives!"

"I'm finally doing the thing I love," she said quietly, gratefully.

I've heard that chefs make the best cheesemakers; they're less prone to follow a script, more likely to improvise. The thought is that a good chef will bring a certain intuition to cheesemaking, as Debbie most definitely did. "Cheesemaking is a craft, not a science," reads a quotation by biochemist Dr. J. G. Davis in *The Great British Cheese Book*. "Whenever in cheesemaking the scientific test results and the judgement of the cheesemaker are at variance, he should always rely on his judgement."

Both Debbie's and my favorite cheese to make was Cardo. It required filling a large vat with fresh raw milk, warming it a bit (to 84.2°F/29°C—it was already warm from the goat), then adding some whey drained from the prior day's curd for its lactic acid bacteria (a practice called backslopping); we would sometimes add starter culture, too, for insurance. (The previous day's whey would hypothetically be enough to inoculate the milk with our microbe friends, but a small amount of added starter ensures the job gets done.)

Then we used cardoons (*Cynara cardunculus*) to set the curd. Cardoons, an edible plant from the same family as the globe artichoke, produce violet flowers—we only had use for the flowers' bright purple stamens, which were like a pile of soft, colorful needles. The cardoon stamens arrived at the farm pre-dismantled and dried; all we had to do was process them into smaller bits. When Debbie first showed me how to weigh and process them—we wanted the resulting texture to be something between a rustling pile of dried flora and a true powder—she poured it onto a seemingly random plastic lid. "It's got to be measured on this. We don't know why; it's what Mary said, so that's what we do." She wrapped the processed cardoons in a cloth and soaked them in hot water, like a tea bag. This cardoon juice—which contained the enzymes we needed for coagulation—was then added to the milk. Again, Debbie used specific, oddball pieces of equipment to do the job. "It's all very technical," she said, voice oozing with sarcasm.

We cleaned up and took our tea break; two hours later, we checked in on the "flocculation" of the curd—the indication that groups of protein micelles have joined. After thoroughly washing our hands,

we'd do the finger test to assess the curd, inserting one finger (usually the pointer finger) faceup into the curd, then slowly lifting. If Debbie wasn't satisfied with how cleanly the curd cut open, we waited until she deemed it ready, anywhere from two to three hours after we'd set the curd. When that time arrived—the quintessential moment in cheesemaking—it was *go time*, and we would prepare for the next step. *The best step.* The reason Cardo was our favorite cheese to make . . .

When it was time, Debbie and I would roll up our sleeves—or shed a layer of clothing entirely—and sink our hands gently into the soft, warm curd. Deeper we would go, until not only our hands, but our wrists, then our forearms were engulfed in the bath-temperature whey and silky curds; it felt like diving into a silk cloud under the ocean. We were breaking the curd and the whey apart, and to reach all corners of the vat, we would go farther— immersing our arms nearly up to our armpits. *My curd baptism*, was how I came to think of it. The room was silent aside from the spa-like *whoosh* of the whey in the tank.

If my movements sped up, Debbie would remind me to slow down—"Calmly, Katie." She was in a meditative state. We would continue breaking the curds into smaller and smaller pieces—we'd lift the chunks into the air on our palms, letting them fall apart into yet tinier pieces as they dropped back into the whey. Debbie instructed me to never make a fist around the curds, which would squish them, but to let gravity do the work; I was to apply gentle pressure only when necessary.

After we separated the curds into approximately pea-size pieces for Cardo (the curds needed to be slightly different sizes depending on which cheese they would become; larger curds were used for making Old Ford, for instance), we moved the curds out of the vat, lifting them from the bath of whey into their final molds. This had to happen speedily, as the curds naturally wanted to knit together; curds are communal, and they begin to unite within minutes. As in many steps in cheesemaking, this one reminded me to quiet my mind and work efficiently. A good cheesemaker needs finesse over haste.

Debbie would immerse a basket, about the size of a pint container for strawberries, into the whey, then sweep it out, bulging full of curds, patiently letting whey drip from the basket's draining holes before tumbling the curds into perforated circular plastic molds the size of a Frisbee. She moved with ease and dignity.

She maintained that same dignity in

After the curd has set, we break it into smaller pieces with our hands.

conversations about the uncertainty at the farm. I'd tell her about some high-octane histrionics at the farmhouse the evening prior and all she would say was "Well, that would explain why the goats were in a foul mood this morning."

I BECAME CONFIDENT IN MY NEW ROLE, moving with celerity in the cheese room and handling the goats without hesitation. I prepared the cardoons for Cardo like a chef preparing her signature dish and flipped freshly set Sleightletts, in their small round plastic molds, with agile fingertips. I hip-checked goats that got in my way when my hands were full.

When I wasn't contemplating milk or getting accustomed to the quirky personalities of the goats (I came to see them like the dogs I grew up with—playful and prone to nuzzle), I was sticking my nose in one of Mary's old books or wandering the countryside around the town. The mild weather and gorgeous surroundings called me to lace up my hiking boots and set out by foot (also necessary, as I didn't have a car).

After a couple of years of living in England, I had fallen in love with it—and the tumbling hills and dirt paths that made a web of public walkways through every county were one of my favorite things about it. Connor and I would choose long-weekend getaways knowing we'd spend most of our time rambling these routes. *Rambling* is the official term—in 1931, a group of walkers, believing that rambling in the countryside was a right and an activity that benefited the whole of

society, organized to create the National Council of Ramblers Federations, and founded the first Ramblers Association in 1935. They successfully campaigned for legislation to protect this interest—regardless of wealthy landowners' private-estate concerns—resulting in the passage of the National Parks and Access to the Countryside Act in 1949 and the Countryside and Rights of Way Act in 2000. As Americans accustomed to private property laws, Connor and I were wide-eyed at the existence of these laws, but enthusiastically grateful, because they exponentially increased our appreciation of the beauty of this fine country.

Goat cuddles on Sleight Farm

There was a public path that cut through the farm, so at any time of day, you could look out the cheese room window and see strangers—some tourists, some local folk—wearing cargo shorts and carrying hiking sticks, whistling as they walked through this curious goat farm on a hill, just one sight as they followed the winding path through various fields, farms, village sidewalks, and pub stops. The daily ramblers trekking through the farm provided entertaining people-watching moments sprinkled throughout the day, and were a reminder of life beyond the farm.

Another help in not taking things too seriously was the teenager I mentioned, Emily, who was on her weeklong Easter school holiday for a portion of my time in Somerset and spent twelve hours a day at the farm. Even when school was in session,

she came by after class let out. Emily was the daughter of Kay, the quiet woman who milked the goats most days of the week. Perhaps that's why I assumed Emily would be shy, too. (One of the first clues I had that Emily wasn't the timid teen I had assumed her to be was when she pointed at the wooden rocker where I had just placed my bum and told me, "That's the chair Mary died in." I never sat there again.) I'm not around kids often, but Emily and I became fast friends—both of us outliers in the farm's crew.

Emily was capable of doing it all, and knew more about goats and the farm than anyone. She'd grown up there; Mary Holbrook had been like an aunt to her. She showed me how to create a bath of mud and feces for the pigs to happily wallow in. She loved the goats like you love your golden retriever, and helped nurse weak kids, swaddling them in blankets and heating up their milk, diligently keeping a timetable of their feeding schedule.

I told her all about Connor, and I knew she was excited to meet him. He planned to come visit over Easter weekend.

"I'll show him around the farm!" she offered.

"Yes, definitely—he needs the special Emily treatment."

He arrived late one evening, having driven a rental car in the height of rush hour to Somerset straight from work in Central London. I had the following day off from my cheesemaking responsibilities, and I couldn't wait to sleep in and awaken leisurely in his embrace. I missed him, but I had been so invested in the farm and overwhelmed by my time there that my life with Connor felt like an alternate universe. In his arms, no words spoken, I remembered. Goat cuddles are great—but they can't compare.

The next morning when I blinked my eyes open a thin sliver, I saw the sun's glow was still soft and pale as it poured into the room. Even when my alarm wasn't set for six, my body woke me up. Knowing I would sooner rather than later start to wiggle with energy to embark on my day, I climbed out of bed to use the loo and let Connor sleep.

As I filled the kettle in the kitchen, it was just before seven; Kay would be on her way to start the day's milking. Emily burst in, full of an energy usually reserved for a giggly sugar-fueled afternoon tea break.

"*Good* morning!" she chimed. "Where's Connor?"

"He's still asleep."

"Lazy!" she shouted loud enough to get through the next room and up through the floorboards into our bedroom.

"Shh. Let him sleep, he drove four hours last night to get here."

"Fine."

I poured Emily a mug of hot water and she stirred in a spoonful of instant coffee, followed by her usual four teaspoons of sugar.

"I've got to catch up on work, so I'll be on my laptop. You can hang around if you want, but seriously, I have to do work," I told her. I could tell this would be a tricky feat; Emily was in chatty mode.

"No problem!"

We walked our coffees into the next room and plopped down on two perpendicularly aligned couches. I cracked open my laptop, but before I had even extended it to its fully open position, Emily yelled, "*Connor!* Wake up, lazy!"

"Emily! Leave him alone!"

"Fine. What are you working on?"

"Mostly emails. Ever since I've been here, I've basically ignored my inbox."

"Oh, poor inbox," she chuckled, her pudgy face twisting into a bigger smile as a loud fart vibrated the couch.

"Emily!" I couldn't help but laugh.

"*Doorknob!*"

"Wait, what?"

"You don't know 'doorknob'?!" she asked in disbelief. "If you fart you have to say 'safety,' and if you smell it, then you say 'doorknob,' and you can hit the person."

Going for a stroll around the farm with Emily

"But you farted—why did you say doorknob?"

She bounded over to the couch I was sitting on. "'Cause I was gonna punch *you*!" She tapped my shoulder with her fist. "For fun!"

"Silly. You know, whoever smelt it dealt it," I said.

"Yeah, whatever. *Connor! Wake up!* Your girlfriend is farting down here!"

"Emily is!" I shouted. Two could play at that game. "And it's *wife*, thank you very much."

We smirked at each other as a voice wafted down from upstairs "Hi . . . I'm up . . ."

When I went up (without Emily) to greet him and apologize for the early wake-up call, he said, "I feel like I'm in a college dorm."

Spot-on. The farmhouse felt like that at times: there wasn't a lot of privacy, and people were constantly roving in and out.

"Are you making babies?" Emily shouted. "Boy or girl?"

The pigs at Sleight Farm; they enjoyed leftover whey from cheesemaking and this Somerset vista

ONE EVENING, AFTER I HAD WRAPPED UP my duties for the day but before Emily's mom had finished hers, Emily and I took a walk around the farm's land. On the far field, where there was no civilization within a twenty-minute radius of where we stood, we stumbled upon a goat that had just given birth to two kids. I mean, it had *just* happened; there was still a mess around the mom's private parts, a goopy fluid leaking from her enlarged lil' goat vagina, and the kids barely had control over their too-long legs. Emily jumped into action immediately. "We need to get them to the barn," she said, certainty and determination in her voice.

"Why? Shouldn't we let them rest?"

"No, they're in danger this far from the rest of the group, and far from the farm. It'll be dusk in a couple hours and they won't make it through the night; they'll get eaten," she explained, as she bent down and picked up both kids in one fell swoop, one in each arm.

"Okay, how can I help?"

She began delegating like a little executive. "Take him"—she lifted the kid cradled in her right arm toward me—"and I'll get the mom to move." She adjusted her energy to that of happy excitement. "Come on, girl! Follow us!" Then to me, her voice returning to a lower tone, "Let's move. As long as we have her kids, she'll come." She was all business.

I cradled the kid as we began our march, making as close to a direct line as we could through the field back to the barn. We needed to cross through two expansive gated plots of land to get there. The kids whined as we walked away from their mom, because the comfort of her uterus was getting farther away by the second. My heart broke for them. "Should we be taking them away from their mom at this point?" I needed reconfirmation.

"Yes, Katie. Trust me." She was probably a little annoyed. "Keep him warm, make sure he's comfortable."

I felt the little guy's chest expanding against mine as he breathed, and I felt his huge heartbeat smashing into the sides of his ribs. *Nervous fella*. Mom was tailing us closely. Within a minute, the kids stopped whining. We made it through the fences separating the fields and got closer to our destination. Emily herded the mom ahead of us as we approached the barn, and when we reached the plot of land opposite, she abruptly halted and said, "Let's stop. Katie—stop here."

"But we're so close to the barn!" I retorted.

"They need to go with their mom." She quieted her voice and plopped the snow-white kid she was holding on the grass near the mamma goat. I followed her example with my black-haired boy.

As we turned around to covertly walk away, my goat started running back toward me (it was more of a stumble gait, but you know he would've run if he could've).

"No, go to your mom!" I commanded as I continued moving farther away.

"He thinks you're his mom now," Emily said.

"What?"

"He felt your heartbeat."

Mammals are amazing.

She swept him up and put him down close to his mom again. This time, mamma intercepted our efforts and put her nose to his, sniffing up and down his body, then doing the same with the white kid. She shoved her swollen udders near them, but they had trouble latching on.

"They'll learn," Emily said.

They were a happy little family again, and I was in awe of my young goat-whisperer friend.

Mary Holbrook, the woman who ran Sleight Farm until her untimely death, had the mystery and charisma that drew in loyal customers like goats to thistles, and built a legacy that won't be forgotten anytime soon. I knew about her when I was behind the slate as a cheesemonger at Neal's Yard Dairy—her name evoked the respect of a saint in the hallowed halls of the cheese shop. My NYD colleague Bronwen Percival knew Mary well, saying, "Mary had a *mystique*."

I had always wanted to meet this woman, whose approach to life was simple: she knew best. I'm intrigued by people with that kind of confidence. She never chased business—she let customers come to her, which of course only increased her allure. Her reputation stood on the pillars of *Mary is an artist* and *Mary listens to her intuition*. Slightly aloof and singularly focused, she became a lauded figure in England's farmhouse cheese world, recapturing the art of cheesemaking as a woman's game.

In England, cheesemaking was historically the duty of the women of the farm. In fact, the word *dairy* comes from the Old English word *daie*, which means "female servant," referencing the woman's role as dairy handler. (I have dubbed these women Milkmaid Power Mammas.) One of the elements that gives British territorial cheeses their characteristic crumbliness is the result of a schedule organized around family life: *Milk the cows and set the curd; leave for a couple of hours to make food for the family. Return to stir and drain; go do the sewing and washing in the home*, and so on.

The tradition of women as cheesemakers traversed the ocean when some Brits left the island for the newly colonized land that would become the United States. The role of women in cheesemaking dates back to the earliest days of the States, too, when it was a woman's duty to perform tasks like milking, churning butter, and, yes, making cheese, while the men were out sowing the fields. It was only later, after the world wars, that cheese became industrialized big business and men stepped in and pushed women out of a field that had previously been their specialty. *Go figure.*

But there are female cheesemakers—like Mary—who have kept the tradition alive. While Mary was an advocate for goats, a British woman named Olivia Mills found her calling with sheep: in the 1980s, she started the British Sheep Dairy Association and wrote the book *Practical Sheep Dairying*, which inspired a fivefold increase in the number of farms making ewe's-milk cheese in the following decade (and has sold in every country in the world where sheep are milked).

So many of my favorite cheeses are made by women that it feels silly to say that cheesemaking *was* a women's game. In recent history in the UK, Lucy Appleby of Appleby's Cheshire and Ruth Kirkham of Kirkham's Lancashire have made remarkable British territorial cheeses (their kin have now taken over their respective businesses).

Here are just a few female cheesemakers on the British Isles who, at the time of this writing, produce my top picks:

- Stacey Hedges and Charlotte Spruce teamed up in Hampshire to make creamy Camembert-style cow's-milk Tunworth (*adore!*) and smaller wheels of Winslade, wrapped in a spruce band.
- Siobhán Ní Ghairbhith makes St Tola, a creamy goat's-milk cheese with hints of citrus, in Ireland.
- Mary Quicke makes traditional clothbound cheddar on Home Farm in Devon; she's the fourteenth generation of Quickes on the farm.
- Carrie Rimes produces Brefu Bach, a small, soft, cylindrical sheep's-milk cheese, in northwest Wales.
- Rachel Yarrow (with her husband, Fraser Norton) makes Sinodun Hill, a goat's-milk yogurt cheese, in Oxfordshire.
- Julie Cheyney makes the soft cow's-milk St Jude and its Époisses-style washed-rind sister, St Cera, in Suffolk.

I could write another book about all the women in the industry I have come to admire. In fact, there's a whole new wave of women enthusiastically entering the cheese scene. The craft of cheesemaking isn't necessarily passed down from mother to daughter in the farmhouse as it was in past generations. But there are still "cheese Jedis, and they reach out to the Padawans like us; they teach us and train us," said one young cheesemaker I spoke with, Ashley Morton, playfully using Star Wars terminology to refer to the mentors (women and men both) who have guided her career in cheese.

"Cheese saved my life," Ashley told me earnestly when we met. Like me, she was an American who followed her passion across the Atlantic. Originally from Harlem, New York City, Ashley was attending the University of North Carolina at Chapel Hill when she hit a roadblock. No longer certain that she wanted to continue her studies in the sciences and medicine, she decided to take a (rather serendipitous) break from school and move back home. It was during this hiatus that she interviewed for a job at Murray's Cheese, the iconic Manhattan cheese shop on Bleecker Street in Greenwich Village.

"I didn't even know there was such a thing as a 'high-end cheese shop,'" she said, laughing, remembering the first time she walked into Murray's. "I grew up middle class, and the cheeses I ate were deli-style, sliced, and only used in sandwiches. The fact that cheese could be stinky—literally!—or super aged, like a Comté, didn't even exist to me."

Her day job at Murray's opened her eyes to artisan cheese, and the many varieties therein—"It was like being in Willy Wonka's chocolate factory, but with cheese!"—and her job turned into an obsession. When she reenrolled in classes at UNC, she also began working at the nearby Chapel Hill Creamery under the

tutelage of the two women who founded it, Portia McKnight and Flo Hawley. There, Ashley began making cheese with milk from their small herd of Jersey cows. "Portia and Flo taught me a lot about what it's like to be on a farm, to feel connected to the animals and the land. They also showed me the care and precision of cheesemaking, and the creativity!" She attributes much of the direction of her career to their mentorship.

She was enraptured by the cheeses she learned about from the UK, France, Italy, the Netherlands, and beyond, but "living in Europe was a far-off fantasy," until she saw an opportunity to move to France (where her grandmother was born). She surprised her family (and even herself!) by crossing the ocean and paving her own path in the industry, dubbing herself "Brieyoncé, the Cheese Maven," and doing consulting and education work from Paris.

"You know, no one expected me to go down this route, but my parents encouraged me to be curious and do anything I wanted to. Sometimes you just have a hunch, follow your instincts, and then magic happens," Ashley says. She'd like to explore cheeses throughout Europe, maybe moving to Switzerland or even the UK. "Visiting Neal's Yard Dairy was like a pilgrimage for me! And I took the train to Devon and stayed with Mary Quicke to see her cheddar-making operation," yet another example of "women who carry the torch and lead the way."

A high priority for Ashley is making cheese accessible for everyone: for people in the shoes she was once in, lacking

Mary Quicke of Quicke's Cheese

an awareness about quality cheeses and feeling intimidated by approaching a cheese counter. To those people, she says, "Take a deep breath—it's just cheese. Relax, and let these people [the cheesemongers] help you out; that's what they're here for." Above all, she hopes people remember that cheese is supposed to be a joy. If Ashley represents the next generation of the cheese industry, it's going in a great direction.

ONE SIMILARITY AMONG ALL THE WOMEN cheesemakers and cheesemongers I've met is that they all seem to have found the path to cheese via an entirely unique and unexpected course.

Mary Holbrook was no exception. She had a PhD in ancient history and archaeology, and she traveled around the world, working on projects like cataloging early scientific instruments in Frankfurt, Germany. Hardly the typical life of a farmhouse spouse. (Her husband, John, was also an academic—a biochemistry professor.)

She started experimenting with cheesemaking later in life, when she and John moved to his family farm, Sleight Farm, in 1967. In the 1970s Mary bought some goats and, uninspired by her role as a museum curator in nearby Bath, began making cheese. Next, she put on her business hat and scaled up.

She was a keen entrepreneur, although money didn't compel her. "She was audited a few times, and they couldn't see that there was any profit motive for her business," Bronwen told me, "but it gave her meaning and something to do and care about. I think it kept her young. At the end of the day, she had enough to pay her bills, so she did what made her happy. People were drawn to her, because really, how many people like Mary are out there? *So* few."

Although she was an academic, she managed to stop short of overanalyzing her cheese. Leen, the cheesemaker at the helm when I first arrived at Sleight Farm, had worked with Mary, and she remembered, "Mary was instinctive with how she treated the cheese. She paid attention, and it's all about attention with cheesemaking. That's what I learned from Mary. It's like cooking in that way." As Leen and I sat together at the long dinner table in Mary's kitchen, she recalled, "Mary followed her own path, which is what you have to do to make good cheese."

"And 'her path' was nonnegotiable?" I asked.

"Oh yes. Mary would never be wrong. But I get it—it's like being a parent: you need to stick to your values regardless of what your kids do. Where I'm from in Belgium, they are more scientific about cheesemaking. They don't know what Mary knew—to look closely, to touch and taste and rely on intuition. That's where the magic is."

Mary rarely, if ever, offered praise, Leen told me, but observing her was a lesson unto itself. Lucky for me, Leen was happy to dole out kind words for a job well done and was forthcoming with what she knew. When I was ladling the curd, she'd coach me: "It's important to cut, not scrape, the curd. It's not ice cream. It's the flick of the wrist. That's it! Great."

Equally kind in the cheese room was Teresa—she had made the hard, aged Old Ford cheese with Mary and stepped up to lead the making of it after Mary's death. When I was bent over the vat with Teresa, she would ponder the best time to add hot water to the curds, "washing" them, as is done when making a cheese like Gouda. (Ever the curious traveler, Mary was shown this hot-water method of warming the curd on a trip to Sicily, where the Italian cheese Provola dei Nebrodi is made in this way.)

"Mary would say, 'Now is the time,' but wouldn't explain why. So this part is a bit of a guessing game," Teresa said as we looked down at the vat of just-flocculated curd. She had huge admiration for the way Mary made cheese. "This is the stage when many other cheesemakers or cheese operations would use a metal harp or put metal strings through it," she said as she pushed her T-shirt sleeves up on her shoulder, "but we use our hands, our bare arms."

She wanted to do Mary's legacy justice. She wanted to continue the work her cheese guru had begun, even though much of it was a guessing game.

The future of the dairy was uncertain while I was there. Everyone working at the farm could make cheese—and make it darn well, considering they followed Mary's orders for years without knowing necessarily *why* they did certain things—but questions about the future of the farm hung in the air like a dense fog, and Sleight Farm desperately needed a leader.

Without one, I was sad but not entirely shocked to hear that the farm's operations closed down later that year. Mary's legacy as the doyenne of British goat's-milk cheese lives on, but her cheeses do not. Her wizardry will go down in history as one of the greats of English cheesemaking.

You don't farm for money. Or to have an easy life.
If you don't enjoy it, I think you'd do something else.
—MARY HOLBROOK

LET'S TALK ABOUT CHEESE TOASTIES

In my first couple of weeks living in London, I had one of the top five cheese toasties of my life. I was at Borough Market when I spotted a stall called Kappacasein (the name refers to the milk protein—all cheese nerds rejoice in understanding the reference). Their toastie included finely chopped leeks, garlic, white and red onions, and scallions—big flavor for a humble cheese toastie. It was a winner: beautifully browned and crispy sourdough bread alongside the crunchy, caramelized bits of cheese that fell onto the griddle as the bread toasted.

If I lost you at "toastie," my apologies. Among the British English words that divert from what I'm familiar with in American English, *toastie* may be one of my favorites (along with *faff** and *cheeky*). It's how they refer to any grilled sandwich, and of course my favorite toastie is a cheese toastie. Cheese toasties are as prized a comfort food in the UK as grilled cheese sandwiches are in the US.

When I make a cheese toastie for myself at home, I want simplicity—I don't want to spend ten minutes on mise en place, chopping items from the allium family and shredding various cheeses before I even slice my bread.

My favorite toastie involves a quality sourdough bread and Kirkham's Lancashire. This cheese has what the Kirkham family refers to as a "buttery crumble," so it's not necessary to shred the cheese; instead, you simply break it apart with your fingertips when putting it on the slices of bread. When you have a cheese that is both crumbly and buttery, that melts willingly with a gentle application of heat and has a bright, tangy flavor, there's not much else you need to level it up. I met Mrs. Ruth Kirkham— one of the ultimate Milkmaid Power Mammas in England as I write this—at a cheese panel and tasting event hosted by the British Library, and was struck by her straightforward sensibilities. She was the wife of a farmer and made some of the best cheese in the country; neither seemed outside the norm to her. I like to think she would approve of how I use her

---

* *Faff (noun): a great deal of ineffectual activity; e.g., "It was the usual faff at airport security." Or it can be used as a verb: "Stop faffing about!"*

cheese in my simple toastie (sometimes with chutney on the side).

The concept of leveling up your grilled cheese is fun—using mayonnaise is a common hack—and can be downright necessary when you're working with industrial cheeses or *meh* bread, but I prefer simply darn good cheese with darn good bread. Therein lies the magical synergy.

The cooking technique is as important as the ingredients themselves, especially to accomplish the textural variety that defines a good toastie. I learned this trick off the back of my friend Rich's practiced bachelor days in the kitchen, when toasties were his plat du jour. (My dad now swears by grilled cheese à la Rich: a smear of mustard on one piece of bread and the addition of sliced tomatoes.)

Here's the method: Over low heat, melt butter, then put two slices of bread into the pan and load each slice with shredded or grated cheddar cheese. (Rich used olive oil—also a good option, though personally I think it imparts too much olive oil–y flavor), lying next to each other rather than sandwiched on top of one another, and cover the pan with a lid. Don't worry—they won't be open-faced sandwiches for long.

Once the cheese has melted, turn one slice of bread onto the other, sandwiching the cheese between them, and turn up the heat for a few seconds, lid off, to encourage extra crunch on the bread—then plate it up. Once you've practiced this technique a couple of times, you'll have it down, and you'll never be faced with a self-inflicted soggy-bread/solid-cheese toastie again.

Note: Refer to pages 58 and 59 for more on cheeses that melt well, and why.

My go-to cheese toastie: a young Kirkham's Lancashire cheese melted on buttery slices of quality sourdough bread with Yorkshire chutney on the side.

Welsh Rarebit (with a Kick)

MAKES 2 SERVINGS

There's a reason the combination of bread and cheese extends beyond country and cultural lines: bread and cheese are a match made in flavor and nutrient heaven. It's instinctive to pair the two. Think about it: bread is rich in carbs, and cheese has a lot of protein and fat. Since ancient times, they have together provided primary components of nutrition. Consider Georgian *khachapuri* (see my version on page 299), Brazilian *pão de queijo*, French croque monsieur, and Lithuanian *kepta duona*.

If bread and cheese go together like two lovers at midnight, like Atlas and the globe, like a moth and a flame—then I would be remiss if I didn't teach you how to make Welsh rarebit, a favorite dish in the UK starring these two ingredients.

Never mind that rarebit is a victim of folk etymology—*rarebit* comes from the word *rabbit*, yet there is no rabbit in this dish. A cookbook from 1747 by Hannah Glasse offers not just a "Welsh rabbit," but also a "Scotch rabbit" and an "English rabbit." Food writers around the world have their own variations. Here's mine—crunchy and oozy, spicy and savory, with a bit of tang.

2 egg yolks

½ cup (100 grams) full-fat plain yogurt (for DIY Yogurt, see page 94)

1 teaspoon English mustard powder

1 cup (100 grams) shredded cheddar cheese

1 fresh red chile (I like Serrano or cayenne peppers), thinly sliced

4 ½-inch-thick (1½-centimeter) slices good-quality sourdough or country-style bread

Worcestershire sauce, for serving

1. Position a rack in the top third of the oven and preheat the broiler (that's the grill, for you Brits) to its highest setting.

2. Whisk together the egg yolks, yogurt, and mustard powder in a medium bowl. Stir in the cheese and most of the sliced chile, reserving about a quarter of the chile slices for topping the bread.

3. Lightly toast the bread in a toaster, then arrange the slices on a heavy sheet pan. Evenly spread a quarter of the cheese mixture over each slice of bread, right up to the edges, and top with the reserved chile slices.

4. Place the pan on the top rack under the broiler. Broil until the cheese mixture is browned in patches, melting, and bubbling.

5. Remove from the oven and top each slice with a drizzle of Worcestershire. Serve warm.

Welsh rarebit may be a staple in British kitchens, but the cheese that's been used in this open-faced sandwich on the British Isles has evolved; the history of British cheese is a topsy-turvy tale. If you look at the eighteenth century, most farms had cows to supply them with milk, and because there was no household refrigeration, any surplus was turned into cheese (often homespun varieties that weren't recorded) to preserve it.

The first thing to rupture Britain's farmhouse cheesemaking was rampant railway growth across the country in the late 1800s. Trains were able to transport milk from rural areas to urban centers before it went bad. During this time (and up until the beginning of the twentieth century), there was also a population boom, and people began to move to cities. This was a scientific era, ripe for a man like Joseph Harding, the "father of cheddar cheese," to introduce modern cheesemaking formulas and equipment that streamlined the process. The Industrial Revolution had hit cheese. This is when we first start to see recipes for cheese, reflecting a societal pursuit of consistency.

Around that same time—the mid-1800s—the world's first cheese factory popped up, in New York State. In its initial year, it was able to produce five times the amount of cheese its counterparts on the biggest farm operations could make. This, plus the increasing transit connectivity, led to American cheddars' increased popularity in England. British farmhouse cheddar producers couldn't compete with the cheap prices of the stuff coming in from America.

Only expediting the decline, the British Agricultural Marketing Act of 1933 established the Milk Marketing Board (MMB) as the legal overseer of milk sales. The MMB controlled who could and couldn't make cheese (not too different from the Swiss cheese cartel behind the popularization of fondue). All dairy farmers had to sell their milk to the MMB, which guaranteed income for the farmers and brought security in a time of heightened anxiety, but it essentially squashed any remaining artisan cheesemakers.

After World War II hit in 1939, the British Ministry of Food was created to "preserve the nation's diet and share it equitably," wrote Patrick Rance in *The Great British Cheese Book*. The ministry dictated that to make the most of England's resources, all milk available to be made into cheese ought to be made into *hard* cheese, because of its ability to travel well and have a longer shelf life. Straight away, soft cheeses were neglected, and milk rationing meant that even England's most beloved territorial cheeses were rarely made. Farmhouse cheesemaking came to a standstill across the country.

In 1954 cheese came off ration and farm production rebounded, with small creameries resuming the production of traditional cheeses. *But then! Say hello to the supermarket!* The birth of supermarket culture (and the factories that provided the goods that filled the stores) massively affected consumer expectations of cheese, including *what cheese should taste like*. A focus on yield, consistency, and efficiency trumped all other concerns.

Remember the Milk Marketing Board from the 1930s? Right, the one that regulated the country's milk (and therefore cheese) production. It was dissolved in 1994. The effect this had on cheesemaking was huge, because without the MMB to support a standard price for milk, dairy farmers faced the low prices offered by the supermarkets. Suddenly, cheese was a valued, higher-profit-yielding option. Just like that, the mid-nineties were primed for British cheese to make a comeback.

To define what a cheese comeback might look like, I talked with Jason Hinds, sales director and part owner of NYD, about his "journey on the cheese ladder"—a reference to the growth theory of the *quality ladder*. What's happened with coffee (another product of fermentation) was his excellent analogy: "Most people are first introduced to coffee via something like Nescafé. But then they move up a rung on the ladder to Lavazza. It's still Robusta beans, but it's better. Then you discover Arabica beans, and the single origins . . . It's a gradation of, say, five levels. You don't arrive at the top. There are levels in between each rung, too, and if you're an interested customer—interested in travel and taste and have the budget to explore—you'll move up the quality ladder."

Jason predicted cheese will follow this path: "The most important part of the ladder is what *happens* on that top rung—when there's enough people there that the demand will be high enough for [quality cheese] to be sustainable. A price that's commensurate with that quality."

The issue Jason sees is that many people still view cheese as a commodity product (it's a straight throwback to the Ministry of Food's dictate during the war), and this becomes clear if you compare cheese to, say, wine, where there's a clear stratification in terms of value and cost, and a progression of the two things in tandem.

"People producing this cheese need to be able to charge the appropriate price, and that's okay if the customer understands *what* they're paying for. Like Rogue River Blue," he says, referring to the hugely popular cheese from Rogue Creamery in Oregon. "He created a super brand!"

Rogue Creamery. In that moment, I remembered there was *another* video project I did shortly after moving to London, aside from the Comté one, that also pushed my cosmic needle in the direction of cheese (although I didn't realize it at the time): a shoot at Rogue Creamery! A video project had taken me to Oregon, where I had petted the cows—free to roam as they wished—and stuck my hands in the curds. I loved every second of it. How had I glossed over this project, which certainly should have alleviated my "trailing spouse" fears? It wasn't my head injury that made me forget about that gig—just goes to show how much a mental rain cloud can block out the sun.

I snapped back to my conversation with Jason.

"You seem hopeful about where it's all going," I said.

"Definitely. Now's the time."

By my third year at NYD, life had evolved a lot since I first slipped on my cheesemonger wellies. I was drawn to return to NYD each Christmas season, like a camp for dairy nerds. I was always glad to be behind the slate again; it felt like a reunion with my favorite cheeses, and with fellow cheese-loving people, too. As time went on, I saw how I equated cheese with connection to my adopted home, how cheese was the base of a community I had formed. I don't mean to hyperbolize these relationships—the simple fact is that we all coalesced around cheese and, in doing so, were ourselves bonded like the curds reknitting in a mold.

Returning to the shop marked an opportunity to reflect on the circumstances of my life over the year prior. It was the reminder to revisit the me of twelve months ago, and it was the realization that one year contains multitudes. I couldn't help but think, *Wow, that first experience as a cheesemonger, I was newly clabbered.*

Clabber has got to be my favorite milk-related verb. (It's a noun, too.) It's when milk ferments and is naturally clotted while souring. When milk clabbers, it thickens to a slush of curds and whey. It's an awkward in-between phase. Like, what are you trying to be, milk? You're not quite milk, but you're definitely not cheese. Clabbered milk was all the rage in the days before refrigeration, and you might even have a form of it in your refrigerator. Got some buttermilk in there? Welcome to the world of clabbered milk.

I like to think of the vast range of fermented milk products, clabbered or cultured, as cheese's cousins. From buttermilk to Turkish *ayran*, a frothy, salty yogurt drink (*yogurt* is a Turkish word, after all). From Iceland's *skyr* to Indian raita. There's kefir, the "Champagne of milks," which uses a SCOBY (symbiotic culture of bacteria and yeast) to ferment, and a Tibetan drink called *tara* that uses a SCOBY, too. And it's not just animal milk that can transform: nut and seed milks can also be fermented.

While cheese is proof of human inventiveness, I see these products as evidence of how we can carry on through

Clockwise from left: *DIY Yogurt (see page 94 for the recipe)* with honey drizzled on top; yogurt and strawberry preserves in a to-go jar; fresh milk; Greek-style yogurt in its container; whey (left over from draining the homemade yogurt to make a Greek-style consistency); labneh with za'atar and olive oil drizzled on top the awkward transitions in life. Who thought this slush could be delicious? Sure, it may not be the elevated art of cheese, but these clabbered cousins offer this advice: *Make it work*. I was a big, walking clabbered human my first year in England. And you know what? I made it work. (But I am glad I continue to ferment . . .)

Other family members—butter and cream—are a result of milk's properties, when the fat and larger particles separate from the liquid buttermilk with the help of gravity or by churning, which agitates the particles until they separate. Crème fraîche? It's just cream that's been fermented.

The second cousins are my favorites, though. Like ricotta. *Ricotta* is Italian for "recooked," because traditionally, it was made using the whey left over from cheesemaking, which was heated a second time (recooked) to form a fine curd. This process is dependent on the type of protein in whey: the serum protein rather than the casein protein (what curds are made of, which gets taken away to become cheese). First, these serum proteins

further ferment, making the liquid more acidic. The whey is then cooked at a high temperature, and the low pH (high acidity) and addition of heat cause a delicate curd to form. This curd is strained further and then enjoyed as ricotta. From the by-product of cheesemaking, more cheese is born!

While it may not be the traditional way of crafting ricotta, I've got to tell you about this home-cook-friendly version I make (using whole milk from my local farmers' market). Heat the milk up to 200°F (93.3°C), take it off the heat, add 2 tablespoons of lemon juice, and stir. Let sit for 10 minutes, then drain the curds in a strainer lined with cheesecloth. You've got homemade ricotta! (You can make paneer the same way, with an additional step of pressing it with something heavy while it's still in the strainer to push out more whey.) Be sure to keep the whey by-product—it's so delicious, I drink it on its own. *Yes, whey.*

When I made cheese at Sleight Farm, it was immediately obvious that the less whey we removed from the curds, the softer the final cheese would be, and the more we removed, the harder the final product. Regardless of what cheese a cheesemaker produces, one thing is certain: whey will be removed. Whether we were crafting the small, soft Sleighletts, which released steady drips of liquid, or the hard wheels of Old Ford, which liberated whey like Niagara Falls, the by-product would be shipped off to the pigs to drink. In life as in food, farmers will be the first to tell you: Let nothing go to waste.

Whey is rich in protein and vitamins, so feeding it to livestock is a great way to put every drop of milk to good use, but there are countless ingenious uses for the stuff. Several of my favorite dairies in England make butter from their excess. There's a power station in France that generates electricity from the nutritious juice. A shepherd in Australia makes sheep's-whey vodka. Everyone's favorite fermentation friend Sandor Katz, author of *The Art of Fermentation*, shares that you can use whey to "bring canned food back to life." All you need to do is "add a little whey and let it sit out for twelve hours and you can ferment beans, salsa, or just about anything."

I've become accustomed to adding the golden liquid to my morning porridge, to soups and stews, to grains for soaking and cooking, to my bread dough, and to smoothies. (Please note: The whey powder you see at the big-muscle-guy store is not what I'm referring to. While that stuff may retain protein, it doesn't contain live cultures.) There are two types of whey: acid and sweet—their name reflects their flavor. The former is strained out of acid-coagulated cheese or yogurt, and the latter is a by-product of making rennet-coagulated cheeses like cheddar.

The discovery of yogurt thousands of years ago was likely a happy accident, but the bigger discovery was that it was easier for humans to digest than the milk from which it was made. Fermentation transformed milk from something people couldn't drink (most humans were lactose-intolerant at the time) into something

they could eat! If you're lactose-intolerant, chances are you can eat yogurt, because the bacteria metabolize the lactose (the milk sugar that some people have a hard time digesting), breaking it down and turning it into lactic acid, which usually agrees better with the body. (Also, *aged* cheeses like Parmigiano Reggiano and cheddar tend to be easier on the stomach for those with intolerances, because as the cheese matures, bacteria break down the lactose into lactic acid.)

Yogurt became popular in Europe only around the end of the nineteenth century, and it wasn't until the middle of the twentieth century that it caught fire in the States. Just recently, the yogurt on American grocery store shelves has become closer to the yogurt found in the rest of the world—thicker and less sweet (think Greek yogurt). Bulgaria, Georgia, Uzbekistan, Kazakhstan, and Iran are all known for eating a lot of yogurt, and each has its own version. And yogurt is a big deal in India and other countries in South Asia, too. My friend Priya Krishna wrote a fun article for the *New York Times* that taught me how important yogurt is in South Asian cultures, where yogurt starters are considered family heirlooms. You can either inherit your yogurt starter, as Priya did, or simply use a few tablespoons of your favorite yogurt from the grocery store or farmers' market as a starter—either will suffice, just make sure it contains live cultures. All you need in terms of equipment are a kitchen thermometer, sterilized jars, cheesecloth, and ideally a Dutch oven.

DIY Yogurt

MAKES ABOUT 4 CUPS (1 LITER), OR LESS,
DEPENDING ON HOW MUCH WHEY YOU CHOOSE TO DRAIN

I've been making yogurt at home for years. It's a habit that began as a cost-saving method to keep pace with my steep consumption. My friends Gwen and Alison, an urban-farmer-and-chef duo with Coriander Kitchen & Farm in Detroit, showed me their recipe, and my response was *"That's all?"* It's easy, and like any food you make yourself, you have ultimate control over the quality of the milk used to make it and the tanginess and texture of the final product.

1 quart (1 liter) whole cow's milk

¼ cup (60 milliliters) plain yogurt or plain Greek-style yogurt (It should have live and active starters, and ideally be organic. Its fat content will not have a substantial effect on the yogurt you make.)

Note: You will need sterilized glass jars for this recipe. Sterilize the jars and their lids by cleaning them first, then immersing them in boiling water for 10 minutes. Or, after cleaning them with hot soapy water, you can place them on an oven rack with the oven set to 350°F (180°C) for 10 minutes.

1. Preheat the oven to 100°F (40°C) and turn the oven light on.

2. Pour the milk into a medium saucepan and set it over medium-low heat. Slowly heat the milk, stirring continuously to keep it from scalding, until it has warmed to 200°F (93°C). Remove from the heat and let cool until it hits 115°F (46°C); this will take 10 to 15 minutes, depending on the temperature of your kitchen.

3. While you wait, prep your equipment: Fill a Dutch oven about halfway with warm water. Turn off the oven itself but leave the oven light on to maintain the ambient warmth.

4. To inoculate the milk with the yogurt starter, place the yogurt in a small bowl, pour 1 tablespoon of the cooled milk into the yogurt, and stir to combine. Pour this mixture into the saucepan with the rest of the cooled milk and stir to combine.

5. Pour the milk mixture into sterilized glass jars. (I like to pour it from a height to create a bit of foam, which will turn into a thick yogurt cream after fermentation.) Secure the lids and place the jars in the warm water in the Dutch oven. The jars should not be submerged, but should be mostly covered by the water—a water level just below their lids is ideal. Place the pot in the oven, as close to the oven light as possible, and close the oven door. Let sit for 5 to 6 hours to start, then taste the yogurt and check its consistency to see if it's to your liking; if not, let sit for up to 4 more hours. The yogurt gets tangier and firmer the longer it stays in the oven, so experiment with how long it takes for the yogurt to reach the consistency and texture you like (I've kept mine in for as long as 9 hours).

6. Remove the pot from the oven. At this point, you can remove the jars from the water, dry them, and store the yogurt in the

refrigerator (it will keep for up to 1 week), or you can adjust the consistency of the yogurt to make it thicker (like a Greek yogurt or labneh) by straining out some of the whey. To do so, place a fine-mesh strainer over a bowl and line the strainer with cheesecloth. Pour the yogurt into the cheesecloth and let stand until the yogurt reaches the desired consistency—5 to 20 minutes. Transfer the strained yogurt to an airtight container and store it in the refrigerator for up to 1 week. I especially like my homemade yogurt with honey or a fruit compote (and I usually add a scoop of nut butter, too).

LEFTOVER WHEY IDEAS

ADD TO BREAD DOUGH

ADD TO SOUPS & STEWS

COOK OATMEAL & GRAINS IN IT

ADD TO SMOOTHIES

What to do with that leftover whey?

You could discard it, sure, but that's no fun!
Remember some of the ideas I mentioned back on page 93?

Sheep in the Lake District, England.

THE CHANGEMAKERS: BLOOMY-RIND AND WASHED-RIND ENGLISH CHEESES

The best way to approach any cheese shop is with an open mind, but you should be able to describe the kind of cheeses you most enjoy or are specifically shopping for that day. I understand how this can seem overwhelming, as more than 1,400 named cheese varieties exist today, but once you know their simple, broad descriptions, you'll be set up for success in your conversations with cheesemongers.

There are five families of cheeses:

- FRESH (soft)
- BLOOMY-RIND (soft-ripened)
- WASHED-RIND (smear-ripened)
- BLUE
- SEMI-HARD and HARD (which can sometimes be further distinguished as hard uncooked or hard cooked)

Traditionally, British cheeses are semi-hard and hard (and some are blue), and generally have a crumbly texture and lactic flavor. Mary Holbrook's fresh goat's-milk cheeses were inspired by what's thought of as the French style, and her washed-rind Cardo wheel was Portuguese style, but by making them her own, she redefined what "British cheese" could be—and she wasn't the only changemaker around.

"YOU'VE GOT TO NAME YOUR CHEESE after something local, haven't you?" said Jonny Crickmore when I visited his farm and cheesemaking operation in Suffolk, south England. He continued, "The Normans, who captured this area under William the Conquerer, were known for their bloomy-rind cheeses—hence Camembert de *Norman*die—so we named our cheese after one of the Norman noblemen who settled in this area of England: Baron Bigod!"

Jonny smiled as the sun hit his bearded face, reflecting the amount of boundless energy he has for the topics of farming and dairy. He is the man behind Fen Farm Dairy, and we stood on a hill overlooking his property on a windy day in February, a couple of months after I finished my third annual shift as a NYD cheesemonger. The long grass around our feet was blown flat by the wind, as though styled by a giant's comb, and enhanced the feeling of seeing something larger than life.

Jonny and his team make the only raw-milk Brie-style cheese in England, and it is widely adored. "Our cheese is a modern British cheese, but the farm is sixteenth century." *That's nearly half a millennium old!* He pointed at the wooden shed down the slope, where his Bungay butter is made, saying, "That house goes with the barn; they've been here for hundreds of years." They were there when Europeans were launching explorations of the Americas. *Wow.*

The area is deeply rooted in the past, and in terms of cheese, Jonny has a rough reputation to rebut. Ever heard of Suffolk Bang? Also called Suffolk Thump, it was a cheese made of skim milk (left over from buttermaking), and, as Jonny tells it, "it was so terrible dogs would bark at it. You could roll a cannon on it!" Jonny was having fun telling me about the infamous product. "People thought Suffolk couldn't make cheese for *bugger all*!" (*Bugger all* = nothing.)

What Jonny is doing with his dairy farm in Suffolk has been innovative and transformational in the British cheese world. It started when he visited a hen farm that had put up a shed with fresh eggs and a coin box; locals stopped by, took however many eggs they wanted, and put money in the box—the honor system. Jonny (who works closely with his wife, Dulcie, on decisions for the business) set

up a similar system with the milk from his cows. "We got thirty pounds for thirty liters of milk. That's when everything changed" in terms of how he realized his dairy could run. He helped other farmers set up their own sheds and vending systems, and started to think outside the box about what other innovations he could attempt with the milk.

Like Joe Schneider of Stichelton, Jonny's lightbulb moment was directly impacted by the offerings at NYD. "Neal's Yard Dairy had all these amazing cheeses made on the British Isles, displayed beautifully on the slate," he recalls, "and right in the middle was Brie de Meaux, a *French* cheese! It felt out of place, but they needed to have it there because no one in the UK was making that style of cheese."

Not *yet*. He saw the void, and he decided to fill it.

To do so, he hired a French consultant, Ivan Larcher, who told him, "If you want to make cheese, you need the best milk," and he was not happy with the high-yielding Holsteins' milk. Jonny re-created the scene for me: "Then he tells us, rather abruptly, 'Zees ees not going to work!' He refused to help us unless we got Montbéliarde cows," the same cows used to make not just Comté, but also Cantal and Mont d'Or. So Jonny went to the Jura in France, the same place I went on my Comté deep dive, and bought seventy-two Montbéliarde cows. Jonny was happy with the change because although Montbéliardes don't give as much milk per liter as Holsteins do, their milk has a higher protein content. All set with his new cows (transported to England via luxury air-conditioned lorry), Jonny started to make an English bloomy-rind wheel.

Bronwen and Francis Percival called it "the UK's first respectable raw-milk Brie" in their book *Reinventing the Wheel*, and once I became gripped with this fascination for cheese in my new homeland, I put Fen Farm on my list of places to visit. By the time I got there, I had made my fair share of cheeses—my fingers intimately knew a knitted curd—but I felt completely ignorant as to how bloomy-rind cheeses were made. What wizardry resulted in that rind?

You may remember from my cheesemaking at Stichelton Dairy that to make the blue's notable streaks, specific bacteria are tipped into the milk at the beginning of the cheesemaking process and encouraged to grow as the cheese matures. In the case of blue cheese, *Penicillium roqueforti* is added to the milk, but for Jonny's Baron Bigod, he adds *Penicillium candidum*, the white mold that grows as the rind ("the fluffy stuff") and *Geotrichum candidum*, another fungus ("the wrinkles"). (This is also the point when he adds the lactic acid bacteria strains—his starter culture—and then the milk is gravity-fed into vats in the room next door, where rennet is added.)

You can't just add those fungi to the milk, then brush your hands off and trust that the cheese will turn into a Brie, with that bloomy rind and viscous interior. Adding the fungal strains is only the beginning. Straight away, Jonny is concerned with keeping tabs on the milk's acidity. Milk is slightly acidic to begin with, and he closely monitors the pH of the milk to determine when to add the rennet, then attentively checks the flocculation to determine the moment they'll cut the curd.

"To get the balance of rennet and acidity is difficult; they have to go hand in hand," Jonny told me over a midday tea and toast, after we'd been in the cheese room. He explained the crucial yet hidden factor at play: calcium. "In milk, yes, you have the proteins, but you've also got all these minerals in there, and one of the biggest minerals is calcium. It's like this: the brick is the protein and the cement is the calcium—the calcium holds the bricks together to make your big wall. The more calcium you have, the more your brick wall is going to be big and strong."

"Structure!" I said, nodding. I love metaphors that help explain science.

"If you dissolve calcium, your structure is going to be weak, and with our kind of cheese, we *want* it to be weak," he explained.

I remembered reading about calcium phosphate in *Reinventing the Wheel*, where Bronwen and Francis describe how "Cheeses with the calcium phosphate left in place are supple; cheeses from which the minerals have been leached away are brittle." High levels of calcium phosphate in a cheese give it the bouncy-ball effect; of course this gooey-style cheese would have low levels of it.

Jonny continued, "What calcium does is it makes cheese rubbery, springy, like Suffolk Bang. Lactic cheeses don't have that quality for that reason—they have low

Young Baron Bigod, just after being molded

Mature Baron Bigod, enjoyed on a cheese plate

calcium. The thing is that rennet locks in about fifty percent of the calcium right away, but acid [created when lactic acid bacteria eat lactose] dissolves calcium." His challenge is to get the balance between the two *just right* to create the soft, melty texture we expect from a Brie-style cheese.

I love Jonny's explanation—and the pressing importance with which he described it—because it shows how every little factor in fermentation is hugely impactful. *Which will be championed and which will be crushed?* That's where the craft of cheesemaking is most felt. I also appreciated Jonny's breakdown, because it was at my level of comprehension . . . which is not far from where Jonny was himself when he started making Baron Bigod.

See, Jonny began his cheese journey as a farmer; he didn't know the first thing about making cheese. He comes from a farming family ("I always knew there was nothing else I wanted to do"), but he's also infectiously curious and entrepreneurial, so after the initial setup support from the French consultant, Jonny taught himself how to make this cheese. He learned from books ("I thought Paul Kindstedt's *American Farmstead Cheese* broke it all down well") and received advice from like-minded artisans ("Joe Schneider helped set me up; my system is inspired by how he does it at Stichelton"). Mostly, though, he learned by doing.

He's rebranding his region as a place for cheesemaking that's a far cry from the days of Suffolk Bang, and that's not nothing. I mean, it's not bugger all.

WASHED-RIND CHEESES LIKE TALEGGIO and Époisses are some of my favorites. When bacteria are encouraged on the rind, the result is a sticky exterior and often smelly and funkalicious cheese (with a bark that's always worse than its bite—these cheeses are rarely as intensely flavored as their scent suggests). They can be soft and runny inside or have a pliable paste.

Martin Gott and his partner, Nicola Robinson, make a washed-rind sheep's-milk cheese called St James. They have a small operation, with around two hundred sheep, called Holker Farm in the Lake District of northwest England. It's here, where the epic craters that hold lakes compete with the lush rolling hills for the "Most Awe-Inspiring View" superlative, that their microdairy sits. Nicola tends the animals and land, and Martin makes the cheese with the sheep's scant 100 to 300 liters of milk per day (depending on the season), enough for the team to make about twelve smear-ripened 9-inch (23-centimeter) rectangles a day. There are a couple of part-time helpers, but when I visited, I saw that it's a much smaller-scale production than many of the other dairies I'd seen. It was about on par with Sleight Farm, where I worked . . . and in fact, that's where Martin cut his teeth making continental-style cheeses, too!

He and Nicola had lived in the same Somerset farmhouse on a hill as I did, but they were there in 2005, while Mary Holbrook was alive. I'll add Martin's reminiscing about Mary to my collection of anecdotes of the mythical creature she was. I said something along those lines after he told me about their dinners together in the old stone abode, and he laughed. "Mary stories are like fairy stories! She was a strong personality!"

Mary rented out land to Martin and Nicola for their sheep to graze, and when they weren't helping her with her goat cheeses, they'd experiment with making molds of curds from their sheep's milk. Their work in the year they spent at Sleight Farm was what they needed to prove to themselves, "There's a business here." They moved to the Lake District in 2006 and have been making the deep-peach-red-rinded St James ever since. It's gained a cult following, partially because of its anti-industrial result: each batch is slightly different than the last. Loyal fans always want to know, *What will this season bring?*

Washed-rind cheeses are essentially what they sound like: the rind is frequently smeared, or "washed" (sometimes with a brine, although St James is wiped with cold water), encouraging bacteria to form on the moist surface. As when I visited Jonny at Fen Farm and was clueless about how bloomy-rind cheeses were made, I wasn't sure how St James got its beautiful orangey-pink, sticky exterior. However, I did my research beforehand and thought I'd impress Martin with my erudition. "At what point do you add the *B. linens*?" I asked, having read that *B. linens* (short for *Brevibacterium linens*) is added to milk or even rubbed on the rind of most washed-rind cheeses.

Except . . . not so at Holker Farm; Martin doesn't manually add *B. linens*. He

St James cheese, held by cheesemaker Martin Gott

This style of cheesemaking is an especially intimate affair: when Martin or his teammates—Malcolm and Nial—rub water on the rectangular slab of curds, they do so with their (clean) bare hands. Observing Martin doing this felt voyeuristic, like watching a lover caress his partner. (Well, not quite so romantic or doting—they've got a lot of cheeses to cover, so they make their way through the stockpile with speed.)

I watched Martin move his hands over the top of the cheese in circular strokes, then dip them in water and rub the sides of the cheese before moving to the next slab. I am reminded of the Korean culinary principle of *son-mat*, which translates to "hand taste." The idea is that the cook's hands—literally, not metaphorically—impart a unique element to the dish; a batch of kimchi whose cabbage was crunched and massaged by one pair of hands has a taste distinct from another batch made with the same ingredients by a different person. There is an affinity for son-mat, especially when it's the hand taste of someone close to you, like your mom. I think of my mom's hands working bread dough at our kitchen counter, and I understand the familiarity and affection. Son-mat is particularly apt in all things fermented, which incorporate the individual microflora of the maker's skin in the "mixed salad" of microbes already present.

explained that the bacteria are naturally in the biodiversity of place—in the grasses the sheep eat and the raw milk, handled with care—and are coaxed out with a water rub three times a week for the first three weeks. "The washing is the key thing," he said. After that, the St James is wrapped and packed—off to cheese shops around the country, where it consistently sells out.

"This style of cheese has been called 'continental,' but I'm convinced it's how early Wensleydales were made here, way back when. It's natural to wash the rind!" While Martin insists he's not making a style of cheese that's new to the island, he is definitely on the frontier of a movement that's gaining popularity.

SINCE FERMENTED FOODS HAVE LONG played a role in our consumption habits, it seems natural that much of the conversation about them circles back to the idea of "how it's always been done." Yet there's a cognitive dissonance between our adoration of tradition and our fear of bacteria (both the good ones and the bad ones).

I love the story of Mother Noella Marcellino, a nun living in Connecticut who produces a semi-soft washed-rind cheese named Bethlehem (I kid you not). She's become a bit of a media darling, having been featured in the *New York Times*, Michael Pollan's book *Cooked* (and the Netflix series of the same name), the *New Yorker*, and more. Her cheese is modeled after a French cheese called Saint-Nectaire, and she makes it according to traditional methods. This includes coagulating the milk in wooden barrels. Today, stainless-steel vats are typically used; they're thought to be more sanitary, which is why health inspectors asked her to cease using wood.

A funny thing happened when she obeyed. The *Escherichia coli* (*E. coli*) levels spiked, proving the porous wooden barrels were the hygienic option because the bacteria in the wood itself kept *E. coli* at bay. "What was happening was that good bacteria were growing in the wood," Mother Noella told Burkhard Bilger in an interview for the *New Yorker*. "It was like a sourdough culture that you keep on using, and it was driving off the *E. coli*."

To prove this to officials, she went and got her PhD in microbiology. With that,

she could guard, by scientific merit, these traditional cheesemaking approaches using raw milk, which she saw as cultural heritage. If the stainless steel didn't work for Bethlehem cheese, "The real question, then, is how and where to make exceptions," Bilger writes in his article. "It comes down to defining reasonable risk."

Mother Noella, whose doctorate was specifically on the fungus *Geotrichum candidum* (yes, one of the strains Jonny uses to make his Brie-style cheese), knows a thing or two about the science behind her craft. With microscope in hand, her habit draped over the lab stool, she could determine that the wooden barrels were not only harmless but contributed to the wonderful flavors of her cheese. That's not to say she doesn't still see God in cheesemaking. She compares cheesemaking to the Eucharist—the transformation of milk into cheese mirrors the transcendence of the sacrament. Bilger adds to her metaphor: "But ripening is more like prayer. You repeat an ancient formula as faithfully as possible, then you wait for something extraordinary to happen—for a visitation that is never guaranteed."

Mother Noella, the benevolent advocate for traditional cheesemaking and raw-milk cheese, ironically found herself in the position of "changemaker" for using cutting-edge science to uphold delicious ritual.

An unexpected but outstanding use of quality aged cheddar cheese: in brownies! See page 111 for the recipe.

Cheddar cheese is the second-best-selling cheese in the world (after mozzarella), according to TasteAtlas. "Cheddar" was first recorded as the name of a cheese in the twelfth century in an official document by King Henry II (he also declared it the best cheese in England). To this day, cheddar is probably Britain's most famous cheese, but unlike Stilton, say, which is a protected designation of origin (PDO), there are cheddar producers from England to the United States, Australia to Canada.

So, although cheddar was born in England, it's not necessarily associated with the Somerset village that gave birth to the cheese and its name. There's a "West Country Farmhouse Cheddar" PDO, but it doesn't own the name cheddar. There's no recipe for cheddar, either, giving cheesemakers the leeway to produce cheese in varying climates around the world and still call it "cheddar."

By the time Americans perfected large-scale production of cheddar in the mid-1800s and started selling their cheaper cheese to Brits (who gobbled it right up), "cheddar" was far beyond retrieval as a protected name.

Cheddar is also a verb for the process of putting slabs of curds on top of each other to press out moisture; the process is repeated several times, giving the cheese its characteristic dense texture. I was champing at the bit to see this in action, and I finally had my chance at Westcombe Dairy, which makes a traditional clothbound Somerset cheddar cheese. It's down the road from the town of Cheddar, from which the cheese you know and love got its name. Like a good cheesehead, I dragged my partner along for the visit.

Connor and I arrived at midday, when the cheesemaking was in full swing. We peered through the window into the creamery and saw two men muscling what looked like huge oars, each stirring a massive vat of curds and whey. From the steam gathered on the glass of the window, it was obviously hot in there, and the men were working up a sweat. After gearing up in hairnets, cloaks, and booties, we joined them in the sauna.

Tom Calver, the dairy's director, was one of those guys wielding an "oar." He welcomed us with a smile and waved us over to join him. Tom's larger vat had several mechanical arms stirring the heated whey and curds, so he mostly worked the edges and corners with his paddle to ensure all the curds were getting jostled.

The contents of the vat would eventually become Westcombe's cheddar cheese. It would be combined with a traditional starter and rennet, then set, cut, and brought to a temperature just under 104°F (40°C). The whole operation was vastly different from the process I had used to make goat cheese at Sleight Farm; it was more like the cheesemaking at Lynher Dairies.

"How do you know it's time to drain the whey?" I asked Tom.

"It's ready when it's ready."

Right.

He elaborated, "I think you can have a little bit of science knowledge and a little bit of common sense, and some confidence—the beauty of cheese is that it's quite expressive. You'll never make the same cheeses that I will; I'll never make the same cheeses as Adam." He gestured over to the other man. "He's making the Duckett's Aged Caerphilly." Adam hadn't stopped stirring since I first spotted him through the window fifteen minutes before.

"You know," Tom said, pausing to think, "cheesemaking is simple. All you're trying to do is create acidity and extract moisture out of milk. So we set the milk

relatively lightly, then we cut the curds into pea-size pieces and we scald and stir . . . both things drive out moisture. You don't want to overstir because then you'll demineralize it, and that calcium content affects the texture. Then we move it to a cooling table, which is like a giant sieve, and the whey goes in the next room over to make ricotta."

"I love your ricotta!" I yelped.

"Ah, do you like it? Wicked." He looked up to meet my eyes and smiled, then turned his attention back to the vat. "What we're left with is the curd particles," he said. The curds, as you may remember, are communal—after the rennet is added, they want to knit together. They'll naturally start to bind into one big, long solid at the bottom of the vat.

That is the point when the cheddaring begins. Tom's team cuts the newly formed solid curd into rectangular slabs about the size of a large serving tray and stacks them on top of each other to draw out moisture and further acidify the curds (as the warmth promotes the growth of lactic acid–producing bacteria). With each restack, the slabs are flipped.

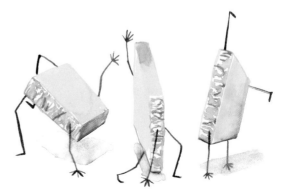

In seventeenth-century England, cows grazed on grasses rich in beta-carotene, which gave their milk an orange hue, so cheese of that color made more money because it symbolized quality. Then cheesemakers discovered they could skim the cream from the top to make butter—but that's where all the orange pigment was, so those cheddar wheels lost their color and its implication of quality.

To get around the issue, cheesemakers added saffron or annatto to the skimmed milk to tint it orange. (Annatto is a natural dye made from the pulp of a seed from the achiote tree; it's also used to color Britain's Red Leicester and Dutch Gouda.) This began the tradition of coloring cheddar in England. "The English cheesemakers were trying to trick people," as Paul Kindstedt, author of *Cheese and Culture,* bluntly told NPR. Most farmhouse cheddars in England no longer use coloring, though.

A similar legend accompanies Wisconsin's famously orange cheddar: the orange-tinted milk that came from pasture-grazed cows was lost when farmers moved to dry feed, so they faked the color, and Wisconsin still fully embraces the squash-orange wedge. Cheesemakers in Vermont and other parts of the northeast have traditionally bucked the trend of adding any coloring, embracing a whiter cheddar.

"And we stack them quite high," Tom said, "so our cheddar slabs become like sheets of pasta or like chamois leather."

In the cheesemaking room at Westcombe, after the cheddaring process is complete—the slabs stacked and restacked until Tom deems the texture and acidity to be where he wants them—he uses a mill to break the slabs into lots of little pieces. "It kind of rips everything apart so you get a larger surface area," he explained. "One of the primary objectives of this stage is to get salt on it to put the brakes on the acidity production from the starter culture."

We walked beyond the ricotta-making station to the pressing room, where the milled and salted curd was put into molds and pressed with a pneumatic ram—*BOOM* goes the cheddar.

To complete the production process, Tom rubs lard over the outside of the cheese and wraps it in muslin (which, with lard, is the traditional binding agent that helps keep the cheese from drying out), then gives it one final press. Then it is time for the maturation room—home to Tina the Turner.

My anticipation before meeting Tina the Turner was through the roof. Let me be clear: I'm talking about a robot. Tina the Turner is the name given to the machine that turns the heavy wheels of cheddar cheese at Westcombe. Tina the Turner has received a lot of attention—including an article in the *Financial Times* by the outstanding food historian Polly Russell, who wrote that this robot is "at the frontline of cheddar innovation in the UK"—so my expectations were high.

We walked to another building with a huge entrance door, which Tom raised open, revealing rows of shelves, each as tall as Jack's beanstalk. The shelves held hundreds of wheels of cheddar, aging to perfection. And there was Tina the Turner, a robot who could extend to three times my height, lift a wheel of cheddar (which weighs about fifty pounds), and flip it over. She should be in the zillionth *Transformers* sequel.

You know when you meet someone new, but you feel like you've met them before? That's how I felt upon meeting Tina the Turner. She was *just like* the automated machines I saw doing the same work in France when I visited the Comté affinage (maturation) cellars.

"She's inspired by the Comté *affineurs* in France," Tom said, referring to the people whose specialty is the art of cheese maturation. He had read my mind.

Clearly. "The thing that strikes me, Tom"—I could feel my journalist voice coming out—"is that you talk about intuition and tradition, but you have mechanical stirrers for the curd and a robot in your maturation room. Not to put you on the spot, but . . ."

"There's nothing artisanal about turning a cheese over. It's backbreaking work. Respect for anybody who does it, but having the robot has been brilliant. What we've been able to do is taste the cheese more. We went from tasting one cheese out of every batch to check to see if it's okay; now we're tasting every single cheddar."

"Quality control," I said.

"Any chef would never dream of sending out a dish they hadn't tasted, but before Tina the Turner, we didn't have the ability to sample from each wheel."

With that, I saw that marrying technology and tradition could make an ideal union. The mechanical stirrers in the cheese room did the bulk of the stirring, but Tom still circled the vat and hand-stirred the corners, getting up close with the curds and paying detailed attention to them. The stirring wasn't on a timer; it was dependent on his intuition.

I COULDN'T GET ENOUGH OF cheddaring, so I visited Quicke's Cheddar in Devon, between Somerset and Cornwall. It was midmorning when Mary Quicke (the *fourteenth* generation of her family to work at Home Farm) and I stood next to each other over the vat and watched her team cheddaring the curds— lifting and flipping the slabs as they got increasingly thinner. She leaned over to me and said, "Cheesemaking is all about taking moisture out," to which I nodded

The cheddaring procedure. Left: *Early in the slab-flipping process, as gravity begins to flatten them;* right: *The same slabs of curds after multiple rounds of flipping them on top of one another*

knowingly. I was enraptured as I watched her assistant dairy manager, Ian, measure the acidity of the whey expelled from the curds after each flip to determine when it was time to mill.

"Why did you decide to make cheddar?" was the burning question I had to ask. "You're not in Somerset—why not make something else?"

"We're in southwest England!" she retorted, as though that should have been obvious enough, and that Somerset does *not* have sole claim to the British cheddar throne.

Queen Victoria, who reigned in England from 1837 to 1901, received a gigantic wheel of cheddar as a wedding present; it weighed over one thousand pounds. If *that's* not enough to prove all of England is boisterously proud of its cheddar, I don't know what is.

Cheddar Brownies

MAKES 24 BROWNIES

Beth, one of my cheesemonger friends at NYD, gave me the idea to put chunks of cheddar in brownies. *Seriously?* I somewhat skeptically made a batch, folding pieces of Montgomery's Cheddar into the fudgy batter. Still warm from the oven, the cheddar chunks were almost like white chocolate bits, "or like cranberries or something!" Connor noted, with their pop of sweet, soft, pliable delight on his tongue.

Chunks of cheddar add a wonderful complementary element to fudgy brownies. Use a mature cheddar for its crystallized structure, which not only breaks into bits more easily, but will take on caramel notes as it bakes.

In this recipe, I say to sprinkle additional cheddar chunks on top as the brownies cool, but I also love topping them with a cheddar brittle. To make the spots of cheddar brittle, add the additional cheddar chunks on top of the brownie batter halfway through baking (at the same time you rotate the pan) and continue baking per the instructions. The added crunch is a fun twist.

These are my ideal brownies now, and *not* just for the novelty factor.

1½ cups (3 sticks/345 grams) unsalted butter

6 ounces (170 grams) dark chocolate (70% cacao), coarsely chopped

2 cups (400 grams) granulated sugar

½ cup packed (60 grams) light brown sugar

1 teaspoon fine sea salt

6 large eggs

1 tablespoon pure vanilla extract

1 teaspoon instant espresso (optional)

¼ cup (30 grams) all-purpose flour

1⅓ cups (115 grams) unsweetened cocoa powder

4½ ounces (130 grams) mature cheddar cheese, broken into roughly ¼-inch (1-centimeter) cubes, plus ¾ ounce (20 grams), broken into pieces, for topping

1. Position a rack in the middle of the oven and preheat the oven to 350°F (180°C). Line a 9 x 13-inch (23 x 33-centimeter) baking pan (at least 2 inches/5 centimeters deep) with aluminum foil (it's okay if the whole pan doesn't get covered—just be sure to cover the bottom and long sides), leaving a few inches overhanging the sides.

2. Melt the butter in a small saucepan over low heat. When it has melted completely, increase the heat slightly to bring the butter to a gentle simmer, stirring continuously, then cook, stirring and scraping the bottom and sides of the pan to pick up any milk solids that may be sticking to the pan, until the butter is golden yellow, smells nutty, and

(recipe continues)

has stopped making hissing and popping noises, 2 to 4 minutes, depending on the exact heat level and the material of the pan used. Remove from the heat and stir in the chopped chocolate. Set aside to allow the chocolate to melt.

3. Combine the granulated sugar, brown sugar, salt, eggs, vanilla, and instant coffee (if using) in the bowl of a stand mixer fitted with the whisk attachment (or combine them in a large bowl and use a handheld mixer). Mix on medium-high speed until thick and fluffy, 7 to 10 minutes.

4. While the stand mixer is busy whipping, combine the flour and cocoa powder in a medium bowl and stir with a whisk to break up any lumps.

5. Reduce the mixer speed to low. Pour in the warm chocolate-butter mixture, then add the flour-cocoa mixture (I spoon in the dry ingredients to gradually introduce them to the batter and decrease the cloud of flour puff that occurs from dumping it all in at once). Mix on medium speed until uniformly combined.

6. Stop the mixer and remove the bowl. Scrape down the sides and bottom of the bowl to ensure that everything has been well incorporated. Using a flexible spatula, gently fold in the cheddar cheese cubes, then pour the batter into the prepared pan, spreading it evenly.

7. Bake for 15 minutes, then rotate the pan and bake for 15 minutes more, until the brownies look set and are barely firm to the touch. Remove the pan from the oven and let cool slightly (just a few minutes), then sprinkle the cheese pieces over the top, spreading them evenly for a nice pop of cheddar color.

8. Let the brownies cool completely (this is the hard part) to allow them to set. Slide a butter knife around the edges of the pan to loosen them, then use the overhanging foil to lift the brownies from the pan and transfer them to a cutting board. Cut into squares, then enjoy your new favorite brownies. These keep well in an airtight container (with waxed paper between the layers) at room temperature for about a week.

The email subject line read "You're Invited: WORLD CHEESE AWARDS," and in my groggy morning state, I rubbed my closed eyelids with the palms of my hands and tried to focus. What had I been invited to do? It was an exciting proposal: I was asked to be a judge for the thirty-second annual World Cheese Awards, and this year, they were happening in Bergamo, Italy.

You might remember I was a fresh-off-the-boat newbie to London when the British cheese Cornish Kern (from Lynher Dairies) won the awards, and my second year in the UK was when Norway's cheese won the supreme honor, just as Connor and I went to spend Christmas in northern Norway. By the time the World Cheese Awards rolled around during my third year living in England, I had found myself in the position of being invited, expenses paid, to judge the event. My trajectory into the cheese world was an evolution I could not have predicted, but this seemed like an indication I was on the right path.

The World Cheese Awards are a rollicking cheese-community reunion (much like the Cheesemonger Invitational and Slow Cheese). Similar to what's done for the Olympics, countries bid to host the annual competition and receive 260 judges from thirty-five different countries—no small undertaking. We were welcomed to Bergamo with the declaration, "Bergamo is not a land of pizza, it's a land of cheese!"

Here's how it works: All the judges are put into groups of three. Each group judges thirty-five cheeses. That year, 3,804 cheeses from forty-two countries were judged, and we scored the cheeses on the criteria of visual appearance of the rind and paste, body and texture, aroma, flavor, and mouthfeel. We were instructed not to penalize cheeses for obvious travel damage, and at the end of our three-hour judging window, we were to mark our "Super Gold" cheese—the highest-scoring cheese on the table.

The Super Gold cheeses chosen by each group eventually make their way to the International Super Jury, which is composed of sixteen of the most respected voices in cheese from around the world (including Jason Hinds of Neal's Yard

Dairy), each of whom chooses a single cheese out of the eighty-four Super Gold winners. The Super Jury then forms a panel and publicly scores each cheese in front of a full auditorium. Cameras, big-screen projections, and an emcee bring the event to life—reality TV–style.

For the first round of judging, I was put with an Italian fella, Luca, and Roman, a Swiss man (from the Italian-speaking part of Switzerland). I had been taking Italian classes and had the opportunity to practice speaking with them as we spent the morning tasting. Luca was team captain and led us through the cheeses, which were spread out on several long tables pushed together. We weren't given any information about where the cheeses were from or their names, only broad descriptions: which animal the milk came from (cow, sheep, goat, etc.) and the cheese's general category (like "mild blue").

We began with the light, bloomy-rind cheeses, making our way up the flavor-intensity ladder through sheep's-milk cheeses like Manchego, then the deeply savory Parmigiano Reggiano wheels (we judged five different wheels of this epic variety), and lastly the potent cheeses like Époisses and wheels with any added flavors (truffle, dried fruit, pepper). We smelled, nibbled, contemplated, and discussed. Luca plugged his nose to accurately identify what he was tasting versus smelling.

To look around the room during the judging was to see hundreds of people saying with their pen and their taste buds that cheese is more than a commodity

product; it's a craft worthy of intense consideration.

The cheese my group selected as our Super Gold winner, to be put up for consideration among the other "best of" cheeses, was a cow's-milk blue cheese with grape leaves that had been soaked in a pear liqueur and then wrapped around the cheese as it aged. It was a delicate yet intact cheese (its flesh kept itself together outstandingly well), with an unusual and compelling flavor profile, neither too blue, nor too flavored by its herbal rind. "It's something special," Luca said, wagging his index finger at it, and Roman and I nodded and went in for another nibble. After we'd tasted and scored all thirty-five cheeses on our table, I adhered the "Super Gold" sticker to its plate.

As it turns out, our pick made it beyond the next round of judging, too, and was one of the top sixteen judged in the big-screen-hyped final judging of the day. When the Super Jury panel sat, this cheese was the last one to be judged—and it was on the heels of an exquisite Parmigiano Reggiano that had wowed the panel and earned lots of sixes and sevens (out of a possible seven points), garnering the highest total score thus far.

As the judges considered this unusual blue cheese wrapped in pear liqueur–soaked grape leaves, the audience communally held their breath. One by one down the line, the judges hoisted their score cards. As the cards flashed over, showing mostly sixes and sevens, there was a buzz in the room: Would it upset the reigning high scorer, the Parmigiano Reggiano?

Drumroll...

The scores were tied! But there could only be one winner. A classic cheese pitted against a modern style with an atypical flavor profile. Traditional versus groundbreaking, but both exceptional—the tie reflected the diversity of quality cheesemaking happening around the world that year.

In the end, the balance tipped to the leaf-wrapped blue—the cheese I had tasted earlier that morning, in a sea of nearly four thousand other cheeses, was crowned supreme champion! *Wow.*

It was only after it had been chosen as the winner that its place of origin was revealed: Rogue Creamery in Oregon, USA. It was not only the first cheese from the United States to win big at the World Cheese Awards, but for it to be from the *same creamery* I had visited years earlier, shortly after I moved to London, the same creamery that had primed me to take on the Comté cheese project, which of course set the stage for all my other cheese adventures—*what are the chances?*

AT THE WORLD CHEESE AWARDS THAT year, I met Jamie Montgomery, the producer of Montgomery's Cheddar, which I often proclaimed to be my favorite cheddar at NYD. The shop's customers affectionately shortened its name to

"Monty's," and more often than not, someone would walk purposefully into the shop and say, "I'm here for Monty's!"

In *The Book of Cheese*, author Liz Thorpe writes, "When it comes to Cheddar, there is no cheese more profound and life-altering than Jamie Montgomery's. For cheese folk, it's the consummate reference point for English Cheddar."

Jamie is tall, with dark hair and a reserved British demeanor that quickly shifts to an easy smile and hospitable warmth; I liked him right away. He is a third-generation producer—the Montgomery family has been making cheddar in Somerset since 1911. Meeting him felt like meeting Martin Scorsese—*I love your work!*—and as a fangirl of his cheese, I was thrilled when he welcomed me to visit his creamery.

His lauded cheddar is made in Somerset, a half hour away from Tom's team at Westcombe, and is also a part of the West Country Farmhouse Cheddar. I took the train from London to Somerset, and Jamie picked me up at the station midmorning. In the car on the way to North Cadbury, where the farm and creamery are, Jamie drove me along narrow roads flanked by lush hedges as tall as elephants. Conversation came easily, and even my simplest questions led to a cascade of anecdotes, like the time Montgomery's was the victim of a cheddar heist(!), or how Jamie assuages his team's fears of any challenges they face—mites, using the right starter cultures—by reassuring them (and himself) that his grandpa had faced the same challenges,

Jamie Montgomery of Montgomery's Cheddar

and if his grandpa could overcome those challenges, they could, too!

Possibly more than any cheesemaker I'd met before, Jamie consistently circled back to an emphasis on tradition—not for the sake of convention or even heritage, but because he believed it made a better product.

When I asked him about why his cheddar is so special and heralded as an outstanding example—if not *the finest* example—of this style of cheese *in the world*, he responded, "I haven't the faintest idea. I just have a list of things I think I mustn't screw up."

"What's on the list?"

"Bedding the cows on straw and avoiding mastitis and listeria and using the right starter cultures. Stuff like that."

The life of a cheesemaker.

"We're doing our best to keep it going," he humbly insisted. Considering that a quick Google search of "Montgomery's cheese" brings up descriptors like "world-class" and "the best," Jamie sure played it cool.

He showed me around the cheesemaking room. Two guys had put the cheddared slabs through a peg mill and were stirring in salt before scooping the little chunks of curd into molds and pressing them with the pneumatic press.

As the head of production, Jamie oversees the entire operation, and most of his time is spent covering the loose ends of the business—he'd be out in the cow pasture fixing a broken fence, replacing rusted troughs, and doing general "firefighting," as he called it.

He walked me next door to "the store," a huge barn where rows and rows of cheese were maturing on shelves that nearly reached the ceiling.

"Where's your robot?" I asked in jest.

He laughed and said, "People ask me if we'd get a robot and I reply, 'I wouldn't have *a* robot . . . I'd have *two* robots!'"

He's a robot guy? Turns out, the only reason he didn't have a twin to Tina the Turner was a matter of budget. For a man who placed such importance on tradition, I was initially taken aback, although I immediately understood his theory echoed Tom's: technology and artisan practices are not mutually exclusive. There's no use in doing artisanal things just for the sake of being artisanal, especially when it results in a poorer product and countless trips to the chiropractor.

He grabbed his cheese tester, colloquially known as the "cheese thief"—the metal tool that allows affineurs to sample a narrow portion from a wheel of cheese and easily cover their tracks—and led me farther into the store. He and I walked through the rows, with shelves of cheese stacked high above our heads. We tasted numerous wheels at various stages of maturation, and batches that used a selection of Montgomery's seven different starter cultures.

"Do you know why we let mold grow on the outside of the wheels?" he asked, and after a moment's pause, he challenged me: "Guess why."

Because it's friendly mold? Because the bacteria positively affect the flavor? Because it's a natural part of the process?

After a back-and-forth of me circling the bull's-eye and him nudging me closer to the answer, I landed on his reason: he goes to the trouble of clothbound (versus plastic, for instance) because it's hugely important for the cheese to breathe . . . but it shouldn't breathe *too* much, or it'll dry out, so he coats the cloth in lard, which keeps the moisture in and stops the cheese from breathing too much. Here's when the mold comes in handy: the mold that grows on the outside of the wheel eats away at the lard, therefore allowing the cheese to breathe—*just the right amount*—as it matures.

"And you know why I wanted you to guess that? Because you've learned it instead of me just telling you."

"You're a good teacher, Jamie," I said, and I meant it. For all the time I spent making cheese at Sleight Farm, and for all my interest in seeing the cheeses made at each creamery I visited, I hadn't given as much thought to the maturation process.

Surely that wasn't the *interesting* part, right?

I had a revelation as I stood surrounded by the wheels of cheese sitting patiently on their shelves, like caterpillars hanging in their cocoons. We humans tend to think it takes an abundant amount of *effort* to undergo transformation, as though we must *earn* a metamorphosis. But at certain moments, no effort is necessary for significant progress to happen. Sometimes, we just need to let go and be patient. Let life do what it does. Let the mold grow, let it eat away at the exterior a bit, and let the cheese breathe. Then wait. Wait for it to become the best expression of itself, which in this case, was some of the best cheddar cheese on earth.

OUR MOVE TO ENGLAND BEGAN A transformation akin to dropping rennet into our lives and watching everything around us coagulate. In the ensuing years, Connor and I held on tight as we were stirred and salted and set into molds. We had no idea how long we'd stay in Europe, but I'd at last found the connection and community I sought. I continued to work on finding myself—and that's where wine comes in.

Here's your cheese party of recipes from this section; and that lone glass of wine beckons you to turn the page for further exploration of it . . .

WHAT CAN WINE NOT EFFECT? IT BRINGS TO LIGHT THE HIDDEN SECRETS OF THE SOUL.

—HORACE

PART TWO

WINE // ITALY

Harvesting grapes at the vineyard of Comelli Winery in northern Italy

FROM THE VINE TO THE BOTTLE

Grapes. Such perfect little bulbs of ripe, sugary juiciness. Look more closely at the bunches, hanging from their vines in the vineyard, and you'll notice a "whitish bloom, visible to the eye, that includes yeasts" (per fermentation guru Sandor Katz). Right about now you should be thinking, *Okay, so grapes themselves contain both sugar and yeast*—and that is your first major clue to the fermentation capabilities of the simple grape.

All that needs to happen next for the grapes to become wine is the application of a bit of gentle pressure, releasing the juices from their grape-skin bindings; the yeasts will intermingle with the sugary juice and have a *feast*! The yeasts munch on the sugars and, just as all living things have by-products from eating, they burp out ethanol (alcohol!) and fart out carbon dioxide. Fine, yeast doesn't actually burp or fart, but you get the idea—fermentation is at work, and this interplay is how grapes transform into wine.

Just about any fruit can be fermented into an alcoholic drink, thanks to that same dance between sugar and yeast, but grapes are special in that they "possess an ideal balance of sugars, acid, and tannins to support yeast growth," Katz explains. More than with any other fruit, "it is easy to fully ferment grape juice into a strong alcoholic beverage to store, age, and ship around the world." Grapes are basically *asking* to be turned into wine.

To put it simply, wine is fermented grapes. Just as $1 + 1 = 2$, you can think of the fermentation of wine as an equation: *Yeast + Sugar = Alcohol and Carbon Dioxide*. Let's break that down further.

Alcohol's organic chemical compound is ethanol, so when you see this fermentation equation in more science-centered discussions, you'll probably see the term *ethanol* show up. When they're talking about ethanol, they're talking about alcohol. And, well, alcohol? We all know about the alcohol in wine (and the hangover that comes with it). The more sugar there is for the yeast to consume, the more alcohol will be produced.

What about carbon dioxide (CO_2)? CO_2 is a gas, and the first few days after harvest, during primary fermentation—

which always takes place in an aerobic environment, meaning the vessel is open to the air—CO_2 floats out of the container. (This is why cellars need good aeration.) In some cases, CO_2 is used during a second fermentation in an anaerobic environment, where it is sealed in the bottle to turn a still wine into that bubbly you toast with during a New Year's celebration.

The simple interplay between sugar and yeast is something humans have experimented with for ages; how and when its fermentation is encouraged or slowed down is a major factor in determining what kind of wine the grapes will become.

A man who was fond of wine was offered some grapes at dessert after dinner. "Much obliged," said he, pushing the plate aside; "I am not accustomed to take my wine in pills."

—JEAN-ANTHELME BRILLAT-SAVARIN

TO SAY "WINE IS OLD" IS UNDERSTATING the reality. There's evidence of winemaking in China dating back nearly ten thousand years, and confirmation of the earliest sign of domesticated grapes, from about 6000 BCE, in the Eastern European country of Georgia. The art of viticulture—growing grapes—quickly spread as the people of the Caucasus migrated in all directions. When people start growing grapes . . . you know what happens next.

"The perfect drink, it turns out— whether it be mind-altering, medicinal, a religious symbol, liquid courage, or artistic inspiration—has not only been a profound force in history, but may be fundamental to the human condition itself," Patrick McGovern says in his book *Uncorking the Past.*

Beyond humans, McGovern points out that animals, such as elephants and birds, "are also known to gorge themselves on fermenting fruit." Humans aren't quite so unique in this predilection; even "robins fall off their perches" post-gorging.

Despite wine's ancient roots, its evolution continues to this day, and here's where it gets interesting, and complicated: as humans evolve, so do the wines we produce. There are diverging methods of production and philosophies behind the decisions on how to make wine. Not all wines are produced in the same way, including how the winemaker initiates the fermentation.

Let's go back to that most basic instance of fermentation beginning: the yeasts found naturally on grape skins (referred to as *native, wild,* or *indigenous* yeasts) consume the sugars in the grapes. Sandor Katz says, "Ripe grapes are so yeast-rich that vigorous fermentation starts almost immediately." *Whoa, a hungry bunch.* However, like all things in nature, there are elements of inconsistency—*just how hungry will they be?* Mother Nature is not predictable, and us humans? Well, we love predictability, so some winemakers add a commercial yeast product to ensure consistency. The yeast they add, *Saccharomyces cerevisiae* (also called baker's or brewer's yeast, the same strain of yeast used in breadmaking), is *predictable*. It sets the rest of the process on a much easier-to-control journey. Wine producers tend to like that predictability, and consumers have come to expect that, too (generally, they assume that a bottle of wine they plan to buy next week will taste just like the bottle of the same wine they bought last week), so for these reasons, this procedure of *adding* yeast has become the standard operation for most wineries around the world. The term *conventional wine* refers to this way of making it.

The thing is, this is fermentation we're talking about! As we learned with artisan cheese, a fermented product is *not* going to taste exactly the same every time. It is antithetical to the process of fermentation, because even beyond the yeasts, there are bacteria that can adjust the final taste and mouthfeel—one example of that is malolactic fermentation (also called malolactic conversion), the process by which bacteria (primarily lactic acid bacteria) convert acids to lactic acids, imparting a buttery flavor or dairy

notes to a wine. This process is commonly encouraged when making a wine like chardonnay.

There's also the concept of terroir, and the role fermentation plays in that. Terroir is a wine's "sense of place," the way it expresses its origins. The *Oxford Companion to Wine* begins its explanation with: "terroir, [the] much-discussed term for the total natural environment of any viticultural site. No precise English equivalent exists for this quintessentially French term and concept." Generally, it's how the wine's flavor and structure reflect the environment (climate, soil, topography—like slope and elevation—and surrounding flora) in which the grapes used to make it were grown.

Oenophiles—wine connoisseurs— point to terroir as the foundation of the drink, and wine writer Megan Krigbaum told me that winemakers are "relying on indigenous yeasts more and more, rather than dumping in commercial yeast. Many say it's crucial to preserving the terroir in wine."

There are many ways that a wine can taste different, aside from fermentation technique and terroir, such as grape varieties. *Vitis vinifera* is the species of grapevine that includes all the grape varieties commonly used for making wine, like sangiovese, merlot, chardonnay, and beyond.

Fun fact: *Vitis vinifera* is also the species of the average table grape, the ones next to the Baron Bigod on your cheese board—though table grapes are plumper than wine grapes, with a thinner skin, and contain less sugar. Same species; different variety. The sugar content is important because (as you just learned) wine is made when yeast consumes the sugars in the grape and transforms them into alcohol (releasing carbon dioxide as a by-product). The riper the grape, the more sugar; the more sugar in the grape, the more alcohol in the wine. (This is why picking grapes at the ideal ripeness is so crucial.)

The type of container in which the wine is fermented or aged will also affect its taste: Was it an oak barrel? A stainless-steel tank? A ceramic amphora?

I've only touched on a handful of the great many decisions the winemaker had to make to create the liquid you're swirling in your glass as you read this (I hope, for your sake). So what at first blush seems like such a simple equation of *how to make wine*, and even of *what wine is*, is revealed to be a messy tangle of vines.

CAN WE AGREE ON ONE THING RIGHT now? *Wine is awesome.* Right? Okay, cool, we're on the same page. That's important, because I'm about to wade into an area of wine that can be divisive.

Currently in the wine industry, the differing paths of winemaking can generally be broken down between the camp that *doesn't add anything* to their wines, and the camp that *does* add elements (such as the yeast mentioned earlier). This divergence exists even before the wine is produced, too, affecting the farming decisions made in the vineyard. There again, the former camp doesn't add anything (chemical sprays such as

pesticides), while the latter chooses to have more command over the process by asserting those tools of control.

There is quite a bit of gray space (in methods and labels and certifications) between these two extremes, but generally speaking, producers in the first camp are known as noninterventionalists, living by the motto "Nothing added, nothing taken away," and their wines are most commonly referred to as *natural wines*. Winemakers on the "adding as needed" side of the scale produce wines dubbed *conventional wines*, and in *some* cases, these are accurately called *industrial wines*.

The latter is presently the more common, modern, global way of growing grapes and making wine.

TO LOOK AT THIS ANOTHER WAY, LET'S consider the Vespa, the motorized scooter that has come to represent Italy the world over. The first Vespa model was presented to the public in 1946, in the aftermath of World War II. The Vespa brought many perks with it (including the emancipation of women in post-Fascist Italy!) and became a ubiquitous mode of transportation, but it shouldn't necessarily be how we equate Italians with transport, full stop, right?

Similarly, modern winemaking methods—spraying the vineyards with herbicides, adding commercial yeast to the wine must, incorporating enzymes to help break down the grape skins, etc.—are not historically how wine was made; they came along relatively recently in history, but have indelibly changed the way people experience wine (consumers' expectations of what wine should taste like) and define the current norms in wine production.

Just as the Vespa is a fairly modern image of Italy and is seemingly ever-present, it doesn't represent *all* the modes of transportation in Italy, nor the *best* mode of transportation for every purpose. When something shiny and new enters a space—whether it be Vespas or modern winemaking practices—it doesn't necessarily cover the whole of the space it enters, and it's not always all good. While we're considering a perspective that takes a broader view of time into account—and the established way of doing something—it's interesting to remember that the

official proclamation of the Kingdom of Italy wasn't issued until 1861, and prior to that, "to be 'Italian' was more of an identification with a number of collective memories, rather than a national memory," says Claudia Baldoli in her book *A History of Italy*. "There are elements of continuity that have shaped Italian identity over the past 1,500 years," which notably included food and wine as some of the most influential cultural unifiers.

Wine and Italy. There's a lot to unpack here. The two are interchangeable to me now, because that country offered me a gateway to the abundant world of wine. Let me take you to the year I stumbled into an unforgettable thicket of vines.

THE COMELLIS

Honk honk! The driver tooted the horn as he navigated hairpin turns, pressing the pedal until it hit the floor as we climbed two kilometers up a steep hill. The path repeatedly switched back on itself, with any vision of what lay ahead entirely obscured. *Be cool, Katie*—this was supposed to be a relaxing Italian countryside escape, after all. At last, we reached the top and entered the sparsely populated town of Colloredo (Colloredo di Soffumbergo), then pulled into a driveway flanked by rolling cascades of vineyards. We'd arrived at Comelli Winery in the far northeastern corner of Italy, in a region called Friuli (Friuli–Venezia Giulia).

I was twenty years old—a full decade before I moved to London—traveling with my best friend, Lara Mancinelli, during our study abroad year. She and I had lived across the hall from each other in our dorm at the Midwest college we attended. When we both moved to Europe for our junior year—she to Florence, I to Geneva—we hatched a plan to meet at Comelli Winery for a reunion.

It wasn't happenstance that we chose

a winery as our meeting place; Lara knew our hosts, Pierluigi and Daniela Comelli, because their son, Nicola, had lived with her family in Ohio during a one-year student-exchange program. The two families became irreversibly linked. When I first met Nicola, a couple of years before I visited Colloredo, he came to our freshman dorm with Lara's younger sister, Maria. They were probably seventeen years old, and were wide-eyed as we took them to a house party. (I'm sure this reinforced multiple outlandish American stereotypes Nicola had. "Do you know how to shotgun a beer?") My memory of him is of a goofy, scrawny kid who could speak decent English.

In Colloredo, Nicola's parents welcomed us warmly to the hilltop, although they had few words in English to communicate with us. Lara had been taking Italian classes, and we relied on that (my French immersion was of little help). We'd be there for a couple of days on our own before Nicola—now a university freshman in Milan—took the train home to join us.

Nicola's paternal grandmother, Nonna Anilla, was there to greet us, too, and nonverbal communication with her was my favorite because it involved her offering homemade baked goods—tortes and cakes and biscuits—like a greeting with confetti of sugar and flour. She lived in nearby Udine and visited Colloredo often. Every weekend she'd come by with freshly baked sweets; in that way, her presence was a constant in the renovated old farmhouse atop the hill.

Nonna Anilla was the last of eight children. Born in 1924, she was eighty-two years old and she stood about the same height as my Italian American grandma, Sally, the top of her curly gray head lower than my shoulders. Anilla was as active and clearheaded as some people half her age, and she had the brawn to scrub a filthy pan spit-spot clean but fingers nimble enough to finely shape fresh pasta dough.

In 1946, a year after World War II ended, her husband, Paolino—Nicola's paternal grandfather—bought the Colloredo property. This was a time when many Italians were moving to cities or abroad to find work, but Paolino had foresight, and he dreamed of what future generations could do with the land. There was a family living on the hilltop when he bought it, and they continued living there until the 1970s, paying rent to Paolino in wine, salumi, and even birds. "The road to get up didn't exist!" Nonna Anilla remembered. "It wasn't easy to get to the top of the hill by car. Everything was kind of a dump."

I couldn't imagine the pristine peak, which had a 360-degree view over parts of Friuli and into neighboring Slovenia, as anything less than stunning, and had never even considered that the wacky, curvy road had only been paved within the last decade. Life up on the hilltop must have felt incredibly isolated from the small towns surrounding its base; and yet up there among the clouds, the small community gathered to make wine. "It was an informal production, and there were always neighbors and farmers who helped out," Nonna Anilla recalled. They grew native grape varieties: friulano, malvasia, and refosco. In between the rows of vines were fruit trees, a garden, and one cow.

By 2006, the year Lara and I visited during college, Nicola's dad, Pierluigi (who goes by Pigi), had taken over the vineyard, where he'd produced wine under the Comelli label since the eighties; he ran it as a side project around his full-time job as a notary. It was still a relatively casual winemaking operation, but Pigi had hopes of raising the bar. He hired a young groundskeeper, Eros, who used his paycheck to help pay for enology school (enology is the study of wine and winemaking), with the thought that he'd step in as head of production one day.

I smile when I remember that I named my Facebook album from that trip "I'm in Love with Eros," referring to all the time Lara and I spent ogling him as he flexed his muscles while doing manual work around the grounds. The name Eros evokes the Greek god of love, sex, and eroticism—*c'mon*, of course we were

The vista from the Comellis' vineyards, overlooking the vines and with a view of neighboring hilltops, with the Italian Alps in the distance

going to swoon. Hilariously, we never even talked to him; it was more fun to have our crush be an inside joke. (An inside joke Facebook won't let us forget.)

Aside from our immature giggle fits, Lara and I were well-behaved guests and grateful that Daniela and Pigi had thrown their doors open for us without hesitation. When Nicola took the train over from Milan, joined by his older brother, Filippo, I was shocked that he was so tall—he had definitely gone through puberty in the two years since he'd visited our university quad. His chest was broad, and he'd grown his hair out à la Paul McCartney on the cover of *Abbey Road*. The time we all spent together on that trip played like a promotional reel for the Italian way of life—strolls among the rows of vines, helping Daniela chop vegetables for dinner as she seared meat and stirred steaming sauce at the stovetop. At dusk we'd lay

a blanket down on the grass among the vines and sip one of the Comellis' white wines—friulano, a grape indigenous to the area—as we watched the sun set on the neighboring towns.

As the sky dissolved from peach to fuchsia over the miles of land below, I couldn't help reflecting on my faded Italian heritage. *Is this what my great-grandparents left behind?* My grandmother's parents had immigrated to the States shortly before she was born and, in their desire to assimilate, never taught my grandma the Italian language, nor did they keep in close contact with family who hadn't moved across the Atlantic. By the time I came around, our Italian roots had been severed, forgotten, or lost. *They're somewhere.* I finished the last sip of friulano, holding the glass by its stem on my cross-legged lap, and said hello to the moon.

131

Friuli–Venezia Giulia, Italy

I RETURNED TO COLLOREDO A DECADE later, the first year Connor and I were living in London. Nicola was now a man—fully bilingual and practicing law in Milan, where he lived with his American girlfriend, Maria—Lara's sister. Do you follow? Sorry, it seems convoluted, but it's just a simple love story: several years after Nicola did the exchange program in America, he and Maria reunited in Italy and, rather unexpectedly, fell in love.

Maria, who had firsthand experience with the challenges of moving abroad for a partner, recognized that Connor and I were new to Europe and thought a jovial Italian Easter celebration would make us feel more settled. She and Nicola invited us to Colloredo to spend the holiday with the Comellis. We'd only been in London for a month, and that crisp spring weekend was the first whisper of home we intuited;

it was a glimpse of the famous familial Italian kindness. (I still hadn't traced the thread of my Italian ancestry, so for the time being, the Comellis were as close as I got to Italian relations.)

The Comellis' property had evolved drastically since my initial visit ten years earlier. It was still breathtaking and elegantly rustic, tucked into the mountains that separate northeast Italy from Slovenia, but the Comellis had done renovations and now ran a functioning *agriturismo*—giving underused farm buildings on the vineyard new life as accommodations for agritourists.

The winery itself, too, seemed to be growing. They made several varieties of red wine and white wine, were represented at Vinitaly, an international wine exhibition and competition held annually in Verona, and exported their wines to high-end restaurants and boutique wine shops in the United States. Eros, the still-hunky former groundskeeper, had indeed become the head winemaker. He oversaw a staff of two, who helped in the vineyard and the cellar.

The transparency with which the winery operated in tandem with the agriturismo—openly showing visitors the steps of the winemaking process—piqued my own curiosity about winemaking. Nicola took me to the cellar—*la cantina*—

and I fell under a spell among the wooden casks and stainless-steel tanks, which held various stages of fermenting grape juice. The space was warm, even with a mammoth fan blowing near the open door, and the scent of the room was subtly floral, undeniably yeasty (in a different way than the cheese shop), and unexpectedly enjoyable. I wanted to stick out my tongue like I was catching a snowflake to see if I could taste anything from the air—the aroma seemed palpable.

Nicola climbed up on one barrel like a monkey to look at the grape skins and juice inside it, fizzing away in a surge of fermentation. That mixture of juice and skins (as well as the seeds of the grapes and, in some cases, their stems) is called the must. He grabbed the handle of a metal paddle and plunged it into the must like a Venetian gondolier. He pushed down on the grape skins that had floated to the top as carbon dioxide was released, collectively known as *il cappello*, "the cap." "It's such a satisfying job," he said wistfully.

Satisfying, sure, and definitely necessary—it's important to keep the cap wet, immersed in the juice. Keeping the juice in contact with the grape skins is called *maceration*. (Maceration = "skin contact.") Doing this not only fends off bacteria but is how red wine gets its color. It's also how the wine gets its *tannins*—the astringent polyphenols found in the grape skins that generate a dry-mouth sensation, like black tea. Tannins give wines their structure; a young wine's tannins will dry out the palate, but as wine ages, its tannins soften.

Maceration isn't *only* used for red wine; it's also used to make what's known as orange wine, amber wine, or skin-contact wine—many descriptors for the same style of wine. To produce this wine, the skins of white wine grapes are left in contact with the juice longer than they are for your average white wine, giving it an orange or amber hue. (Some of the most influential orange wine producers, Josko Gravner and Radikon, are also in the Friuli region.) In making both red wine and orange wine, the skins are eventually discarded and the remaining liquid is matured.

"So," I began, as I watched Nicola continue to push down the cap, "what, exactly, happens to turn grape juice into alcohol?"

Nicola loved playing teacher. "Simple. The yeast eats the sugars in the grape juice and converts that sugar to alcohol."

"Right," I said bashfully, "I think I knew that."

He continued the lesson as he helped me up onto the barrel: "Carbon dioxide is the other main by-product of fermentation, and that's why we keep the cantina well ventilated. People can pass out . . . or even die if there's not air circulation." *Oh, snap.*

I followed Nicola's lead and clambered above the cap of the next barrel, which he hadn't punched down yet. It felt like I was standing over a heated vent, because as microbes work, they create energy. Temperature is an important factor in

fermentation—a warmer environment encourages activity (bacteria will be more active and yeast will work harder), and cooler temperatures slow down fermentation—so as the microbial transformation occurs, it self-propels. I held my hand over the barrel of fermenting grapes, in which the yeast was actively making alcohol and carbon dioxide, and I could feel the heat emanating from the exciting bustle below. The magic was happening!

Nicola handed me the paddle, which had a flat metal bottom perpendicular to the handle, and invited me to press with all my might against the solid layer of grape skins until I broke through the

With Nicola Comelli, pushing down on grape skins **135**

Pushing down the grape skins—"il cappello"—during primary fermentation

intense surface tension of the cap. I let out an unexpected grunt, and Nicola chuckled. "It's difficult at first! This step is something that's done every day during this phase of fermentation," he explained. "We punch down the skins so they remain wet and in contact with the juice. It's how the wine gets its color and texture."

After that first puncture, the rest of the punching-down process was easy, and like Nicola said—it was satisfying. The liquid below me was alive.

It can be hard to escape the perceived snobbery of wine, which may prevent you from asking questions when you're still learning the basics. We all need a Nicola—a friendly wine aficionado—to introduce us to vinification. Nicola himself wasn't a winemaker or a certified sommelier; he was an employment lawyer, but the family vineyard was his true passion. He was in love with every stage of the process; when he entered the cantina, he inhaled deeply and exhaled dreamily. "I love that smell."

Me too. I vowed to return.

IT WASN'T LONG BEFORE I HAD THE chance to do so: six months later, Connor and I went to Colloredo for Nicola and Maria's wedding at the old chapel overlooking the vineyard. Of course Lara was there, too, and I was sure our younger selves would have done backflips at the cause for this reunion. That visit to the Comellis' fortified an idea I'd been contemplating: *What if I helped the Comellis with their next grape harvest?*

EXPERIENCE IT LIKE A CHILD

Eating a meal at a table in Italy—leisurely following your bites with sips of wine and moving through the courses like a raft on a meandering river—is a distinct experience. It's not just the people and environment that make it special; it's just as much the actual nourishment. Food writer, cookbook author, and photographer (and Rome resident of two decades) Kristina Gill told me, "Italian food is not particularly sophisticated—but that's the beauty of it, right?" Like a teacher explaining fractions, she broke down the elements of four pastas dishes that make up the most popular Roman recipes: *carbonara*, *amatriciana*, *gricia*, and *cacio e pepe*. All of these have essentially the same handful of ingredients: cheese, egg or tomato, and cured pork . . . "It's *three* things that can taste like *fifty-seven* things," Kristina said. "With Italian food, you're able to make a symphony out of very simple, pure ingredients." (The same idea applies to grapes becoming wine.)

To take Kristina's simplicity meets symphony idea one step further, let's think about what that does to the human who consumes it. In *Pasta, Pane, Vino*, author Matt Goulding quotes an observation by Anthony Bourdain about the emotional quality of Italian food: "One should experience it like a child, never like a critic, never analytically." For a food to put you in your wide-eyed inner child's shoes? That is, simply, a gift.

What immediately comes to mind for me is sitting at the Comellis' large, circular dinner table with a bowl of cheesy polenta in front of me, blissfully washing it down with the Comellis' red blend, Soffumbergo, which uses the native refosco grape variety, as well as merlot and cabernet sauvignon, each of which is aged separately and then blended in the bottle. The resulting wine is earthy and spicy, like tobacco fields and dried fruit.

Daniela Comelli's polenta, one of the dishes she frequently made, was proof of Bourdain's point: it cradled me with each spoonful. When I asked her for the recipe, she pointed me to the gold standard: Gianni Cosetti's cookbook, *Vecchia e nuova cucina di Carnia*, which the famous chef wrote as an homage to his native Friuli. "He's the one who has made simple Friulian cuisine important," Daniela told me.

In his writing, Cosetti specifies how to top polenta—a typical dish from northeast Italy—based on the season, and which wine pairs best with that variation. In summer and winter, Cosetti suggests a glass of malvasia to pair with foie gras–topped polenta. In springtime, friulano (formerly known as tocai friulano), with asparagus tips on top of the dish. In autumn, thin slices of white truffle atop the polenta, with sauvignon blanc to wash it down. (Having the dish *without* wine was clearly not an option.)

At grocery stores in northern Italy, the polenta aisle has as many options as the cereal aisle in American stores. Daniela reaches for white polenta if she plans on topping it with fish and yellow polenta to go with meat. (Cheese pairs with both kinds of polenta.) At an average shop in the States, you probably won't be faced with multiple options—as long as it's not the instant stuff, just go with it. Most Italians who live in the Friuli region make polenta often enough that they have a motorized stirrer and a copper pot called a *paiolo*, the traditional basin for cooking polenta. Don't worry; I don't have those things and you don't need them to make this, either.

In most Italian cookbooks, you'll find the abbreviation "q.b.," which is short for *quanto basta*, meaning "however much is needed," "as needed," or "however much you like" (a little like when American cooks write "to taste"). It's a principle from the book *La scienza in cucina e l'arte di mangiar bene* by Pellegrino Artusi, a classic culinary resource in Italy first published in 1891. I love this kind of direction when I'm reading, or even writing, a recipe because it's a reminder to trust your senses, and everyone's are a little different. If you want to drench your dish in olive oil, do it. If you love black pepper, go crazy with it! Basically, do what you want, do what feels right. *Quanto basta!*

Friulian Polenta

Polenta can take many forms, and this version (which Cosetti called *toc' in braide*, or "dip in the farm") has a pool of cheese on top. (I know this isn't the cheese section, but there's no escaping some overlap.)

The cheeses Cosetti calls for are *formaggio di malga* (a pliable hard cheese that's quite strong and salty), *caprino* (a fresh goat's-milk cheese), and *ricotta fresca* (fresh ricotta). While the ricotta may be easy to source, I suggest easier-to-access Gruyère in place of formaggio di malga, and any fresh goat's-milk cheese as a substitute for caprino.

POLENTA

4¼ cups (1 liter) water (see Note on page 141)

2 cups (500 milliliters) milk

1 teaspoon fine sea salt, plus more as needed

1⅓ cups (200 grams) finely ground cornmeal (it might be labeled "polenta" at the grocery store; avoid the instant variety)

SAUCE

11 ounces (300 grams) cheese (a combination of Gruyère, fresh ricotta, and goat cheese), shredded or broken into smaller pieces

½ cup (120 milliliters) milk

TOPPING

4 tablespoons (½ stick/60 grams) salted butter

⅓ cup (50 grams) finely ground cornmeal

Fine sea salt and freshly ground black pepper (optional)

1. Make the polenta: Combine the water and milk in a large saucepan and bring to a simmer over medium heat. Add the salt, then gradually pour in the polenta, stirring vigorously with a wire whisk or wooden spoon to avoid clumping. Reduce the heat to medium-low and cook, stirring fairly continuously, for 40 minutes (or according to package instructions, which can vary), until the polenta is thick and almost creamy in texture and begins to pull away from the sides of the pan. Try a bite; if the individual grains still feel firm, add a little more water and whisk it in well. As it cooks, make sure you're scraping the bottom, corners, and sides of the pot so the polenta doesn't catch and burn.

2. Meanwhile, make the sauce: Fill a medium saucepan with 1 inch (2.5 centimeters) of water and bring it to a boil over medium heat, then reduce the heat to maintain a simmer. Place the cheeses and milk in a medium heatproof bowl and set it over the pot of water. Let the cheeses melt together, stirring every so often to combine them with the milk, until you have a smooth liquid. If the sauce is ready before the polenta, set it to the side until the polenta is almost done,

(*recipe continues*)

at which point you can reheat the sauce on the stovetop, while whisking, to ready it for serving.

3. Make the topping: Combine the butter and finely ground cornmeal in a small saucepan, and cook over medium heat, stirring as the butter melts. Cook, stirring occasionally, until toasted and golden, 3 to 4 minutes. Remove from the heat. (In *Vecchia e nuova cucina di Carnia*, the directions refer to this as *la morchia*, which literally translates to "the sludge." While that might not be a charming description, it is accurate! Rest assured, it is totally delicious spooned onto the polenta as a condiment.)

4. When the polenta has finished cooking, taste and season with salt as needed, then remove from the heat and serve immediately. Divide it among individual bowls and pour the sauce over the top, followed by a spoonful of the topping. Season with more salt and pepper, if desired, and serve.

Note: You could also use whey instead of part/ all of the water for cooking the polenta!

TUFFY

When I was a kid, it was a big deal when "Uncle" Jimmy Tufaro came over to visit. The son of two Italian immigrants, he'd served in the Merchant Marine—the tattoo of a curvaceous woman on his bicep proved it—and went on to found a steel fabrication plant in northeast Ohio. By the time I was ten years old, he was a squat, white-haired retiree with stories as grand as a dragon's tail. We called him our uncle, but there should've been a "great" in there—he was my grandma's brother. (Just to make things confusing for a little kid, I have an uncle Jimmy, too—my mom's twin brother.)

Uncle Jimmy didn't come over often. The half-day drive between our homes in different corners of the state was one we were more likely to make (not frequently, truth be told). I couldn't remember the last time he had visited, and from my mother's bread baking in anticipation of his arrival, and compulsive cleaning, I could tell it was an Occasion, with a capital O.

The whole family gathered with Uncle Jimmy and his son Danny, my mom's cousin, in the living room; the windows were open and the screens kept out the active rural bug population. I sat on the floor at my dad's feet and looked up at Uncle Jimmy, who seemed to be a towering figure, matching his lore in the family.

"Show us your tattoos!" my brother, Brian, and I requested after he was seated.

He grinned and began rolling up his sleeve. "You wanna see her dance?" he asked in his deep, froggy voice (something like Marlon Brando's sandpapered timbre

in *The Godfather*). His biceps, though no longer particularly muscular, was bronzed and thick, much like his stocky physique, and had a hula dancer inked on it.

"Yeah, dance!" Brian and I laughed giddily. In some combination of arm swivel and muscle twitch, he made the lady "dance." The anchor tattoo on his broad forearm couldn't boogie in the same way, so I have to excavate my memories to visualize that ink.

FOR A GREAT-UNCLE WE BARELY SAW, HE had an all-encompassing warmth, able to touch every person in the room with his presence, which was the essence of the Tufaro side of the family. When my mom spoke of him, she usually ended with a comment of admiration: "He's a gem," or "Sweet and dear, that's Uncle Jimmy."

During the Depression, he'd ridden railroad cars and supported himself with nickel boxing matches. He'd left his immigrant family's home as a teen and passed several years barely scraping by, doing the hobo hustle. That struggle gave way to serving in the navy; later, he founded the metal fabrication plant, where he himself worked and also employed his sons, Danny, Joey, and Nickie. His nickname, "Tuffy," was inspired by the alliteration of his last name and his toughness (oh, and the time he fell into a deep concrete hole and hit his head, but lived—walking away from the incident with a skull fracture). His external toughness was how he survived, but his kindhearted ability to make every soul around him shine has become his legacy.

It was in his nature to power through life as a burly man, but if you lifted the lid a bit, you'd find an aura of unconditional acceptance. (My dad tells the story of how Uncle Jimmy unequivocally welcomed him into the family, saying, "If you're good enough for our Susie, you're good enough for us," and giving him a big hug.)

After he passed away, a few years following that breezy day when he visited us in southeast Ohio, I remember his children Danny and Patty would wrap me in hugs that felt like Uncle Jimmy lived through them. Even when I grew up, they lifted on their tiptoes to give me kisses on the cheek, opening their arms wide as the timeless symbol of welcome and love.

My mom's cousins were proudly Italian American in a way that didn't carry on in my grandma's lineage when she married my grandpa Wayne. Uncle Jimmy, on the other hand, married Concetta (Connie) Novello, also the child of Italian immigrants. Their kids, in adulthood, threw large parties to make Italian food en masse. Every winter Danny hosted a sausage-making party, where he and any willing helpers would make three hundred pounds of pork sausage for smoking and drying. Each fall, Patty opened her garage and had all the Novellos come over with basket upon basket of fresh tomatoes to can their secret recipe for tomato sauce, a joyous and messy tradition that was even featured in the local newspaper.

Patty was especially close with my grandma, her "Aunt Sarah" (they always used Grandma Sally's Americanized given name). She admired my grandma for her

FaceTime, when she spent Sundays with my mom—the youngest of her Von Trapp bunch. At ninety-four years old, her bright personality still found its way through the cracks, but she was no longer able to sustain a conversation. I told her about my visits to Italy, but she couldn't connect them with anything meaningful.

"That's great, honey" was her vacant response.

"Italy, where your parents are from! Isn't that cool?" I'd say, trying to elicit some emotion or memory (or both) from the depths of her dementia. Grandma's decline underlined the slow fade of my Italian heritage, like a sidewalk-chalk drawing that's been out in the elements.

I desperately longed to know what she thought of my desire to find her parents' birth certificates, and I wanted to share that I'd booked a flight to return to the Comellis' in September to help with the grape harvest. La vendemmia, *here I come.*

independence and smarts—Grandma was near the top of her high school class and was college-bound. As a woman in 1943—the daughter of immigrants!—that's no small feat.

Like her brother Jimmy, my go-getter grandma Sally lived her long life with a rare mix of Tufaro toughness and warmth. As Connor and I packed up to move to London, her health and mental acuity were declining. Once, shortly after we'd moved, Patty, who frequently called her to check in, rang Grandma. "Hi, Aunt Sarah! It's Patty."

"I'm sorry, who?" Grandma didn't remember her niece. When Patty hung up the phone, tears fell from her eyes as she grieved. Aunt Sarah, strong and fierce, who had raised nine children while working full-time, was slowly leaving us.

About a year later, after I'd worked my first Christmas as a cheesemonger at Neal's Yard Dairy, Grandma moved to my hometown, where she could be better taken care of. Connor and I called on

THE HARVEST

Autumn pulled in like a high-speed train, and before I knew it, I was on my way back to the vineyard in Colloredo. I had taken six months of Italian classes in preparation; it was important to me to attempt elementary communication to better connect with the people I encountered.

When I arrived at Comelli Winery, I parked the car and exhaled audibly. I'd driven up that steep, curvy road and pulled into the driveway at nine o'clock in the evening. I pried my sweaty palms from the steering wheel as a protective howl ricocheted off the maroon stucco walls of the house and into the abyss over the vineyard. I stuck a leg out of the door and greeted Maia, the Comelli's large dog—a Bracco Italiano with long ears and droopy lips. *"Ciao, Maia, basta!"* I said as I emerged from the car. (*Basta*, which means "enough" or "that's all," was a word I had learned well when I was with the Comellis over Easter. At dinner Maia persistently lifted her long nose to the kitchen table; to discourage this behavior, *"Basta!"* was the dinnertime refrain.)

Daniela, the matriarch of the Comelli family, walked up behind her dog. "Katie! *Come stai?*"

"Bene. Ma sono stanca." Good, but tired. She stepped to greet me with arms wide open and welcomed me with a hug. She ushered me inside, sat me down at her kitchen table, placed a bowl in front of me, and ladled in hot broth with buttons of tortellini swimming in it. She'd simmered the broth over ten hours—low and slow—anticipating my arrival. My heart melted straight into that bowl of soup; I was so grateful. After I slurped up every drop, I crawled right into bed.

THE GRAPE HARVEST—*LA VENDEMMIA*— can feel like catching Harry Potter's golden snitch, because it's up to Mother Nature (in cahoots with the winemaker) to determine the optimal time to pick the grapes, and once they're picked, there are no do-overs. I'd be in Colloredo for a week strategically aligned with when the pignolo grapes—an indigenous red wine grape variety—would *probably* be ready to be harvested, but there were no promises.

Harvested pignolo grapes

Eros, the winemaker, had already harvested all the grapes for the white wine, and some of the red wine grapes like merlot, too. Pignolo was the last grape variety to be harvested that year.

I spent the next several days in the cantina with Eros, tasting the batches of fermenting wine, the grapes for which had been picked in the weeks prior, mid-August. The white wine grapes were always the first to be ready for harvest, then the reds—with the pignolo grapes taking the longest to ripen fully. I kept my fingers tightly crossed that I'd have the opportunity to experience the pignolo harvest.

I liked spending time in the cantina. The pleasantly yeasty aroma of the wines fermenting in the tanks would become the norm after a few minutes as my senses acclimated. I'd enter, greet Eros with "*Buongiorno!*," and stand to the side watching him in silence as he tinkered with the tanks and smelled each batch of juice as it fermented. In a matter of minutes, he'd call on me to hand him a light, or turn off a pump. One time, when he was pumping fermenting grape juice from the bottom of a tank back over the cap of floating grape skins on top (a process called *rimontaggio* in Italian, though it's often referred to by its French name, *remontage*), he invited me to climb up to watch, and after he was certain my glasses wouldn't fall into the tank, he handed the pump to me to direct the deep purple grape juice over the cap. This had the same effect as "punching down" the

A Babo mostimeter—a hydrometer used to measure sugar in the grape must

Eros Zanini, winemaker at Comelli Winery

cap, as I had helped Nicola do the year prior: when the skins float to the surface of the juice, you "punch down" or "pump over" (two different ways of doing the same thing) in order to reintroduce the juice to the skins. This needs to happen for the color and tannins from the skins to leach into the juice.

Eros explained to me that tannins are an indication of the type of grape used in the wine—certain varieties are known for having high or low tannins—and pignolo, the grape I had come to Italy hoping to harvest, is known for its high tannins, its robust mouthfeel.

Sometimes it was just Eros and me puttering around, and sometimes his helpers, Christian and Michele, were working alongside us. In a last-minute turn of events, Lara often joined us in the cellar, too.

Lara—who, you may remember, is my best friend and my connection to the Comellis in the first place—spent much

of that week in Colloredo because it just so happened that she had planned to visit Maria and Nicola in Milan for the month, and when she heard I'd be in Colloredo, she decided to meet me there.

It was more than a bonus or an added perk: her Italian-language proficiency made my cellar time with Eros much more productive. Despite my six months of Italian classes in London, if Lara hadn't been there, I would have spent most of the week miming. I wanted so badly to speak the language—the few sentences I could add to a conversation rolled gratefully off my tongue—and I was determined to continue learning beyond la vendemmia.

Aside from being my indispensable and pro bono translator, Lara was also my companion for swims in the pool and evening trips to Cividale del Friuli, the nearby medieval town founded by Julius Caesar in 50 BCE, for a Campari spritz aperitivo.

Near the end of the week, I watched as Eros walked through the rows of the vineyard, closely inspecting the hanging pignolo grapes. He gathered the Brix levels (in the wine world, sugar levels are measured in degrees Brix, abbreviated as °Bx), comparing the readings from the refractometer to help decide if the grapes were ripe enough to pick. Eros was looking for the grapes to reach their ideal sugar-to-acid ratio. He thought a couple of additional days in the sun would be good, but only if the weather stayed as sunny and warm as it had been. The forecast suggested the coming forty-eight hours would get colder and wetter—not

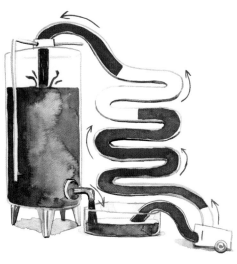

Rimontaggio

Even lizards love pignolo grapes.

Eros prepares for the harvest.

ideal. Colder days slow grape ripening, and too much rain means the grapes plump up with water, which causes their acidity levels to drop.

Eros was usually calm and collected, but his face betrayed the worry he must have felt. One chance was all he had for this year's pignolo vintage—one shot to not mess it up. So he consulted Emilio Del Medico, his wine adviser, who worked with a handful of wineries in the area, including New York restaurateur and *MasterChef* judge Joe Bastianich's vineyard, about twenty minutes from Colloredo. When Emilio came over, Eros introduced us in the cellar.

"The two most important times in winemaking," Emilio told me with an air of gravitas, "are the moment you pick the harvest and the first twenty-four hours after the harvest. Everything rides on those decisions."

The pressure was on.

"Tomorrow, pignolo is ready to pick."

Daniela shared Eros's decision with me the evening before the harvest was to begin. It was my first wine harvest ever, and I had no idea how quickly, how seemingly impromptu, the verdict could be made.

"The harvest is like *il parto*"—childbirth—"so we say Eros is giving birth tomorrow!" Daniela smiled.

In celebration, Lara and I popped open some *spumante* (sparkling wine) and snacked on umami chunks of cheese from a wedge of fresh-cut Parmigiano Reggiano (which inspired my eternal adoration for

Prosecco, the effervescent Champagne-esque wine that's put in your Bellini, is from northeast Italy, and the history of its name is riddled with semantics.

Historically, the prosecco grape variety was used to make prosecco wine in the Veneto and Friuli–Venezia Giulia regions of Italy. As the popularity of the wine grew (like when Paris Hilton had a canned prosecco brand circa 2008), more places around the world started making it and its following skyrocketed.

Italian authorities wanted the same control over the name "prosecco" that Champagne had—in which only that style of wine made in the northeastern region of Champagne, France, can be called Champagne.

To protect the name—and the inherent monetary value of being able to use that name—the Italian authorities decided to put up the armor of a DOC/DOCG designation, the same kind of appellation law that applies to cheeses like Comté and Stilton. The only problem was that prosecco was a grape variety, not a geographical term, as is necessary to create an appellation law. In an innovative move, the Italians rechristened the grape variety "glera" and located a town in Friuli called Prosecco to stake as the geographic region.

As of the 2009 vintage, Prosecco was no longer the name of the grape (which couldn't be protected), but it was the name of a place (which could). The new laws stated that for a wine to be labeled as "Prosecco," it must be from one of the designated appellations in/around the town of Prosecco, Italy, and be made with 85 percent glera grape.

Author Jason Wilson talks about this bizarre history in his book *Godforsaken Grapes* and concludes with an assumed eyebrow-raise and shrug, "No matter that the Friulian village of Prosecco wasn't really known for its sparkling wines. No matter that no one in the Veneto ever really called the grape Glera."

Bubbles in sparkling wine are created by dissolved CO_2. Although it's possible to pump CO_2 into a wine (like the carbonators some of you may have on your kitchen counter to turn still water into seltzer), most high-quality sparkling wine producers use the power of fermentation to harness the CO_2 that is a by-product of yeast consuming sugar. There are two commonly used methods to create sparkling wine during a secondary fermentation process: tank fermentation and bottle fermentation. To break down these basics, I've enlisted the expertise of wine consultant Tanisha Townsend.

Katie: Tanisha, can you give me the basic breakdown between Prosecco and Champagne?

Tanisha: The quick and dirty? You got it. The main difference is Italy (Prosecco) and France (Champagne). Another difference is the grapes used: Prosecco uses mainly glera grapes. Champagne uses chardonnay, pinot noir, and pinot meunier.

KQ: All three grapes are always used to make Champagne?

TT: No; sometimes it's the two reds, sometimes it's the one white. When you see "blanc de blancs," that's 100 percent chardonnay grapes. "Blanc de noirs" means it's made from the two red grapes or one of the two reds. They have two very distinct tastes. If you prefer it to be richer, fruitier, more full body, you'd probably prefer blanc de noirs. If you like it to be crisper, more citrusy, then blanc de blancs are for you.

KQ: Another huge difference is the way they're made, right?

TT: Exactly. Typically, Prosecco uses the tank method [also called the Charmat method or *metodo Italiano*], where they do the secondary fermentation in a tank to give it the bubbles, and *then* they'll put it in the bottle. Whereas in Champagne, they put still wine in the bottle and then add the yeast and sugar to the bottle, so it undergoes secondary fermentation in each separate bottle [this is called the *méthode champenoise* or traditional method, and it's also how Cava—the Spanish sparkling wine—is made].

KQ: Right, because when the yeast consumes the sugar, one of its by-products is CO_2 . . . and if there's nowhere for it to escape, it becomes sparkling wine! To recap: tank method = secondary fermentation occurs in the tank; traditional method = secondary fermentation happens in the bottle. Got it.

that simple combination). Since we were in northeast Italy, of course our bubbly of choice was Prosecco.

The grapes we'd be picking the following day—the pignolo grapes— produce what's known as the "noble wine," the red wine known simply as pignolo. A grape variety indigenous to the region, it's a beloved one. Daniela said of the wine, "Pignolo can be for Friuli what Barolo is for Piemonte." By this she meant that pignolo wine *could* become famous, revered, and sought after, like Barolo (a wine made from nebbiolo grapes). Like nebbiolo, pignolo grapes are high in tannins and produce a wine that is robust, rich, and textured, with a delicate balance of acidity and a long finish.

Evidently pignolo is a famously finicky grape. The literal translation of *pignolo* is "fussy," which I supposed made sense, although wine textbooks point to the grape bunch's resemblance to a pinecone as the accurate etymology (*pigna* means "pinecone" in Italian). They are a great grape to age in oak, because resting in the barrel can soften their tannins and the harder edges of their flavor. The Comellis aged pignolo in barriques—the wine world term for oak barrels of small capacity (225 liters), as opposed to huge casks—for a minimum of three years, followed by one year in the bottle.

In terms of how it's best enjoyed, "Pignolo needs food," Daniela had said as she slid a plate of cheese and crackers closer to me when we opened a bottle at dinner earlier in the week. "At first it's strong, but after a glass, you come to love it."

Aside from pignolo, the Comellis harvested other native grapes, like picolit, a white grape variety made into a sweet dessert wine, with a deep amber color and notes of apricot and honey, and the red wine grape refosco dal peduncolo rosso, an ancient variety thought to have grown on that land for more than a millennium, and of course friulano, which food critic Florence Fabricant called "an Italian white that makes friends easily." I enjoyed learning about these wines—new to my tongue—and I sensed the pride the Comellis felt for those vines. Among all of them, I counted pignolo as my preferred bottle. I was ready for the harvest.

IT WAS BEFORE EIGHT O'CLOCK IN THE morning; the sun was still low in the sky, hiding behind trees and buildings. I walked from the agriturismo apartment where I slept into the hillside vineyard it overlooked. Eros was moving empty barrels from storage into the cantina and Michele and Christian were in *la vigna* placing big red crates throughout its rows. These would soon be filled with bunches of grapes.

As I approached the rows of pignolo grapes, I began to hear the chatter of a dozen people speaking in enthusiastic Italian, a tune of overlapping conversations. I introduced myself with a wave and a smile: *"Ciao, sono Katie."* In a matter of moments, gloves and clippers appeared in my hands; I was ready.

A harvest will vary based on many factors: the size of the vineyard, whether the grapes are handpicked or machine-

The grape harvest at Comelli Winery

In the vineyard with Felicia

my case, in basic Italian) as we worked. Felicia, Christian's wife, positioned herself next to me with a big smile and a hug and helped get me oriented. She couldn't speak English, which helped me see the whole experience as a language class on top of a grape harvest.

We made our way down the rows like a gang of ants following a trail of food. It was a true team effort, and with camaraderie established, the time flew. The sun heated things up quickly, and before I knew it, we were shedding our jackets and sweatshirts. I placed a tidy bunch of grapes in the red crate and looked in it to see bugs climbing up the walls of the rigid plastic, escaping the crush of the grapes where they had previously nestled. *Bugs mean healthy soil*, I had to remind myself to keep from squirming.

The grapes hung at the height of my stomach or lower, so less than an hour into clipping, my back started to hurt, and I had to adjust my stance (which I constantly tweaked during the rest of the morning as new parts of my body piped up in complaint).

I never felt the truth of the adage "Many hands make light work" more than I did while cutting the grapes. When we began a new row, I'd look down the length of the plot and think, *This is going to take a while*, but inevitably we'd put down our overflowing red crates and I'd marvel at how quickly we'd made our way through it.

Around midday we finished, tired but cheerful. We walked toward the main building together as a crew, some people lagging behind to light a cigarette or pet

harvested, and the style of wine that will be made, among other considerations. Like many agricultural businesses, vineyards often hire migrants to do the labor of the harvest—this is true everywhere from cherry farms in Michigan to asparagus farms in Belgium—but the workers at this harvest were an exception to the rule: they were local friends and neighbors. Comelli Winery is small as far as industry standards go, and ever since Grandpa Paolino bought the land almost a century prior, the harvest had been established as a community endeavor.

All morning we clipped the grape bunches from their vines and chatted (in

Maia. As we approached the main room of the agriturismo office—the windows and doors were open, the sunshine pouring in—I heard pots clinking and clanking, and smelled the rich scent of Bolognese.

Daniela had been cooking up a storm while we were in the vineyard, and when I peeked into the room, I saw Lara in there with her flawless posture and graceful movements (an entire childhood as a ballerina will do that) setting the long dining room table with plates, forks, and wineglasses.

A half hour later, everyone had reconvened around the table. Eros poured wine—people drank either red or white to accompany the feast of cheese and salami, bread and mortadella, and *penne alla bolognese*—dispelling the myth that (in Italy or anywhere) one must drink certain wine with certain foods. Although red is typically thought to complement that kind of a meal, the heat of the day and the exertion of the morning inspired most of the table to ask for white wine—friulano.

Daniela called our attention and lifted her glass—we all followed suit—as she thanked us for our work and offered a toast: *"Salute!"* Eros popped the bubbly before we had even finished our first glasses (*down the hatch!*), and he walked around the table for a prompt refill of our quickly emptied glasses. I didn't get *ubriaca* (drunk), but I was happily tipsy as I picked up my fork to dig into the meal.

We ate gratefully, unabashedly motivated by our growling stomachs and the feast before us. The meal wasn't over until everyone deployed pieces of bread to sop up the extra sauce on their plates—an end-of-meal ritual known as *fare la scarpetta* ("make the little shoe"). The annual romp in the vineyard was closed for pignolo, although the fermentation had just begun.

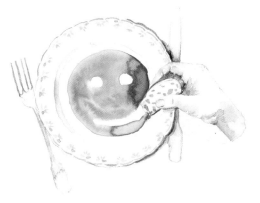

Spaghetti all'Ubriaco (Drunken Spaghetti)

When Italians discovered the joy of using their favorite beverage (wine) to cook their favorite food (pasta), variations of this plum-colored pasta dish became a standard meal. *Spaghetti all'ubriaco*—"drunken spaghetti"—isn't as inebriated as it sounds: the heat burns off the alcohol in the wine. In cooking the pasta with the wine, however, the noodles are imbued with a subtle sweetness and depth of flavor.

A medium-bodied dry red wine works well here, but honestly, I've used a wide variety of leftover reds. (The origin of this dish is considered to be Tuscany, so if you want to stay regional, you could uncork a Chianti or some other wine made primarily with sangiovese grapes, one of the most important grapes in Italy and grown abundantly in Tuscany.) Ideally, it would be a delicious red wine you would happily drink—and sometimes I do pour myself a glass and cook with the rest—but I also think the adage "Waste not, want not" is perfectly applied here: if you have an opened bottle that's past its prime for drinking, this is the perfect use for it.

I make this version with nuts, cheese, herbs, garlic, and red pepper flakes. I love garlic, so I use a lot. If you don't love a garlicky pasta, use fewer cloves. Ditto with the red pepper flakes. These simple ingredients are all you need to put together an addicting, lip-smacking plate of pasta.

I find these deep-plum strands of spaghetti completely irresistible, as sexy as a satin sheet.

Coarse sea salt

12 ounces (340 grams) dried spaghetti

¼ cup (60 milliliters) extra-virgin olive oil

4 small garlic cloves, thinly sliced

½ teaspoon red pepper flakes

1 cup (250 milliliters) red wine

½ cup (1.6 ounces/45 grams) freshly grated Pecorino Romano cheese, plus more for serving

¼ cup (45 grams) finely chopped nuts (I like pine nuts, walnuts, or almonds)

⅛ teaspoon freshly grated nutmeg

Fine sea salt and freshly ground black pepper

Sprigs of parsley, for garnish

1. Fill a large pot three-quarters full of water and bring it to a boil over medium-high heat. Add a generous amount of coarse salt (the adage "It should taste like the sea" is a good gauge of how much). Cook the spaghetti for 2 minutes less than the instructions on the package for al dente. (You don't want it to be completely cooked because it will continue cooking in the red wine later.)

2. While the pasta is cooking, heat the olive oil in a large, high-sided pan over medium-low heat. Add the garlic and red pepper flakes and cook, stirring, for 1 minute, or until the garlic becomes fragrant. Pour the wine into the pan with the garlic and stir. Remove from the heat while the pasta finishes cooking.

3. Drain the pasta, reserving 1 cup (about 250 milliliters) of the pasta water.

4. Add the pasta to the pan with the wine and garlic over medium heat and stir. Cook, occasionally stirring gently, for 2 minutes, or until the pasta is al dente and has absorbed most of the wine, taking on a plum hue.

5. Remove the pan from the heat and mix in the cheese and nuts. Stir in a tablespoon (or more) of the reserved pasta water; its starchiness mixes with the fat in the cheese to create a silky coating on the noodles. Finish with the nutmeg, season with salt and pepper, and stir to incorporate well. Taste and adjust the seasoning if you think the dish is asking for it.

6. Serve garnished with parsley and topped with more cheese, and enjoy slurping down the drunken noodles.

IT'S A GRAPE PARTY

Italy is one of the world's largest producers of wine (neck and neck with Spain and France). Wine has been made and consumed on the Italian peninsula for thousands upon thousands of years, and "the boot" is perhaps the most fruitful land when it comes to native grapevines. "The microcosm of Italy alone has the richest mosaic of indigenous grape vine varieties on the planet, with over 1,500 known varieties, of which 361 are written in the roll of varieties utilized in the production of wine," states Walter Filiputti in *The Modern History of Italian Wine*. Multiple Bible-size books have been written about Italian grapes—a topic worthy of its own encyclopedia.

Italian wines were dealt a blow in the mid- to late nineteenth century when phylloxera struck—a microscopic aphid that completely ravaged vines across Europe, and the world. Phylloxera was a major setback. Then, after the world wars, many Italian growers planted international varieties of grapes, which led to a period of wine production that left many of Italy's native grapes forgotten—

and by the mid-twentieth century, some varietals were going extinct.

One man credited with inspiring winemakers in Italy to recover their indigenous varieties was the late Luigi Veronelli, a wine philosopher of sorts. Wine writer Megan Krigbaum told me, "Veronelli is basically God to winemakers in Italy," because he promoted the idea that Italy's grapes were something to celebrate and emphasized the idea that wine can showcase otherwise unseen local cultures. As a result, "The last couple decades, Italy's star has been rising—it's beginning to be important again on the international stage," Megan said.

"However you divide [Italy]—twenty regions, ninety-four provinces, 8,090 communes—the units contrast," writes Burton Anderson in his book *The Wine Atlas of Italy and Traveller's Guide to the Vineyards*. "This variety accounts for local colour and mass confusion. How many wines are there in Italy? How many grape varieties? Figures have been given, but nobody knows."

If Italy has such an overwhelming number of indigenous grapes, how can anyone keep tabs on them? That's one of the challenges Italian producers face in reaching the average buyer. Some people argue that the appellation system is needed for just that reason: just as some British cheeses have protected designation of origin (PDO) status, Italy has similar regulations (in cheese: Parmigiano Reggiano has *denominazione di origine protetta*, or DOP), and there are also rules around European-produced wines.

Italy marks their wines *denominazione di origine controllata* (DOC) or, following even stricter regulations, *denominazione di origine controllata e garantita* (DOCG). I asked Megan for clarification on these classifications. "DOC and DOCG are regionally designated areas that have laws that dictate what can be grown, how it can be grown, how the wine is made, and so on," she said. There's also *indicazione geografica tipica* (IGT), which is meant to accommodate producers who make good wines but use nonnative grape varieties or otherwise don't meet DOC standards. "IGT has become increasingly important for producers who are growing indigenous varieties but just don't agree with the DOC restrictions," Megan said.

The Italian system, introduced in 1963, was modeled on the French appellation system, which was created in the 1930s and designates wines (and other French products, such as butter and cheese) as *appellation d'origine contrôlée* (AOC) or *appellation d'origine protégée* (AOP). The specifications are meant to protect something special, to defend against fraud, and to give consumers a

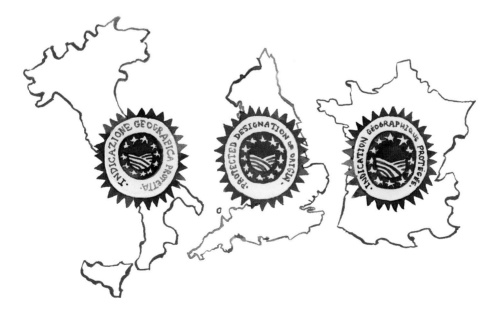

consistent product. This means there are a lot of rules: vine varieties are specified, and so are things like levels of alcohol, acidity, and winemaking practices.

Appellation designations have been a contentious quality standard, though, as Megan suggested. In the 1970s, before the broadest designation (IGT) was created, ambitious producers in Italy began to label their best wines "*vino di tavola*"—table wine—which was the lowest category of wines, now known simply as "*vino*." (It's *vin de table* in France and *vino de mesa* in Spain.) This was a rebellious move; they purposefully downgraded their product because they didn't agree with the restrictions of the appellation system.

If this all feels confusing; you're not alone. The wine world is a mind-boggling web of words. "The bigger problem, maybe, is just the nature of wine taxonomy," pointed out wine critic Esther Mobley in the *San Francisco Chronicle*. "We refer to Chardonnay from Sonoma as 'Chardonnay' but Chardonnay from Burgundy as 'white Burgundy'; to Chenin Blanc from South Africa as 'Chenin Blanc,' but 'Vouvray' if it's from a specific part of the Loire Valley. Nearly every bottle demands a different syntax."

It's word soup! Don't be hard on yourself if you can't pick up a bottle of Barolo, without any prior experience with it, and think, *Ah, yes, this is made with the nebbiolo grape!*

NEVER SAID NEBBIOLO

Eros made an astute decision to do the harvest that day, because the following day brought *la bora*—the powerful wind that famously rolls over the Slovenian mountains next to Colloredo—and it blew in fast! People scurried inside like the plague was descending, shuttering windows and lighting candles. La bora, which originates from weather patterns as far away as Russia, has inspired children's fables and vineyard fears alike for centuries. The sky was ominous and heavy, and the boisterous gusts rattled windowpanes and slammed doors. Better for the grapes to have been safely in the cellar than on the vine. We harvested on Friday, and Saturday morning la bora moved in just as Lara and I hopped on a train to Milan.

Milan was a complete one-eighty from the idyllic ten days I'd spent in Colloredo. Its urban environment featured loud neighbors, trams and taxis, and visits to vintage clothing shops. Our meals didn't have Daniela's homespun generosity, but we gathered in the kitchen most nights that week for our red sauce dinner parties.

Our versions of *pasta amatriciana* and *pasta alla Norma* took center stage, washed down with Comelli pignolo or Soffumbergo. We opened so many bottles of wine that I learned there are two ways to say "corkscrew" (a word so important it necessitates multiple terms): *cavatappi* and *apribottiglia*.

During the day while everyone was working, I explored the city alone. Like a fly on the wall, I witnessed the unspoken rules of café culture by watching other tourists make the dreaded mistakes: asking for to-go cups, requesting flavored syrup, and wanting milk in their coffee after eleven o'clock in the morning. (You can get away with the latter, but you *will* be judged.) I'd get my *caffè* and *cornetto* (croissant) and consume them standing up at the bar. Gelato was a daily treat, and I eventually caught on that breakfast would always be sweet. (If you're a savory morning person—bring nuts.) In the evening before dinner, I was all about the Campari spritz and reveled in the nonchalant way everyone seemed to indulge in the aperitivo ritual.

Spending time with Lara, Maria, and Nicola—all of whom are nearly bilingual—I badly wanted to speak Italian better than I could, and they were patient coaches. I flipped through my flashcards every morning and every evening, scribbling the random assortment of additional words I had learned throughout the day. *Sei furba* (you're sneaky), *albicocca* (apricot), *un filo d'olio* (a drizzle of oil—literally "a string of oil"). The words felt like a silk ribbon flowing from my tongue—I built out my vocabulary like a fleet of boats on the ocean.

At the end of the week in Milan, the four of us piled into the car to make our way to nearby Piedmont (Piemonte), one of Italy's most revered wine regions, with property price tags to prove it. As the car hummed along, I looked out the window and melted into the comfort of watching the rolling green hills pass, bathed in warm autumn light.

As we approached the heart of the area, we saw there were vineyards in every direction; grapes appeared to be the only crop growing for miles. Nicola called wineries to determine where we could go for a tasting and a tour. His voice rode the roller coaster of the Italian language—a cascade of rolling Rs and vowels. He hung up after the third call. *"Dai!!"* he said, exhaling. *C'mon!!* No luck with that vineyard. "California wineries are so organized; like, they have time slots, depending on how many wines you want to taste," he said, exasperated. "It's not really like that in Italy." The more pertinent truth was that we hadn't thought to call ahead before that morning—you do need to make appointments to visit wineries in Piedmont, and we were late to the game. This was how I stumbled into Piedmont without knowing I was entering the nebbiolo heartland.

Nicola connected with a family-owned winery offering a tour, and it was there that I had my first real encounter with nebbiolo—one of Italy's most adored grapes. "Nebby . . . what?" I asked Nicola.

"You've never said nebbiolo?" he asked, shocked.

The late-ripening, early-flowering nebbiolo grape is an Italian powerhouse: it's what comprises the superstar wine Barolo and the beloved Barbaresco (both named after towns in Piedmont). Although nebbiolo is one of the most renowned grapes in the wine world, it's fair to say that a bottle of Barolo is more recognizable than the grape from which it comes.

When you see a wine named Barolo or Barbaresco, you know it's been made with 100 percent nebbiolo grapes. Three-fourths of the nebbiolo vines around the world are planted in Piedmont, and since I'd never been to Piedmont before, it's not entirely surprising that I wasn't familiar with nebbiolo. Of course, the further into the Italian wine world I ventured, the more I realized what a significant grape it is. Sommeliers and wine writers talk about it with glowing superlatives.

After visiting G.D. Vajra, a vineyard in Barolo, and getting a tour of their cantina and production areas, we walked into the sunny day, felt the warm Piedmont sun on our shoulders, and went to their tasting room next door. I sipped their red wine Dolcetto d'Alba (made of dolcetto grapes, whose name means "little sweet one," although the wines produced from it are nearly always dry) and smiled at the harmony of flavors swirling in my mouth. Then I tasted their Barolo and felt like the stool had been pulled from under me—I was slow-motion falling into a world of a richly seductive wine. *Holy cow.* It was like the difference between a soft, pleasant peck on the cheek and a profound kiss that sweeps you off your feet. This was the latter. *I get why it has such a following.*

After the tasting, we found a trattoria with outdoor seating in nearby Verduno; the ideal stop for lunch. It was a warm, sparkling afternoon, and would probably be one of the last crystal-clear days before more autumnal weather moved in. Nicola ordered a Barbera d'Alba (barbera is another key grape in Piedmont, and Alba

is a city just north of Verduno). The wine matched the day: it was bright, complex, drinkable, and nuanced, with traces of a cherry-inspired sweetness.

We drained the bottle as we ate our antipasti, and then ordered a Barbaresco and enjoyed fresh agnolotti pasta—a regional spin on ravioli. The subtle hints of rose, fennel, and leather from the drink were like little side-dish waterfalls of flavor to accompany the pasta down the hatch. *Both this Barbaresco and the powerful Barolo were made with 100 percent nebbiolo?* I was stunned. *But they're so different—how?* Experts point to terroir as the main difference: the nebbiolo grapes for Barolo are planted on a different angle of slope and are exposed to microclimates determined by nearby rivers, altitude, and so on. This will cause the grape to react to fermentation differently than its siblings grown in other terroir.

One of the reasons we opted for Barbaresco with lunch was that it was the more affordable of the two (caveat: it's not *always* less expensive). The thing that makes Barolo so expensive (and the same goes for some bottles of Barbaresco) is that it takes *a lot* of time to be ready to drink, and you know what they say—time is money. Barolo is extremely tannic when it's young; time softens the strong tannins, so it ages for three years after it's harvested and before it can be released. For eighteen of those months, it must be aged in an oak barrel. To be a Barolo Riserva, it needs to wait *five* years after the harvest to be released. Wineries store bottles of each vintage until they're ready to be consumed, and that's a sunk cost until the timer goes off. Barolo may be expensive to produce, but it's a good return on investment.

Barbaresco doesn't need to age quite as long; it can be sold after two years of maturation. Both wines are complex, but Barolo is fuller, whereas Barbaresco is a bit brighter. There used to be a saying that Barolo was the wine of kings and Barbaresco the wine of queens. Sexist, but you get what they were going for.

Alba, another principal city in Piedmont, is situated near the center of the Langhe wine region—there's been evidence of nebbiolo vines being grown around Alba since at least the fourteenth century. To try a taste of great value from this outstanding region, look for Langhe Nebbiolo, a red wine that is often made from fruit of the same vineyards as Barolo, but will only set you back $20 to $25 (on average), versus $40 to hundreds of dollars for a Barolo.

The explosion of Piedmont's popularity for its excellent wine has been swift and sturdy. If we had had more time in Piedmont, we could've explored some of the region's other grapes. It's fair to say that some of its lesser-known grapes are worth investigating, too. No grape is to be ignored in a country as fruitful as Italy.

We left the trattoria, immersed in a slightly buzzed cloud, and explored the rolling cobbled streets of the town before we found a soft patch of grass, where we dozed in the sun. The next day, I said goodbye to my friends—although I should've known it wouldn't be long before I'd see Maria and Nicola again. Ever since Connor and I moved to Europe, our paths crossed theirs more and more often.

MAKING MY WAY: UNDERSTANDING NATURAL WINE

Back in London, I enrolled in the Wine & Spirit Education Trust (WSET) Level 2 course and learned about wine-producing regions and grape varietals around the world. I learned tricks, like how to ascertain acidity (after you sip, put your chin to your chest, and if saliva wants to drip from your mouth, that's an indication of high acidity), and untangled some of the confusing naming conventions, such as that pinot gris and pinot grigio are two names for the same grape (in France and Italy, respectively). Most of it was merely memorization—which grapes are grown where and why. There was *so*

much to learn, and I was just beginning to peel back the top layer of the lasagna (a hundred-layer lasagna).

"There's a lot of faff on wine labels to get you to pay higher prices," one of my teachers said, which reminded me of the appellation debate . . .

Remember how back on page 160 I mentioned that some producers purposefully buck the appellation designations (in Italy, that's DOC/DOCG) and opt instead to take the "lesser" label (IGT)? They do this because of their view that the bureaucratic systems behind those designations completely miss the mark in accurately helping consumers choose a product that is representative of the terroir, and of quality winemaking. In some cases, a DOC/DOCG-marked wine is more expensive than a higher-quality wine without the designation.

Among the admired producers in Italy who have chosen that path is Elena Pantaleoni.

I spoke with Elena, one of the leading proponents of natural wine, whose estate, La Stoppa, is in the hills of the Emilia-

Romagna region of northern Italy. Beyond appellation designations, she refuses to put the "organic" certification label on her bottles, even though she has been organically certified for many years. She shuns these labels because she thinks they are misleading—they are too easily manipulated to trick the consumer into buying something that *seems* like an indication of quality but is all too often just a marketing tool.

Several trusted friends spoke incredibly highly of Elena, and I was nearly giddy when I had the chance to meet her. I was curious, too: why had she chosen this path of natural winemaking, which many people considered avant-garde? When we talked, she was friendly and cool, with a confident, understated air I've come to admire, and she helped put all this in perspective for me.

"I like to talk about *wine* instead of 'natural wine,'" Elena said. "What I make is wine. All the industrial wines should be named as industrial products; we should not need to define our way as natural. Wines have been made for centuries in the way that I make wine, and just in the past fifty to fifty-five years (depending on the place) everything has changed. So it's a very short story compared to how long wine has been made—thousands and thousands of years. It's amazing how people can forget.

"At a university, for example, if you study enology and viticulture, there isn't a compulsory course on the *history* of viticulture, of wine. But if you know history, you can put everything in the right

spot. They invented enology to correct the defects/mistakes/flaws of wine. Fine. But in just fifty years, this has become *the way* to make wine. So now I have to call my wines 'natural' and I am the 'avant-garde'? Like it's something very modern, but it's nothing modern."

In my talks with Elena, so many of the same lessons I learned in my fermentation adventures with cheese resurfaced, such as respecting the roles of time and environment. Elena's perspective is that nature is much more powerful than our will, and that it takes *time* to make wine well.

"If you see things from the industrial perspective, to be different is something that is bad—*deformita*, we say in Italian," she said. "It depends on expectations." For her, wine is interesting *because* it can change.

I spoke with Helen Johannesen of Helen's Wines in Los Angeles, a retail wine shop with two locations (including a nook in the back of the hit restaurant Jon & Vinny's; she's business partners with Jon Shook and Vinny Dotolo, two stars of the LA dining scene). With her wine shops, Helen sees one of her biggest responsibilities as educating her customers: "It's about education, but it's also about perception."

The perception of wine—what it is and what it should be—is at the heart of many of these discussions. As such, it's important to look at who is setting these expectations. "I'd be invited to these really elite tastings, and I'd be the only woman in the room. And everyone was white," Helen told me. "There is a [wine world] culture precedent, which goes down to what you wear, and how you talk, and how you move your arms. Those were rules that I did not believe in and chose not to abide by." When she was first starting in the industry, she thought, "'I can look professional, but I don't have to wear a suit—that's dumb. I don't have to dress like a man to be good at my job.' Now it's amazing how much is changing. But it's still got a long way to go."

She believes the change has got to start at the top, and as the owner of a popular business in LA, she's doing her part to reach out to all kinds of people who show an interest. "You don't need to know everything; if you have the passion, let's learn together."

She agreed, as did every other wine expert I interviewed, that Italy is a particularly challenging country to get a proficient grasp of, because of the quantity and variety of indigenous grapes. You must immerse yourself in the culture to understand this vast offering of wines.

Back in Emilia-Romagna, Elena Pantaleoni told me, "In Italy, especially in our area, we are used to wine always having been a part of our meal; to consider wine exactly as something you eat. So if you consider wine as you do cheese, or pasta, or a vegetable—it's part of the tradition and culture of the place, but it's also a part of the nature and climate and soil."

Her whole point, and her life's work, is to treat wine as an expression of the identity of a place—of the soil of her land and the grapes native to that soil.

BETWEEN MY TRIPS TO ITALY, I SPENT AN inordinate amount of time at the British Library immersed in books about fermentation, and that's where I met wine and food writer Carla Capalbo. A frequent writer for *Decanter* magazine, Carla is considered an expert in Italian wines.

"Go south," she said. "The real story about Italy is the south. Go further down, to Puglia, Sicily. Don't do what's been done before—what's the new frontier? I'd say it's natural wine."

I knew she was right.

"Try to find a person who has interesting reasons for doing what they're doing and has made some hard choices about it."

I remembered Carla's words when I learned about Mimi Casteel, a winemaker, farmer, and scientist in Oregon. "For most people, when they think of terroir, their mind goes straight to soil," Mimi told me. "They have a vision of soil that's freshly plowed by a horse—bare, brown soil, and almost fluffy, but that's not all terroir is."

I called Mimi after seeing a video of a presentation she gave to a room of wine writers and industry professionals. She spoke with a deep conviction about the issues facing wine's sustainability in the vineyard. I was almost entranced listening to her, and I knew I had to get her on the phone.

Mimi has a master of science degree and professional experience as a botanist and ecologist in addition to her current status as farmer and vintner, all of which arms her with the knowledge to make a thoroughly convincing argument: namely, that the agricultural system needs to put the health of the soil first. She is a scientist, emboldened by her passion and practicing what she preaches.

At her vineyard, Hope Well Wines, Mimi is farming in a wholly regenerative way that has, until recently, been considered extreme in today's agriculture systems. She doesn't irrigate, nor does she till, in order to boost the habitat. The way she farms creates a unifying nexus of living organisms on her land that are "communicating with each other. If we're repeatedly disturbing the soil, then the habitat is disturbed, and those communication networks need to be rebuilt, restored. We're missing out on what terroir could be." The result? The wine tastes better, she says—and it seems others agree: "The fact that Casteel's methods make better wine is almost beside the point," writes Leslie Pariseau for *Punch* magazine, "but one worth considering nonetheless."

There's no denying that agricultural practices have an effect on climate change, and likewise, "Climate change is certainly having an effect on the shape of the world wine map," states an article on the popular wine website JancisRobinson.com. "Between 2000 and 2016 the biggest percentage increases in vineyard area were all in cooler countries: China, New Zealand (where vineyard area quadrupled between 2000 and 2016), the UK where it doubled, and Canada."

Talking with Mimi about the urgent need for winemakers (all farmers, really) to reconsider their farming practices

inspired me to think of terroir—and wine—differently. If we don't value sustainable farming, we've got a problem. This understanding was the groundwork for my inquiry into the topic of "natural wine." I waded in with caution.

If you've heard about natural wine, you may also be familiar with the confrontational tone that can accompany it among certain wine-loving crowds.

How is it that natural wine can be such a contentious topic? Perhaps it's because those opinions often characterize a culture or a set of values—so natural wine represents much more than the wine itself.

THE DOGMATIC RHETORIC OF THE "conventional versus natural" can muddle the issue. As I mentioned before, the big difference comes down to production methods in the vineyard and cellar, including the use of additives—such as diammonium phosphate, folic acid, and enzymes, all aimed at aiding or hurrying the fermentation process. (Generally speaking, natural wines do not have any additives.)

One of the challenges was that there was no concrete definition for what natural wine is, and it seemed even advocates couldn't agree on a rule book. The nuances of this discussion were numerous and subtle. *Minimal intervention wine*, a term sometimes used interchangeably with *natural wine*, was even less defined than its counterpart.

In April 2020, France became the first country to approve an official label

Vineyards in Piedmont

for natural wines, and other countries will likely do the same. (One of the most well-known natural wine proponents, Isabelle Legeron, said she *hopes* other countries will follow France's lead.) *Wine Spectator* reported on this update, saying that the label defines natural wine as being made with certified organic grapes that have been handpicked and fermented with native yeast. In the cellar, the winemaker cannot use any additives or certain modern techniques (such as pasteurization). It also states that growers are allowed to add a small amount of sulfur dioxide prior to bottling, but that this inclusion must be indicated on the label.

"Biodynamic wine" is not the same as natural wine, although the two have a lot in common in the wine-production Venn diagram. Biodynamic wine is distinguished by its underlying philosophical, even spiritual, principles. Austrian philosopher Rudolf Steiner is credited with developing the set of beliefs known as biodynamics, a homeopathic way of working with the land, in the early 1900s. It's all about matching Mother Nature—her rhythms, her seasons, the phases of the moon. (Following moon cycles and planting according to a waxing or waning moon is not a new practice; indigenous cultures around the world plant this way, and the *Farmers' Almanac*

publishes lunar planting calendars.) Ritual and ceremony also play key roles.

I tumbled down a rabbit hole. I read books by the influential natural wine advocate Alice Feiring. I consumed countless podcasts and articles. I learned about Masanobu Fukuoka's *The One-Straw Revolution*, his philosophy of "do-nothing farming," and how he preached to revegetate and reinvigorate lands that had once been fertile but now had more in common with deserts. There were so many hotly contested ambiguous zones that I felt as if I needed a hazmat suit.

The topic of sulfur is a particularly gray area. Sulfur has been vilified in the natural wine movement, but it has an important role in preserving wines by preventing oxidation and inhibiting the growth of undesirable bacteria. Sulfur has become a bit of a bogeyman, but it's not dangerous (in small quantities), and it's actually a by-product of fermentation. Yeasts naturally produce sulfur dioxide as they metabolize, and therefore it is, and has always been, a part of winemaking. (It's been attacked in recent years for causing headaches, stomach pain, and respiratory irritation in some people, which may be true in cases when it was added to wine in excess, and with other additives.)

There was something interesting afoot. I hatched a plan for my next trip to Italy.

ROME: LEARNING THE LANGUAGE

It had been eight months, almost to the day, since I had clipped grape bunches at the wine harvest. I felt a gnawing eagerness to explore my Italian heritage, and haste seemed appropriate: every time I talked with my ninety-four-year-old grandma, born of two Italian immigrants, her memory dwindled like the last savored sips of a beloved bottle of wine—each conversation was a reminder of the second hand of the clock moving insistently forward. *Tick, tick, tick.*

It added a new urgency to my Italian language studies in London, and as I prepared to embark on an expedition in Italy, I signed up for an immersive language study in Rome to kick off the trip. Sure, most people I'd encounter in Italy would probably speak basic English, but I felt that to rely on that would be to miss the opportunity to connect with people I had so much to learn from.

I made a plan; it entailed spending a month in Italy, starting in the center in its capital, Rome, then traveling south, more or less. It was a loose plan, with an itinerary that would be largely developed once I was on the ground. I wanted to make sense of my recent onslaught of wine learning and scratch the ancestry itch.

Those were my reasons for going to Rome, but everyone visits Rome with a different purpose. There's the Vatican for the religious and art lovers among us, the Colosseum for the history fans and wannabe gladiators, and the food scene for us gluttons. Regardless of motivation, antiquity oozes from every corner, from every table, and through each door hinge. It's inescapable in Rome.

Rome sits in a region called Lazio, and in terms of wine, it's mostly known for its white wines (those made with malvasia and trebbiano grapes especially). But as the country's capital, Rome attracts bottles from some of the most respected producers in the country—it's a hotbed of exceptional Italian wine. I needed to start digging, and this seemed like the perfect launchpad, especially considering Maria and Nicola had recently relocated there from Milan. I called Maria to tell her about my trip, and she enthusiastically offered their apartment as my home base.

Rome's Trastevere neighborhood

Les Vignerons wine store in Rome

As soon as I landed, I learned that Roman life in July involves sweating a lot. At 90°F (32°C), the summer weather was much hotter than anything I'd experienced in years, and this set the scene for heavy usage of the nomenclature *glou-glou* (pronounced *gloo-gloo*). A French term adopted by Italians, Americans, and the wine world as a whole, it means "highly drinkable" (hence the onomatopoeia, like "glug-glug" in English).

One of my first days in Rome, I visited an enoteca in the Trastevere area called Les Vignerons, "the best stocked natural wine shop in central Rome," advised an article from *The Infatuation*. I perused the shelves and picked up a bottle with an illustration of a boxer dog on the label. "That is glou-glou!" the man working at Les Vignerons told me. "So easy to drink, one bottle per person!" I had a feeling

"glou-glou," the words that sounded like baby talk tumbling from his mouth, could be a ploy to sell bottles, but it is indeed accepted wine parlance, and he successfully sold me a few glou-glou wines.

I first heard about Les Vignerons from an article online written by Katie Parla, a Rome-based food and beverage writer. Originally from New Jersey, she'd called the Eternal City home for sixteen years when I contacted her to speak more about the Italian wine scene. Katie is something of an expert on Italy, with more than a few cookbooks on the country's food under her belt and certifications in Italian wine, so I was hopeful about what I might learn through her eyes.

She cut to the chase, and in so many words suggested I go to Sicily (the same advice Carla had given me): "Sicily has been making and exporting wines all around Italy for hundreds of years, but there are some new producers doing exceptional work." *Noted*.

ROME GRABBED MY HEART LIKE A

desperate *vignaiolo* clutches his grapevine in one hand and a rosary in the other. I wanted to feel better connected to this country, my heritage top of mind, and I freely slipped into my little routine. I got good at the *due baci*—two kisses, one on each cheek—as a greeting and a goodbye. I'd switch between saying *salute* and *cincìn* (pronounced *chin-chin*) as a toast, glass in hand. I embodied the little hints to locals that I wasn't an average tourist: I weaseled my way through the rush hour crowd in the metro saying *permesso* rather than the oft-misused *scusi*.

Nicola and Maria's apartment was a thirty-minute walk from my language school, near the Roma Termini train station. Classes were a hoot—we would sing along with Italian pop songs and play versions of Simon Says with our new vocabulary. I became friends with a Russian woman in my class, Elena, who couldn't speak a word of English. I don't speak Russian, so the only way we could communicate was in our shared language, Italian. We spoke like two-year-olds, but it didn't matter. We got lunch after class and had our toddler-style conversations in public spaces where native speakers looked at us with bemused glances.

On the metro, shuttling around the city, I would do the Italian homework outlined by my teacher, then write

Aperitivo with Nicola, Maria, and friends

Katie and Nicola in Rome

introductory emails to vineyards I hoped to visit later in the month: *Sono interessata a visitare la tua vigna la prossima settimana . . .* The evenings usually included an aperitivo or dinner with my hosts and their friends—extracurricular Italian lessons that stretched beyond the classroom, and beyond language itself.

Even in an Italian home, the rhythms of the dinner table echo those of an osteria or trattoria: dinner begins around nine o'clock (or later), and the *antipasti* are presented first, followed by the *primi* (soup, pasta, or rice), *secondi* (the mains, typically meat or fish), *contorni* (vegetables or salad), and, last, the sweet *dolci*. (I never did get used to having my salad *after* my pasta and main.)

Usually at Nicola and Maria's apartment, we'd have the antipasti, primi, and contorni, but skip the secondi. We always had a glass of wine with the meal, and often some sweet nibble as our dolci.

One evening, Maria and Nicola invited a coworker and her boyfriend, Guy (pronounced the French way—*gee*), over for dinner. The guests brought a red wine, Morellino di Scansano (which is how I

learned Scansano is the name of a village in Tuscany and morellino is the local name for the sangiovese grape. The label is code for sangiovese grapes produced from a coastal area of Tuscany. This piecing together of information became a game for me with each new bottle of wine).

While we sipped our fermented sangiovese juice, Guy talked about how in Cameroon, his home country, wine was previously unknown but was becoming a product VIPs were offered. This led to a discussion about emerging wine markets like China, and eventually turned to the growth of natural wine.

"I understand the importance of going back to the roots and rethinking how we do things, and that less is more," Nicola said, "but the wine process is a process that's made by humans, you know? You can't think that wine is some magical thing that's created with no human interaction or no human addition. I mean, like, the Romans used to put sulfur and copper in their vineyards. There's always been intervention."

Ancient Romans did love their wine. There was a wide range of varieties offered, and a diverse market for them—from the Roman elite to the poor. There have been thousands of amphorae (vessels used to transport wine) recovered from sites throughout the empire, which offer proof of the widespread consumption of wine.

Wine was also used for multiple purposes aside from quenching thirst: *The Oxford Companion to Wine* notes that it was significant "in medical treatment,

and much of the information about the color, quality, and effects of particular wines owes far less to the tasting books of Roman connoisseurs than it does to the notes of the doctors."

Clues in ancient Roman texts and from archaeological excavations suggest that the Romans usually made white wine rather than red (after experiencing the city at the height of summer heat, I think I understand why—they wanted something refreshing), and that it was almost always sweet, which historians determined based on frequent references to a late-season harvest, when the grapes would have plumped up nicely with sugary juice. The stages of winemaking weren't drastically different from what they are today—people trod on the grapes, pressed them, and fermented the juice. "No other people in history have done so much as the Romans to advance the culture of wine," Burton Anderson writes in *The Wine Atlas of Italy*. "They devised oenological methods so ingenious that some feats weren't matched again until the seventeenth or eighteenth centuries when Europeans began to look beyond the mysteries of God and nature to view wine as a science."

Historical clues come from the work of poets like Horace and Ovid, and erudite texts like Pliny the Elder's *Naturalis historia*, one of the single most significant books that has survived to the modern day. It showcases an outstanding breadth of knowledge regarding nearly every aspect of life in ancient Rome, in which the social sphere was stratified but dinner was an important cultural ritual for all and one where wine was drunk, usually from clay cups.

Lucius Junius Moderatus Columella, a Roman soldier who became a farmer and a prolific writer on agriculture, also offered hints at the role of wine in Roman society in his twelve-volume work *De re rustica*: "We consider the best wine is one that can be aged without any preservative; nothing must be mixed with it which might obscure its natural taste. For the most excellent wine is one which has given pleasure by its own natural qualities." He goes on to discuss some of the many additives used in wine, from modifying acidity with chalk and marble dust to using boiled wine must as a sweetener and preservative to adding seawater or salt during fermentation.

Which brings me to Nicola's point that there's always been intervention *of some sort* in winemaking. A general assumption of modern-day drinkers is that the traditional way of making wine is purer, but a closer look at historical documents shows that additives were sometimes used during winemaking thousands of years ago, too—only with different kinds of additives than those we have today.

The next evening, at an osteria, I brought up this topic again: "Comelli Winery is making moves to be an organic vineyard, right?"

"Yes, and I think it's good we're doing that," Nicola said. The only reason they had not already pursued the certification was the expense (which is steep for a small producer like them).

Dinner out in Rome

"What would you ideally want to label the wines as?"

"Ideally, I would try not to label myself. I think it's aggressive to say you're a natural wine, whereas other people are unnatural. Maybe I'm too shy, in a way."

"What about biodynamic?"

"Well, there's two different worlds, the vineyard and the cellar. So you never know whether people are biodynamic in the vineyard, or cellar, or both. It's confusing. To become organic, it's only in the vineyard; you can still do whatever in the cellar."

We could've discussed this convoluted realm all night, and we nearly did. I loved these conversations with him about wine, because although he had opinions, he was open to being challenged, and willing to explain his reasoning.

He shared an article with me, titled "So Everything's a Natural Wine Bar Now?" In it, writer Leslie Pariseau puts natural wine establishments in America under a microscope. She talks about the map of growth for natural wine in the United States: predictably in bars in New York and California, but also in Houston and Minneapolis, Boston and Miami, and many more. Some of these venues proudly declare themselves "natural wine bars," and others carry natural producers

in a more understated way, alongside ambitious culinary offerings.

Pariseau quotes Jon Bonné, who points out the oxymoron that is the current status of natural wine as a trend: "If everything's a natural wine bar, then we've sort of lost the fight. If homogeneity is the villain in the story of natural wine and the places that venerate it, what happens when the natural wine bar is no longer a rarity?"

My point of reference is to consider this as I do farmhouse cheese. Just like with artisan cheese, in which each wheel will be distinctive (even when it's the same producer making the cheese with the same animals), each bottle of natural wine is, almost by definition, not only unique but irreplicable. Without stabilizers and preservatives added, this diversity is a basic element of what constitutes natural wine.

Sitting at the osteria table going on midnight, belly full of pasta, with all the windows open—welcoming in any fresh air to relieve the oppressive heat of the day—I was content. The ability to exchange contrasting views and still enjoy each other's company reminded me of my mom's ability to talk about politics from a place of curiosity. Nicola predicted, "If Americans are getting into natural wine, then Italians will follow in ten years." It would appear that's the way it's going.

Pasta e Ceci (Pasta with Chickpeas)

MAKES 4 SERVINGS

Some of my favorite food memories from Italy are standing in Nicola and Maria's kitchen, wine in hand, helping them prepare the cuisine they know so well. "Italians don't use onions *and* garlic in a dish," Nicola told me. "It's one or the other." *French culinary training, step aside.*

Pasta e ceci (pasta and chickpeas) is a dish you can find all over Italy, although how it's made varies greatly depending on which part of the country you're in. "There are hundreds of ways to make this dish all around Italy," Nicola said as he reached for a tin of anchovies, "and Romans use anchovies, so we use anchovies." You won't even be able to taste "anchovy" in the final dish; they just add a savory depth of flavor.

I asked what wine he would pair with this. With the chickpeas and rosemary, I felt like it was asking for a cozy red, but I could see how it could be considered a lighter pasta dish, too . . . What would my wine-obsessed, flavor-discerning Italian friend say? "People who do wine pairings are fifty percent bullshitting," he tossed off as he put the pasta into the pan with the chickpeas. There you have it. Enjoy this dish with a guilt-free glass of whatever wine suits you in that moment.

6 cups (1.5 liters) vegetable broth (homemade or store-bought)

2 tablespoons extra-virgin olive oil

1 teaspoon red pepper flakes (or less, to taste)

3 smallish or 2 large garlic cloves, gently crushed and peeled

1 rosemary sprig, cut in half, plus a few needles for garnish

Fine sea salt

2 oil-packed anchovy fillets

1 (14-ounce/400-gram) can chickpeas, drained and rinsed

3½ cups (300 grams) dried ditaloni pasta (preferably Garofalo brand) or other pasta, such as conchiglie (small shells)

Freshly ground black pepper

Grated Parmigiano Reggiano cheese, for garnish

High-quality extra-virgin olive oil, for garnish

1. Warm the broth in a medium saucepan over medium-low heat. (You want it to be just about simmering when you combine it with the other ingredients in step 3.)

2. Heat a large, heavy-bottomed pot over high heat, then add the extra-virgin olive oil and heat for about 30 seconds. Add the red pepper flakes, garlic, and rosemary sprig and stir. (If you use the recommended amount of

(recipe continues)

179

red pepper flakes, it may make you cough a bit as it sizzles.) Reduce the heat to medium-low, stir in a light sprinkle of salt, and cook for 1 minute.

3. Add the anchovies to the pot and stir (they'll break apart quickly in the hot oil). Add the hot broth and the chickpeas and bring the broth back to a simmer, stirring. Simmer for 15 minutes, or until the chickpeas are warmed through and softer in texture and some of the liquid has evaporated. Remove from the heat.

4. Fish out the whole garlic cloves (or tell your guests to beware, in case there are any garlic-averse eaters among you) and the rosemary sprig. Using an immersion blender, blend about a quarter of the chickpeas directly in the pot. (This is not an exact science; I just eyeball it, blending until I've blitzed more than a few chickpeas but less than half the pot.)

5. Return the pot to low heat and add the pasta. Cook according to the package instructions until the pasta is al dente, typically 10 minutes. Turn off the heat and have a little taste. Does it need more salt? If so, add that and a bit of black pepper, too. The mixture should be brothy enough that the pasta rests in a shallow puddle, so add up to 1 cup (250 milliliters) more water if most of the liquid has cooked off. Cover the pot and let stand for 4 minutes.

6. The pasta e ceci is ready to be plated! Spoon into shallow bowls and top with black pepper, a few rosemary needles, and grated Parmigiano Reggiano. Drizzle high-quality extra-virgin olive oil on top and serve.

Zucchini Carbonara

MAKES 4 TO 6 SERVINGS

Maria learned this dish from her Italian host mom, Mimma ("the most incredible cook!"), in Como, where she studied abroad during a gap year after high school. This carbonara is different from the carbonara you might know: the classic version is made with guanciale (or bacon) and eggs mixed with grated Pecorino Romano or Parmigiano Reggiano, which creates a delightfully creamy plate of pasta. I love Mimma's version, which adds grated zucchini and omits the guanciale.

This recipe calls for both pecorino cheese and Parmigiano Reggiano—pecorino is a bit saltier; Parm is a little sweeter and nuttier. I enjoy this combo of them for their subtle flavors differences, but if you have only one of them on hand, that's fine; just double the quantity to make up for the absence of the other.

My favorite thing about this dish is how silky the simple sauce makes these noodles. It's not magic, it's science: that texture is the result of an emulsion between the egg-and-cheese combination and the starchy pasta water. Pasta water is key; you should always scoop out a cupful before pouring the rest down the drain—it will improve just about any sauce or other addition to the pasta. (And make sure you salt the water well before cooking the pasta—salty pasta water imparts much more flavor! Italians absolutely swear by using coarse sea salt—the big granules of salt, called *sale grosso*—for pasta water. I've followed suit in the recipes in this book.)

2 tablespoons extra-virgin olive oil, plus more for drizzling

1 white onion, finely diced

1 large zucchini, coarsely grated

1 garlic clove, smashed and peeled

¾ teaspoon red pepper flakes

Fine sea salt

Coarse sea salt, for the pasta water

12 ounces (340 grams) dried spaghetti

2 large eggs

¼ cup (20 grams) grated Parmigiano Reggiano cheese, plus more for garnish

¼ cup (20 grams) grated Pecorino Romano cheese, plus more for garnish

Freshly ground black pepper

1. Heat the olive oil in a large skillet over medium heat. Add the onion, zucchini, garlic, red pepper flakes, and a pinch of salt and stir. Cook, stirring frequently, until the onion is translucent and the zucchini is soft, about 5 minutes. Take off the heat and let the pan cool. Remove the garlic clove.

2. Fill a large pot three-quarters full of water and bring it to a boil over medium-high heat. Add a generous amount of coarse salt (the adage "It should taste like the sea" is a good gauge of how much). Add the spaghetti and cook until al dente according to the package instructions. Drain the pasta, reserving 1 cup (250 milliliters) of the pasta water (let it cool

slightly so it won't scramble the egg when you combine them!).

3. Whisk together the eggs, Parmigiano Reggiano, Pecorino Romano, and a pinch of pepper in a large bowl. Add a couple tablespoons of the pasta water to temper the egg mixture, then add the pasta and toss to coat. Pour the contents of the bowl into the skillet with the zucchini and mix well, adding a splash more of the reserved pasta water if needed to help make a smooth sauce.

4. Divide the pasta among bowls. Serve garnished with a drizzle of olive oil, some pepper, and a bit more grated cheese.

AGE AIN'T NOTHIN' BUT A NUMBER . . . RIGHT?

Coffee and chocolate are two of my other favorite fermented products that not everyone associates with fermentation. Like the grapes, coffee cherries and cacao pods are picked, then undergo a process of fermentation, although their process is slightly different. Let's take the cacao pod as our example: once freshly picked, the beans are spread out on tarps or mats and covered with leaves so they don't dry out before they fully ferment. The beans are encased in a moist, fleshy layer that's full of sugary starches, and this sugar is converted into amino acids and peptides, which is how fermentation hugely impacts the flavor of the final chocolate product.

When Danish chocolate maker and former chef Mikkel Friis-Holm tasted a chocolate he'd just made, he noted that it had a lot of tannins. Then he had a lightbulb moment: *Like wine!* Which inspired him to try *aging* his chocolate. He recounted this epiphany to writer Jenny Linford, who told the story in her book *The Missing Ingredient*: "This is exactly the same sensation I get when I drink a young red wine with lots of tannins.

Usually those tannins will transform . . . and that is exactly what happened after a year and half with this chocolate! The very fresh unripe plum-flavour notes had matured to ripe, almost prune notes, like a port. The spiciness, which had been like an angry bee that wants to get out, was still there, but it had mellowed. It was the best chocolate I had on the shelf."

Who knows? Maybe in a decade we'll see chocolate sold by vintage year!

But not all wines age well. Wines age best when they are high in acidity and (for red wines) high in tannins because those features will soften and smooth over time. Other important elements to look for are high alcohol content and fruit-forward flavors. Red wines typically age better than white wines, although some whites, like Madeira and chardonnay, are known for aging well.

The color of a white wine becomes more intense and darkens due to oxidation, whereas red wine loses color and gets paler in intensity as the pigmented tannins become sediment. Flavors change and new flavors develop as wines mature, which can either be delicious or less than ideal. "Once in-bottle most wines do not improve," said my WSET class manual. "Their fruit flavors start to fade and are replaced with vegetal notes. A few wines are able to mature and improve over the course of several years and sometimes decades."

Regardless of how long you're keeping a wine before you open it, it's best to store bottles somewhere cool, away from direct sunlight. That's why ancient Romans stored wine in catacombs (underground cemeteries!—*creepiest wine cellars ever*). Whether you're aging a wine or simply storing it, minimal disturbance is also important. Bottles laid horizontally on the top shelf of the closet is an easy and fuss-free storage method.

What about sherry? And port? Aren't they types of wine? Do they age well?

Sherry and port are fortified wines, which means they're high in alcohol; both age for around two years in their production. Because of the production method used for sherry, it won't really improve with additional aging in the bottle, whereas some varieties of port have to mature in-bottle for at least *twenty years*, and often even longer. (Tannins are part of the reason for that: port is made with red wine grapes, while sherry is made with white wine grapes.)

Sherry is produced in southern Spain: a simple dry white wine is made and then, after fermentation is complete, alcohol is added to the wine before it is aged. Sherry is aged using the solera system, in which the fortified wine moves through a succession of oak casks at set intervals as it matures. Only a portion of the wine in each cask is transferred to the next, so the casks contain a blend of wines of different ages, and they blend together as they age, which means the resulting sherry is a mixture of vintages. Since the solera system ensures that your sherry has a variety of ages in it, there's no need to continue aging it.

There are different styles of dry sherry—fino, oloroso, and amontillado—and the specifics of the maturation process determine which style it will become. There's a fascinating method used in the making of fino sherry, and partially in the making of amontillado sherry, in which the liquid ages under a thick white layer of yeast, known as flor. This protects the sherry from oxidizing. With oloroso sherry, the wine ages in contact with oxygen, which results in a brown color and flavors of dried fruits and caramel.

Port, which is produced from grapes grown in the Alto Douro region of Portugal, is born much like any other red wine—after the harvest, the grapes are gently crushed and the skins macerate in the juices to extract color and tannins. But then! Fermentation is not allowed to come to completion—a grape-based spirit is added to boost the alcohol content, which kills the yeast and interrupts fermentation. The wine is then matured, traditionally in an old-oak cask. The resulting port is sweet and high in alcohol. There are ruby ports and tawny ports, which get their names from their respective colors, the result of extended oxidative aging.

Port may also be designated as "vintage port." The term *vintage* has a very different meaning when you're talking about port than it does when you're talking about wines. With wine, "vintage" refers to the year the grapes were harvested. When it comes to port, the "vintage" label is an indication of a particularly fantastic harvest year, and producers will only declare that a port is vintage after it has aged in the barrel. "Vintage Ports are not made every year and Port producers only 'declare' a Vintage Port in the best years," clarified my wine course manual. (Read: vintage ports are expensive. But also incredible.) Bottles of vintage port can be aged for a maximum of two and a half years in barrels (or stainless steel) before being bottled, then require anywhere from ten to forty years of aging in the bottle before they are considered *just right*. (People who love port are clearly not commitment-phobes.)

Two elements that are sprinkled in this conversation and many others in this book are temperature and oxygen. Separately and in their interplay with each other, they are very important, and I'm going to take a moment to give them the extra love they deserve, with some help from Benjamin Spencer.

"Some of the most interesting characters we get from wine can be because of temperatures: too cold, and you get more vegetal flavors; too hot, and you can kill the yeast and the fermentation does finish, and you get a sweet wine," he told me, when I caught him on a video call. He was calling from his warm, sunny Sicilian backyard, as I sat hunkered down in my London apartment on a chilly, overcast day. Our chat about temperature struck a chord, as I sipped my hot tea and watched him wipe sweat off his brow.

"Temperature control is hugely important," he continued, "and the other big one is oxidation. Fermentation is a walk on a tightrope between oxidation and reduction, which is the lack of oxygen, which can suffocate yeast during fermentation." We know that oxidation is used purposefully at times (whether it's the oxygen necessary for yeast to thrive, or to give a tawny port its signature color or to develop the flavor notes of an oloroso sherry), but when would a producer want reduction? "Cheesy or rubbery aromas are the result of reduction; a little bit of reduction in a chenin blanc is beautiful," Benjamin said. But reduction is definitely not always ideal, and needs to be used purposefully.

It's also possible to introduce too much oxygen during fermentation, Benjamin notes: "Overintroduction of oxygen can blow off a lot of the primary aromas and flavors, and also the heat that's necessary to ferment the grapes."

Temperature and oxygen—the tango they dance with each other on the stage of fermentation is one of give and take, always attempting that perfect balance. If the choreography is a success, then it's a performance not to be missed— whether it be sooner (most white wines) or later (vintage port). Age is nothing but a number, as long as the dance is enjoyable.

THE FAT ONE

I took a weekend trip to Bologna from Rome—two hours north by train—to experience the capital of the Emilia-Romagna region. Its nickname, La Grassa ("The Fat One"), reflects the plethora of culinary delights it offers. It is the birthplace of the eponymous Bolognese sauce and a culinary bastion for local specialties like Parmigiano Reggiano, balsamic vinegar, tortellini, tagliatelle, and the sparkling red wine lambrusco.

I was a solo traveler in this enchantingly historic, energetic, and youthful city. My first night there, I found an off-the-beaten-path pasta restaurant and ordered *tortellini in brodo*, in which the small, beloved navel-shaped pasta, stuffed with meat and cheese, was served in a face-meltingly rich broth. Snatched from their umami hot tub, the tortellini curled on my tongue like they'd found home.

Since I was in the spirit of celebrating Bolognese cuisine, I ordered a bottle of lambrusco. At that time, I didn't know the stereotypes that often come with lambrusco ("it's too sweet," "it's cheap" . . .), nor did I know how untrue those generalizations could be. I sat outside and sipped my effervescent ruby wine and slurped my belly buttons of pasta as I admired the antediluvian towers attached to the buildings around me and the lengthy colonnades, connected porticoes that create a covered web of walkways all around the city. As I slurped, I felt grateful that the pasta, and the city itself, had made it to the present day so seemingly unchanged (the ancient architecture within the historic city walls has been preserved).

I decided to explore to walk off dinner, and my feet took me to a wine bar, Enoteca Bibe, right outside the city center. It offered a highly curated list of wines from small producers around the country; it drew me in like a slurp through a straw. Straight away I met Sofia, a woman a couple of years younger than me who owned the shop with her father (who easily could've been Santa Claus). She had thick brown hair pulled up in a bun, black-framed glasses, a "Where's Waldo" red-striped shirt, and an apron tied around her

Carlo and Sofia, father-daughter owners of Enoteca Bibe in Bologna

waist. To acquaint me with the selection, she pointed to the shelves lined with bottles, each section labeled with a region of Italy.

I noticed there were two different labels for Emilia and Romagna. *"Perché?"* I asked, pointing. Sofia switched to proficient English and told me locals consider Emilia-Romagna to be two parts: to the west, Emilia, which produces the vast quantities of lambrusco; and to the east, Adriatic-facing Romagna, which proudly produces sangiovese. "Romagna people are happier people," she said (and never mind that she was from Romagna).

The curation of her wine selection focused on the people behind the wines, farmers running small vineyards and producing exceptional products. She said she preferred the term *artiginale* (artisanal) over natural for the producers who make wines with minimal intervention. "I feel that calling something 'natural' is an excuse for bad wine," she explained. I pressed further, my interest in the semantics of this debate piqued; I was fascinated that everyone seemed to have their own definition of the "natural" label.

Sofia had gone to viticulture and enology school and acknowledged that she preferred when wines were made without many chemicals or additives. "If you know a lot about enology, then you don't need to use enology. The correct way is somewhere in the middle. Makers must have *buon senso*. They must think in a good way— using their head and heart to work the land."

I liked her vibe. I decided to do a tasting.

She first poured me a Pignoletto from Emilia-Romagna, a spumante that some say could rival Prosecco. (Italian sparkling wines are labeled *spumante* or *frizzante*— indicators of how bubbly the wine is. Spumante = sparkling; frizzante = semi-sparkling. The secondary fermentation determines the pressure buildup of CO_2 and affects how sparkling a wine becomes.)

Her dad brought out a plate of freshly sliced mortadella and flashed a big, jolly smile as he set it down in front of me. "Sparkling wine is good to drink with something fatty or heavy, like the food of Bologna," Sofia said.

Next was a white wine. The label read both "Tenuta il Plino" and "Albadiplino." I'd never heard of either of those names, so I had no idea what to expect. "This is made from one hundred percent Albana grape," Sofia explained, "one of the most important white grapes here."

"What's all the other stuff on the front label?"

"Tenuta il Plino is the name of the producer." She pointed to the name, then moved her finger to "Albadiplino" and said, "This is the wine's fantasy name. They are put on bottles for personalization."

Fantasy names are basically nicknames a producer gives the wines; they're neither a designation of place of origin nor a grape varietal . . . just an added name. They're fun once you have some favorites and know what's behind the label, but they're yet another veiled hurdle to wine proficiency.

Next, she brought a bottle of Emilia-grown barbera, a grape famously produced in Piedmont. "Barbera is known for its acidity, but this is less acidic than Barbera from Piedmont."

I sipped. "I see what you mean. What food would you suggest pairing with this?"

"I don't like the universal combinations. There's no such thing. It's personal," she said. "With an important wine"—*important wine!* I liked her more

by the minute—"like a Barolo, for instance, I don't like to eat anything with it."

"That's not very Italian of you, is it?" I retorted. "One thing I've been told every time I'm in Italy is how important food is with wine."

"That's what I mean when I say it's very personal! But yes, we Italians talk about food while we're eating."

"I do, too!" I nearly shouted.

"Yes, you're Italian," she agreed.

We concluded the tasting and I said my farewells. I walked into the warm Bologna night, my feet lightly tapping the cement, the waltz of a slight buzz; my hunger still happily satiated from those belly buttons of pasta I'd gobbled up.

Legend has it that Venus, the goddess of love, once stayed at a tavern near Bologna. The innkeeper, after spying on her through a keyhole, rushed to his kitchen and created tortellini, inspired by her navel.

Tortellini in Parmigiano Reggiano Brodo

MAKES 8 TO 10 SERVINGS AS A STARTER OR 4 AS A MAIN
SPECIAL EQUIPMENT: MANUAL PASTA MACHINE (OPTIONAL, BUT PREFERRED)

Tortellini, one of Bologna's prized creations, are traditionally stuffed with a mix of meat (typically pork of some kind: pork loin, raw prosciutto, mortadella) and Parmigiano Reggiano cheese. When I'm at home, I prefer making a cheesier filling, like what I saw the sisters who run the pasta shop Le Sfogline in the city center—the tortellini queens of Bologna—make to fill their *tortelloni*. (Tortell*oni* are the slightly bigger version of tortell*ini*.)

The flour used to make pasta in Italy, *semola di grano duro* (durum wheat), can be difficult to source outside the country, which is why I use all-purpose flour in this recipe. I get a richly yellow dough like I had in Bologna by using a higher ratio of egg yolks to egg whites. This promises moist, rich noodles with a vibrant yellow color.

I've found the most effective way to get the dough to the proper thickness (or rather, extreme thinness) is to use a hand-crank pasta machine, which is the one piece of special equipment I recommend for successfully making this recipe.

As you finish wedges of Parmigiano Reggiano, save the rinds to use for this broth! It can be made days or even weeks ahead of time (and frozen until ready to use).

PARMIGIANO REGGIANO BROTH

8 ounces (220 grams) Parmigiano Reggiano cheese rinds (about 2 cups)

1 small yellow onion, quartered

1 large carrot, cut into ½-inch (1½-centimeter) chunks

3 cremini or white button mushrooms, cleaned and quartered (optional)

3 garlic cloves, smashed and peeled (optional)

2 bay leaves

½ teaspoon whole black peppercorns (optional)

Coarse sea salt

PASTA DOUGH*

2 cups (240 grams) all-purpose flour, plus more for dusting

6 large egg yolks

1 large egg

1½ teaspoons extra-virgin olive oil

1 tablespoon whole milk

TORTELLINI FILLING

1 cup (250 grams) fresh ricotta cheese

½ cup (50 grams) freshly grated Parmigiano Reggiano cheese

½ teaspoon freshly ground white pepper

½ teaspoon fine sea salt

Pinch of freshly grated nutmeg

Zest of 1 lemon

¼ cup (13 grams) finely chopped fresh parsley

TO SERVE

Rice flour, for dusting

Coarse sea salt

Grated Parmigiano Reggiano cheese

Lambrusco (optional)

* adapted from Thomas Keller *(recipe continues)*

1. Make the broth: Combine the cheese rinds, onion, carrot, mushrooms (if using), garlic (if using), bay leaves, and peppercorns (if using) in a large stockpot and fill it with water. (Use at least 3 quarts/3 liters of water to make enough broth for all the tortellini you'll have.) Bring the water to a boil over high heat, then reduce the heat to low and simmer for 2 hours. Toward the end, taste the broth for saltiness and add salt if you think it needs it. (The Parmigiano Reggiano rinds will lend saltiness to the broth, so people with a high sensitivity to salt may feel it doesn't need more, but I usually add at least a couple tablespoons of salt—it makes a difference to my taste buds!)

2. Strain the broth into a large bowl and discard the solids. If you'll be using the broth immediately, transfer it from the bowl back into its emptied pot and set aside. Otherwise, let it cool to room temperature, then transfer it to an airtight container and store it in the fridge for up to a week or in the freezer for up to 3 months.

3. Now the fun part: make the pasta! Mound the flour on a clean work surface and create a big well in the middle with your hands. Put the egg yolks and the whole egg into a bowl, then pour the eggs into the well in the flour (cracking them into a bowl first ensures you don't get any eggshells in the dough). Add the olive oil and milk. Using your fingertips, break the yolks, then begin mixing in a circular motion with your fingertips, slowly incorporating flour from the edges of the well into the egg mixture in the middle. Before long, you'll start to see a dough forming. Continue mixing to bring the dough together, using a pastry scraper to lift any flour stuck to the work surface. Once the dough is well combined, use a kneading motion: first bring the dough together with the palms of your hands to shape it into a ball and then press the ball down and forward with the heels

of your hands. Repeat this for at least 10 minutes. Don't shortcut here; set the timer and put on some music or a podcast, then knead, knead, knead! (If you prefer, instead of mixing it by hand, you can make the dough using a food processor fitted with the blade attachment or a stand mixer fitted with the dough hook. Combine the ingredients in the food processor or mixer bowl and process or mix on medium speed until the ingredients are well combined and the dough forms a ball, then transfer the dough to the counter and knead briefly—about a minute—by hand until you have a smooth dough round.)

4. Wrap the dough thoroughly with plastic wrap so it doesn't dry out. Let it rest for 1 hour on the countertop. (The dough can also be stored in the refrigerator up to overnight; bring it to room temperature before rolling it out.)

5. While the dough rests, make the tortellini filling: Combine the ricotta, Parmigiano Reggiano, white pepper, salt, nutmeg, lemon zest, and parsley in a medium bowl and stir until well incorporated. Cover and store in the refrigerator until you're ready to fill the tortellini.

6. If you're using a pasta machine, set it up and flour the rollers; dust your work surface with flour as well. Unwrap the dough and flatten it into roughly the shape of a rectangle, then feed it through the pasta machine on the widest setting. Narrow the rollers by changing the machine setting by one notch, then pass the dough through the rollers again. Continue this process, narrowing the rollers each time (you'll just pass it through once on each setting), until you get to the second-thinnest gauge (or the thinnest, if you're keen to test your culinary dexterity!). You can cut the long sheet of dough into sections and work with one section at a time,

if that's more manageable. (If you're not using a pasta machine, use a rolling pin to get the dough as thin as you can.) Place the sheet(s) of dough on the floured work surface and cover with a few clean, damp kitchen towels to make sure the dough doesn't dry out.

7. Working on a floured surface, use a 2¼-inch (6-centimeter) square ravioli cutter or a sharp knife to cut out squares of dough (if you have more than one sheet of dough, work with only one at a time and keep the others covered with a damp kitchen towel). Cover the dough squares with a damp kitchen towel to prevent them from drying out. Gather any scraps of dough, bunch them together into a ball, roll it out again, and cut more squares until all the dough has been used.

8. Form the tortellini: You want to work quickly here, as the tortellini will be easier to assemble if the dough is still quite fresh and moist. Line a couple of plates with parchment paper and dust them with rice flour. Remove the tortellini filling from the refrigerator and scoop ½-teaspoon dollops into the center of each pasta square. Working with one square at a time, orient the dough so one corner is facing you, then pull that bottom corner over the filling and place the point just a sliver below the top corner, forming a triangle. Gently press these points together along the edges of the dough triangle to seal them, pushing any air out of the center as you do this. Wrap the two pasta arms to the left and right of the filling around your pointer finger, overlapping the ends, and press to adhere them together. Place the tortellini on one of the prepared plates and repeat with the remaining squares. If the dough dries out a bit and doesn't adhere well, dip your

finger in some water and wet the edges of the squares so they will stick together. As you craft the tortellini, occasionally sift rice flour over the newly shaped tortellini.

9. If your broth has cooled, heat it up to a light simmer.

10. Bring a large pot of water to a boil over medium-high heat. Add a generous amount of coarse salt (the adage "It should taste like the sea" is a good gauge of how much). Add your tortellini a handful at a time, making sure not to crowd the pot too much, and cook until all the tortellini in the pot have floated to the top, about 1 minute, then turn off the heat and let the them sit in the hot water for 3 minutes more. Using a slotted spoon, transfer the tortellini to individual serving dishes. Bring the water back to a boil and continue with the remaining tortellini.

11. Top each serving with a few ladles of the broth, finely grate some Parmigiano Reggiano on top, and enjoy with a glass of chilled lambrusco, if you like.

Note: These tortellini freeze well! Transfer the assembled tortellini, still on the parchment paper, to a sheet pan and freeze until solid, then move them to a freezer-safe airtight container and store in the freezer for up to 2 months. To cook frozen tortellini, just boil for a bit longer, 2 to 3 minutes; when they float to the top, turn off the heat and let them sit in the water for 3 minutes before plating.

Caffè freddo with Elizabeth Minchilli

WINE RULES AND NON-RULES

Back in Rome from my weekend away, I met Elizabeth Minchilli at a small shop in the Rione Monti neighborhood for a morning *caffè freddo*—a slushie-inspired caffeinated beverage that perfectly suited the already intensely hot day. Elizabeth is an American who has lived in Rome for most of her life, is married to an Italian, and has raised her children there. She's written books about Roman architecture and Italian food and leads culinary-focused tours around Italy. She befriended writer Elizabeth Gilbert while Gilbert was on her *Eat, Pray, Love* journey, the "eat" portion of which appropriately took place in Rome. (Elizabeth knows just about *everyone*, I'd find out.)

At the shop counter, when Elizabeth ordered her caffè freddo, she asked that something be added; I couldn't quite make out what she said. The woman working the counter nodded knowingly, and Elizabeth asked if I wanted it in mine, too. *"Sì, certo,"* I said. I had no idea what I was agreeing to, but I trusted that if Elizabeth was getting it, it wouldn't suck. When I tasted my drink, it was a dance of sweet and

bitter, energizing and cooling all at once. I asked Elizabeth what she had ordered, and she revealed it was a *caffè freddo con granita*—an iced coffee with a dollop of coffee granita.

We took our drinks to a small two-top table near the sunny entrance of the café and our conversation swiftly moved to wine. "How do you guide your guests on which wines to drink when they visit Italy?" I asked, knowing she must deal with a lot of those questions from her tour groups.

"There are no rules. And no judgment," she said earnestly. "But if you're in Piedmont and it is truffle season, then you should order a nice Barolo. If you start by drinking the wines of a place, that's a good place to start." She continued, "My experiences with wine come from two of my best friends, who happen to be on diametrically opposed sides of the wine opinion spectrum. My friends, who I've known for most of my career, are Alice Feiring and Monica Larner."

My eyes must've bulged out of my head at this mention of two foes spending time together. Like Batman and the Joker deciding to forget their differences and hang out.

"Monica, of course, works for Robert Parker, and Alice wrote the book against Robert Parker," Elizabeth explained. "Monica and Alice get along fine! It's not always such a head-on conflict."

I was shocked to hear this. With the three women in one room, I would've guessed Elizabeth had to play the role of conflict-resolution coach. Alice is perhaps the most well-known and loudest champion of natural wines in America, and I've heard her say in interviews that she won't even drink conventional wine, and insists natural wine holds the "moral higher ground" because it prioritizes organic and sustainable farming. (Alice's anti-Parker book that Elizabeth mentioned was *The Battle for Love and Wine: Or How I Saved the World from Parkerization*, published in 2008.)

On the opposite end is the camp of Robert Parker Jr., the tremendously influential American wine critic whose 100-point scale for rating wines changed the international wine industry (some people, like Alice, would argue that it homogenized the industry). Monica moved to Rome in the early 2000s to be the Italy correspondent for *Wine Enthusiast* magazine, and later joined Parker's *Wine Advocate* team (he's since retired from the publication). In her work, she has inherently propagated his standpoint, favoring conventionally produced wines with bold, ripe flavors and significant amounts of oak and alcohol.

"Where do *your* opinions lie?" was the obvious question to ask Elizabeth, imagining her at a dinner table flanked by Alice and Monica.

"I'm somewhere in the middle. For me, it's about the culture and what's around it."

"Is natural-versus-conventional a thing in Italy?" I asked.

"Natural is becoming a movement, that's for sure."

NO MATTER HOW DILIGENTLY I MAKE THE case for "drink what you like," and insist that, as Elizabeth says, there are no rules, I've talked with enough friends and family to know that you, dear reader, will probably be disappointed if I leave it at that.

There *are* guidelines for pairing wine with food, and there are reasons for those. If you're keen to learn by following the "rules," they're as good a place to start as any—eat and drink and decide if you agree! (In what situations would you break the rules? When do the pairings fit adequately?)

Without getting too specific—few food and wine pairings are universal—the generally accepted commandments are:

- The wine should be sweeter than the food.
- Sweet wines low in alcohol (like a riesling) generally pair well with spicy foods; wines high in alcohol can increase the burn of spiciness.
- Typically, white wines are used to create a contrast with or complement the acidity in the food, whereas red wines are used to make a match to the weight and texture of the food.

- Wines high in acidity (like pinot grigio) pair well with fatty or oily foods.
- Foods with high acidity need wine with high acidity.
- Sweetness and umami in foods tend to make wines taste more acidic and bitter.
- Dishes with a lot of salt and acid tend to make wines taste sweeter and fruitier.
- Wines high in tannins go well with fatty dishes (e.g., a bold cabernet sauvignon and a steak are considered a perfect pairing).

Certified sommelier Paolo Cantele of Puglia's Cantele winery told me, "Italian wines tend to be high in acidity, which means you have to pair them with food." So there *is* a logical, sommelier-endorsed explanation of why Italian wines are so good with whatever is on the dinner table. *See?! I knew there was a reason!*

If you're stressing about this stuff, remember to keep this in mind:

Study after study shows we're all vulnerable to the power of persuasion, from fancy labels to verbal cues. No one—neither expert nor amateur—can consistently differentiate between fine and cheap wines or distinguish the diversity of flavors within them. Our appreciation of wine and other drinks and foods is as much a construct as any other sensory experience.

—SIMRAN SETHI, *BREAD, WINE, CHOCOLATE: THE SLOW LOSS OF FOODS WE LOVE*

BEFORE I PARTED WAYS WITH ELIZABETH in Rome, I asked what she meant when she wrote, "The entire concept of Italy is more a state of mind than a geopolitical reality."

"Everybody thinks Italy is one unified whole," she said.

I nodded. "The boot."

"The boot, exactly. And it's not. It's only been a country for one hundred fifty years. Talk to someone from Piedmont, and to assume that he has anything in common with someone from Puglia is ridiculous. I mean, Sicily is like an entirely different country."

"Does that parallel with the wine world in Italy, too?"

She raised her eyebrows and lifted her pointer finger. "You guessed it."

I'd put this diversity of districts to the test; I had been in Rome for ten days and was preparing to pack my bags to leave again. This time I'd go to Umbria and follow the wine stream down to Puglia (Apulia in English), hoping for more information about my ancestry.

Ciambelline al Vino (Wine Cookies)

I loved Rome and was sad to leave it so soon, but I did learn a recipe there that has had a lasting impact on my (kitchen) life: *ciambelline al vino* (which literally translates to "wine doughnuts"), a traditional cookie from Lazio. They originated in the hills just outside Rome, where they're also known as *ubriachelle*, "drunken ones." These crunchy little treats are not to be confused with *ciambellone*, an Italian version of a Bundt cake, best enjoyed with afternoon tea. Ciambelline al vino are traditionally enjoyed dipped in (what else?) wine. They are to wine what biscotti are to coffee.

You could be drunk and still make these: they're *that* easy. The recipe calls for equal quantities of wine, sugar, and olive oil, plus about six times as much flour—*e basta!* That's essentially it. Use red or white wine, whatever you have on hand.

If you're overwhelmed by the choice of which wine to choose (like my friend Sam, who helped me test this recipe and had a glut of options thanks to her quarantine stockpile), here are some tips: The flavors of whichever wine you choose will *very* subtly (really, barely) be present in the final cookie. What makes the biggest difference is the tannins of the red wine and the sweetness and acidity of the white wine. The tannins in red wine add a pleasant balance to the sugar in the ciambelline, whereas a sweet white makes for a simple cookie that's fantastic without being too saccharine. Your wine decision will not make or break your enjoyment of this cookie. (Note: Most rosés will give you a result closer to that of a white wine in this recipe.)

I add a pinch of salt and some baking powder, because salt in desserts is heaven and the baking powder gives them a little textural boost. Traditionally, fennel seeds are sprinkled in, too. I love these with or without the fennel seeds—go with what your palate tells you, or what you have in your pantry. I've also gotten in the (some would say quirky) habit of adding cacao nibs when I make ciambelline with a sweet white wine, because I think the bitter nibs add a nice balance to the slightly sweeter version of the cookie.

When it's time to eat them, you could do as the Romans traditionally do and dunk them in wine, but they're also perfect with a cup of coffee or tea.

½ cup (125 milliliters) red or white wine

½ cup (125 milliliters) extra-virgin olive oil

½ cup (110 grams) sugar, plus up to a ½ cup more for coating

Pinch of fine sea salt

1 teaspoon baking powder

3 cups (360 grams) all-purpose flour, plus more for dusting

2 tablespoons fennel seeds or cacao nibs (optional)

(recipe continues)   **201**

1. Combine the wine, olive oil, ½ cup (110 grams) of the sugar, the salt, and the baking powder in a large bowl. Mix with a wooden spoon, gradually adding the flour as you stir. When you've added most of the flour, but not all of it, stir in the fennel seeds (if using), then add the remainder of the flour and mix well. The dough should come together and peel away from the sides of the bowl easily.

2. Lightly flour a work surface and place the dough on it. Knead the dough until a smooth ball is formed; this will take a minute or two of working the dough. (Sprinkle more flour on the work surface and over the dough if it sticks to your hands.) Place the dough in a clean bowl and cover with a clean kitchen towel. Let rest on the counter for 30 minutes.

3. Position two racks in the middle of the oven and preheat the oven to 350°F (180°C).

4. Roll the dough into a long, thin log, about 1½ inches (4 centimeters) thick and 14½ inches (36 centimeters) long. Cut the log into ½-inch-thick (1½-centimeter) rounds.

Working with one round at a time, roll the dough between your hands or on the work surface into a rope about ½ inch (about 1 centimeter) thick, bring the two ends together to form a circle, and press them together, one on top of the other, to adhere. Set aside and repeat with the remaining rounds of dough.

5. Pour the additional sugar into a small bowl. Gently press each cookie into the sugar, coating both sides. Place the cookies on parchment paper–lined sheet pans as you go, keeping ½ inch (1 centimeter) of space between them.

6. Bake for 10 to 15 minutes, until the cookies are slightly golden, rotating the pans 180 degrees and switching their positions on the racks halfway through. Remove from the oven and let the cookies cool on the pans on wire racks before eating. (They're best eaten at room temperature.) These keep well in a sealed container at room temperature for up to 1 week or in the freezer for up to 3 months.

IN VINO VERITAS

"Look, the car drives itself!" We were hurtling down a curvy country road outside Perugia, and my Umbrian host wanted to show me how smart his car was. He removed his hands from the wheel as I braced myself. We'd both had a few glasses of wine, and the red flags waved frantically in my head. *What is going on?* As I opened my mouth to protest, sure enough, the car autocorrected and kept us on the road. After a couple of these alarming hands-off demonstrations, he said, "Everything is predictable," making a statement perhaps more about his view of the wine world than the car's safety mechanisms.

The driver was Danilo Marcucci, a rising figure in the wine industry—a man my local farmers' market wine merchants, Oli Hudson and Sam Rogg of Natural Born Wine, introduced me to. Earlier that day, wearing tight black jeans and sporting manicured facial hair, Danilo had walked me around vineyards (his own and several for whom he consulted) and spoke in grand, sweeping statements about viticulture and life.

Wine writer Marissa Ross wrote in *Bon Appétit* that Danilo was the "Yoda of Italian natural wine. Or maybe the Batman." (How about Obi-*Wine* Kenobi? Sorry.) The comparison to Yoda is reflective of how Danilo speaks, grammatically scrambling words in a sentence mosaic that reaches for profundity.

I had never heard of Danilo (and hadn't yet seen the Yoda-comparison article) when Oli and Sam connected me with him. Only afterward did I realize I was to spend a day as his Luke Skywalker, a natural wine Jedi in training. I didn't know what I was getting myself into, and that's how I found myself strapped into his futuristic car, tipsy, barreling down a rural road in Umbria.

There's a Latin adage, *in vino veritas*—"In wine lies the truth"—which is a reference to the lowering of inhibition that accompanies intoxication, and the age-old inclination of humans to show their true colors or be more candid under the influence. The alcohol in wine is at once its appeal—a social lubricant, a de-stressor—and simultaneously the crux of many of the industry's challenges.

It's a paradox I wrestled with as I delved deeper into the wine world. After leaving the relative comfort of Nicola and Maria's apartment, I had moments of doubt and vulnerability as I raced through Italy, meeting as many wine producers as I could. It was like the feeling I had that first night in the Somerset farmhouse, alone somewhere unknown, and my mind went to worst-case scenarios. There were times in my journey as I'd be walking along, when—with a *snap!*—it felt as if someone had replaced my shoes with roller skates, and my feet were flying out from under me, my arms splayed out to the sides, as I tried desperately to regain my balance.

These moments, sprinkled throughout my trip, made me miss Connor. When I left for Rome, we had just hit our two-year anniversary. For some reason, I thought we wouldn't be getting each other anniversary presents (I don't know where I got that idea), and when he placed a gift bag in front of me, I realized my mistake. *Whoops.*

But wait . . . that's not all. His birthday was the following week, and I'd be abandoning him, waving to him from Lazio. Even though I had conferred with him before buying that ticket to Italy a week before his birthday, I felt bad. He was remarkably understanding and supportive of my dream to write this book.

Purchasing a one-way flight and not having every step, every accommodation, and every meeting booked ahead of time went entirely against my normal mode of operation. I had some appointments sketched out, with gaping blank sections between. I didn't know when I would be returning to London, and I didn't know where in Italy I would end up. I was learning along the way and the newest information directed my decisions in real time.

When I arrived in Perugia—the capital city of the Umbria region—pulling into the station on a direct train from Rome, I knew Danilo would be waiting to pick me up. What would the rest of the day have in store? I had *no idea*, nor any certainty about where I'd rest my head that night, aside from Danilo's assurance that he had set up my accommodations. I put myself in his hands, the hands of a man I'd never met before—it was only unnerving when I stopped to think about it, but that's the trust inherent in travel.

If it hadn't been for Sam and Oli's recommendation, I don't think I would've given much thought to Umbria as a wine destination. It's the fourth smallest of Italy's twenty regions and one of the few landlocked ones, making it a harder sell for tourism. In terms of climate and geology, it's similar to the region directly to its northwest, Tuscany, which produces five times as much wine.

Tuscany and Umbria share similarities, but Tuscany has been covered exhaustively—ad nauseam, some might say—by wine writers and journalists. It made sense I should explore the lesser-known Umbria, the underdog, led by Danilo, who carried the

Danilo Marcucci in his vineyard

torch for the dark horse, Italian natural wine.

Upon my arrival, I climbed into the passenger seat of his car and he drove me to the first stop of the day, Conestabile della Staffa, his wife's family's vineyard, where he made wine. Aside from that winery, he was a consultant to a dozen other winemakers, usually helping small conventional producers move to minimum-intervention, organic production.

Once we got to the vineyard, I took out my notebook. He saw I was poised to take notes and began Yoda-ing. "Liquid earth, my wines are."

"Liquid *heart*?" I misheard him through his accent.

"Not heart—earth." He crouched down to touch the ground. "Each place has its own language. This earth is clay and

limestone, and also calcareous gray stone, and I figure out how to work with it. I'm the Google translator of soil."

We went to the cantina, where Danilo had set out bottles from about a dozen of the winemakers he worked with. We sipped, and Danilo talked. I was there in such a different capacity than I had been at the Comellis; I was visiting as a journalist, writing a lot of notes, and when Danilo came up for air, I tried to understand the context of his work.

We opened a wine, a fizzy rosé made from the Gamay del Trasimeno grape with ciliegiolo grape blended in, from Tiberi, one of the wineries he consulted for. It was a pét-nat—short for *pétillant naturel*, a French term for a style of sparkling wine made by bottling the wine *before* primary fermentation is complete (as

A rosé "pét-nat"

The cantina at Conestabile della Staffa

opposed to the méthode champenoise I mentioned before, which occurs during secondary fermentation), capturing the remaining CO_2 created in that anaerobic environment.

Pét-nats usually have smaller, more effervescent bubbles than in-your-face carbonation. The term might be chalked up as trendy, right along with glou-glou, but "As a repackaged name for an ancient concept," Zachary Sussman writes in *Punch* magazine, "the trend has brought renewed attention to ancestral-method wines with deep historic roots in the rural areas of France and Italy where they've been produced for generations—long before anyone ever coined the term 'pét-nat.'"

Danilo said, "*This* is wine," then he paused. He swirled the glass and took

another sip before finishing his sentence: "Clean and clear."

"Clear—that's not what most people think of when they think of natural wine, right? Isn't 'cloudy' usually associated with it?"

"They think of foggy and maybe even syrupy," Danilo agreed. "We are the new revolution of natural wine. Ten years ago, it was unclear and dirty, but our mission is for people to not know it's natural."

This acknowledgment of how the average wine drinker in Italy and America thinks of natural wines was also an understanding of the importance to move beyond it.

By the time we tasted our way through the lineup of wines, it was early afternoon, and we left for another meeting, another tasting. This is when

Danilo showed me his car's fancy self-driving system. Then more cantinas and more drinks. I wondered if this amount of drinking would be considered a typical day in the life of a wine journalist. I realized I should've used the spittoon more often, but no one else was, and I was desperate to give the appearance that I knew what I was doing.

Our final meeting was with "the shepherd winemaker," Giovanni Battista Mesina. He stepped out from a cozy barn to welcome us as his affectionate farm cat purred at our heels. Giovanni didn't speak English, which made me even more grateful I was fresh out of intensive language learning—I could communicate the basics with him.

His winemaking operation, in a small shed beside the barn, was a snug space, just big enough to make thirteen thousand bottles yearly. His fermentation room was the size of my bedroom—barely enough space for a cement container in which his red wine fermented and a fiberglass tank where it aged, and a stainless-steel tank for his white wine.

As he showed me around the space, he lifted the lid of another large basin to show me its contents: olive oil! He had just pressed the olives from his olive trees. (Giovanni had sheep and *also* made sheep's-milk cheese! For family and friends rather than for profit. I felt an immediate kinship with this soft-spoken farmer who DIYs so much.)

He and Danilo walked me out to the vineyard, which sat atop one of the highest hills in the area, overlooking the valleys of the neighboring village. It was as beautiful as any Tuscan postcard, and I stood paralyzed for a moment, looking at it in awe. Danilo played hair stylist with the vines and Giovanni inspected his vermentino grapes (his favorite white variety, from Sardinia).

He recounted his transition from making conventional wine to natural wine. "It's harder to make natural wine," he said. "You can't just add chemicals to fix things, and so it's never going to be exactly the same!" *Why do things always have to be the same?* "Copper and pesticides were bad for the sheep—I had to make a change." (Note: Interestingly, most certified organic growers spray copper sulfate in their vineyards to combat mildew, although some are beginning to reevaluate.)

We walked back to the cellar, passing herds of sheep and the dogs that looked after them. Cosetta, Giovanni's wife, set the table for us, with a spread of their homemade cheese and homemade charcuterie, and of course bottles of Giovanni's wine, I Vini di Giovanni, which had a label (made from grass!) with hand-drawn sheep on it. (The hand-drawn-label vibe of natural wines has become a meme in the wine world.)

We sipped his Vermentuzzo, a golden-yellow white wine made of vermentino grapes that have been fermented in their skins (an orange wine). It was incredible—complex yet refreshing, dry but tasting a bit like sweet pineapple, and its minerality left an impression of having tasted an Umbrian rainfall. I sat across the table from Giovanni, listening to him explain his process, utterly amazed at what he created.

The four of us sat together—talked, snacked, and sipped—and I must admit to feeling happy to have Cosetta in our company; I'd spent the entire day surrounded by dudes. It was nearly evening, and I felt the truth that the wine world is still largely a man's world. I had held my ground and smiled as I chatted, meeting after meeting, even if at times I felt like a dog going for a walk in the rain—a bit bothered but playing it cool and shaking it off.

Giovanni poured his wine into our glasses. *"Il vino fa parte della nostra cultura,"* he said. *Wine is a part of our culture.* Wine is essential. His identity was entirely intertwined with his craft, and with the bottles that stood in front of us on the table.

Having finished my glass of Vermentuzzo, he poured his Rozzo, a medium-bodied red wine made from 100 percent sangiovese grapes, earthy, with plum notes—a wine that felt intimately pleasant.

The Italian word *sangiovese* is from the Latin *sanguis Jovis*, meaning "blood of Jupiter." Just as Jupiter is the largest planet in our solar system, sangiovese grapes are the most widely planted red grape variety in all of Italy. They are most commonly associated with Tuscany, but they're planted all over the country and will have vastly different outcomes depending on where they're grown and how they're fermented. They're one of the most malleable grape varieties in terms

of vine-to-wine expectations. For this reason, sangiovese grapes are frequently blended with other grapes—such as in Chianti, which includes at least 70 percent sangiovese grapes—with the other varieties chosen for their balancing qualities of tannin and fruit.

I swirled Giovanni's Rozzo in my mouth, doing that hilarious thing wine people do (which I used to make fun of): inhaling a bit of air and swishing the liquid around my tongue and palate in a (not so quiet) show of how far I'd come in my wine learning. I was interrupted from my sangiovese ecstasy when Danilo piped up, "Good wine, good life, *good women*!" and raised his glass. Cosetta rolled her eyes and smirked, *"Uomini." Men.*

That summed up my thoughts, too, after spending a day with a rotation of nearly a half dozen all-male winemakers. I was so aware of being a woman that day; more than I had been in the many other situations I'd been in with all men. *Why?* The thought came and stayed, nuzzled behind my ears, as I finished the glass of wine.

"MY LOVE FOR SANGIOVESE STARTED during my time living in Italy," wine consultant Cha McCoy told me. "Before I moved to Italy, I had box wine in the refrigerator—particularly white zin, as it was my ex-boyfriend's choice—and I didn't know anything about wine!" What happened next—moving to Italy for business school—indelibly altered her path.

"Italian food and wine is a religion!" she said, and for her, it was infectious.

She intuited what Giovanni expressed to me. When she moved back to America, she created an event series she calls The Communion with the purpose of demystifying wine, where she offers wines to taste (and bread to munch on). Her gatherings are inclusive and focus on educating wine lovers who may not be interested in attending the elite industry's typical monochromatic functions.

I felt hopeful when Cha told me, "I am connecting with more women and people of color every day, which is amazing to learn their stories and know we [women and people of color] exist no matter where they are located."

I pulled up my email and sent a note to Arianna Occhipinti, a wine producer in Sicily whom multiple trusted friends in the wine industry had told me about. A female winemaker who had grown to near rock-star status: visiting *her* vineyard became my North Star as I continued traveling farther south.

FAMILY ROOTS

If Italy is shaped roughly like a high-heeled boot, you'll find Lecce in the bottom portion of the heel. I'd been to Lecce, in the southern portion of the Puglia region, once before, to visit my friend Michelle Fix—the sister of one of my and Connor's dearest friends. Lecce on a sunny day—which is most days—is blindingly splendid: its limestone buildings reflect the sun in a 360-degree seduction. I understood why Michelle had moved there and never left.

It's all too easy to fall in love with the slower southern pace of life, the local dishes like *orecchiette con le cime di rapa*, a small, round pasta with bitter greens, garlic, anchovies, and peppers, and custard-filled bites of the sweet, flaky pastry called *pasticciotto* to accompany your daily espresso fix. Baroque architectural monuments are heavily sprinkled around the city, and their bright structures emerge from the ground like the teeth of southern Italy getting ready to bite into a piece of pizza.

When I arrived at the train station, Michelle was there to meet me. She was to be my bilingual buddy for the next few days; I had enrolled her help in setting up some of the vineyard visits. Before that, I was looking forward to getting some answers about my ancestors from Vincenzo, the immigration lawyer she'd connected me with.

Straight from the train station, we went to meet with the *avvocato* (lawyer). We sat in his steaming law office; Michelle pulled a fan from her purse and waved it at her neck to cool down, generously redirecting it toward me every few minutes. Even though the windows were open, the air was still and felt pregnant with humidity, and anticipation.

Based on the data I had given him, Vincenzo had managed to locate the birth certificate of my great-grandmother, my *bisnonna*, in government records in nearby Calabria, but he couldn't find my *bisnonno*—great-grandfather.

The information I had for bisnonno Nick Tufaro was based on guesses. First off, Vincenzo began, "There is no name 'Nick' here. His name was Nicola in Italy." So there's one assumption—*but what if he had grabbed the American name Nick out of thin air and his Italian name was Luigi or something?* The second assumption was his exact place of birth, Tursi, and the third guess was regarding his birth year—I had told Vincenzo it was 1897. Vincenzo came up empty-handed when he searched with that information.

"What are my options?" I asked.

Vincenzo turned to Michelle and began speaking in Italian. Michelle looked at him intently as she continued fanning herself and said, "*Sì. Sì.* Okay, *sì.*" She turned to me and relayed the information: "Italian citizenship is based on this thing called *jure sanguinis*, which basically means citizenship through blood."

"I have jure sanguinis through my bisnonna and bisnonno?"

"Well, only through your great-grandfather," she said. She turned to Vincenzo for clarification. They had a quick exchange—*okay, sì*—and she continued, "Before 1948 women could not pass citizenship to their children, only men could—so if you're interested in exploring dual citizenship, then having your great-grandmother's birth certificate is not enough. You need Nicola Tufaro's birth certificate."

People (me included) tend to forget that Italy is a new country. While its history is profound and the stuff of legends (as evidenced by Rome's Colosseum and even the ancient wine archives I've referenced), Italy the nation is an infant as far as European borders are concerned. March 17, 1861, was Italian unification day, when Vittorio Emanuele II became king of the newly coalesced country. Prior

to this, there were no Italian citizens, because Italy itself did not exist! Great-grandparents may seem like a long way back to reach for citizenship, but further than that and there wouldn't have been an Italy to tie roots to at all.

Michelle and I determined to roll the dice and see if we could track down bisnonno Nicola Tufaro's birth certificate. It was a long shot, but Tursi, the town with the best chances of having the paperwork, was a little over two hours away, so we put it on the itinerary.

THAT EVENING, MICHELLE, HER HUSBAND, Domenico, and I went to a trattoria for dinner. Domenico ordered us a bottle of red wine, a blend of primitivo and negroamaro grapes. "Both are native grapes," he said with the pride of a local. Primitivo and negroamaro are both red wine varieties that are high in tannins and bold in flavor—typical of southern Italian wines—and the blend was a brazen welcome to the area. Typically, grapes are blended to balance each other—a grape with deep ruby color might be mixed with a grape that is lighter in appearance, or grapes might be mixed to find an equilibrium of flavors. With primitivo and negroamaro, it was like my tongue was sandwiched between these audacious grapes—in the best way. "Susumaniello is another local, antique grape they're bringing back," Domenico said. "Try to have some while you're here!"

I nodded as I tucked into the antipasti spread—marinated and grilled summer vegetables, olives, mini balls of mozzarella tossed with rosemary leaves and olive oil—and sipped my wine, already anticipating what I'd order for my main dish: orecchiette.

Orecchiette is a pasta shape born in Puglia and thought to look like ears (*orecchie*, which is where it gets its name)—it's one of my favorite pastas. I'd been hankering for a bowl of orecchiette in Lecce like a grade-schooler awaits Christmas morning, and when my hosts recommended an even more specialized pasta dish featuring orecchiette on the menu—*maritati*—I had to try it.

Maritati literally translates to "married," and it's a combination of two pasta shapes: orecchiette and minchiareddi, a thin, rolled rod the length of the space between two knuckles on your pinky finger. The fact that they were called maritati—a clear indication of their phallic and yonic counterparts—made me chuckle. With a naughty smirk, I inwardly

cheers'd to Connor and dug into the pile of pasta.

THE NEXT MORNING MICHELLE AND I went to Tursi, and had plans to visit a couple of wineries on our way back to Lecce. The scheduling was determined by the times the *comune* (town hall) office was open—two hours in the morning, two days a week. This felt like my only shot.

Tursi is in the vicinity of Matera, in the Basilicata region, which is famous for housing an ancient city of cave dwellings carved right into the mountainside. As we approached my purported ancestral town, I was shocked to see some of these same mountainside caves.

We saw the sign that said TURSI and passed a man on a tractor puttering in the opposite direction, out of town. We turned into a nearly vacant parking lot in front of an old off-white Soviet-looking building.

We entered the single-paneled door and stood in front of reception, which was behind a glass pane. It was eerily quiet in the building and it seemed that, other than the receptionist, there was no one else around. Michelle explained to the woman why we were there, which prompted her to—silently—stand up, go into the room behind her, and return moments later to motion us through the next door.

In room beyond, we saw a small man sitting behind a large bureau desk, flanked by floor-to-ceiling bookshelves. He invited us to sit opposite him, removed his glasses from the bridge of his nose, and listened attentively as Michelle explained our aim, and our predicament of working with uncertain information. He seemed unmoved by our earnestness, but his response in Italian broke the disconcerting silence of the space, "Which year would you like to see?"

"1897," I said, starting with the year I had given the lawyer in Lecce. He disappeared around the corner, into another room. Michelle and I looked at each other with raised eyebrows and a *fingers-crossed* glance. The man returned with a relatively thin but gigantic book, the size of his entire torso, and set it on the table. It contained all the births in Provincia di Tursi during 1897.

He opened the book and located the "T" section, turning the large page with a *whoosh*. He replaced his glasses atop his nose and peered through them as he followed his pointer finger down the page, saying, *"Tufaro, Tufaro, Tufaro . . . non Tufaro."* He closed the book with a thump and looked up at us.

"We should try another year," I said. "Can he look at the next year, 1898?" Michelle politely made the request and he again disappeared into the next room,

returning with another massive book. This time, *"Tufaro, Tufaro, Tufaro . . . aha"*—I held my breath, trying to read the angled cursive writing upside down—*"Elena Tufaro. Non Nicola Tufaro."* I sighed and requested the following year, 1899. Same disappointment.

I looked at Michelle questioningly, almost awaiting her instructions. I wasn't hopeful and I didn't want to take more of this guy's time. "We could try one more year," she said.

"Yeah, we should," I responded. "Last one—let's look at 1896."

I thought I could sense a sigh from our helper behind the desk, but he agreed. It was a repetition of events: book appears, glasses on nose, pointer finger traces, "Tufaro, Tufaro, Tufaro." Then his finger halted. "Nicola Tufaro," he said, and looked up at me over his glasses. "Nicola Tufaro," he repeated.

I felt electricity jolt through me, as real as if I were holding a wire that had just been shocked to life. I looked at Michelle in disbelief and screamed, *"Nicola Tufaro!"*

A Cake to Celebrate!
(White Wine and Olive Oil Cake with Red Wine Buttercream Frosting and Boozy Mascarpone Filling)

MAKES ONE (9-INCH/23-CENTIMETER) DOUBLE-LAYER CAKE

To celebrate successfully finding my bisnonno's birth certificate, I wanted to make something special and indulgent, but not too challenging. Even if you're a shy or newish baker, you can knock the socks off dinner guests or a birthday buddy with this cake. It's Connor's absolute favorite. Lara had made a version of it from Food52 (crowd-sourced from a home baker named Midge) for Nicola's birthday in Milan the year before, which I have adapted to be even boozier and more colorful. It's a stunner.

You could call this a "drunken cake," but we've already used that naming convention for some of the other dishes in this book, and let's get real—none of these dishes have any significant traces of alcohol in them. They're supremely flavorful and super fun. This cake is inhaled so fast, it's a winner every time. If there are any pieces left over, have them for breakfast the next morning with coffee. You'll be all, *I woke up like this.*

CAKE

Butter, for greasing

2½ cups (300 grams) all-purpose flour, plus more for dusting

4 large eggs

2 cups (400 grams) granulated sugar

1 cup (250 milliliters) white wine (fiano is a favorite white wine from Puglia, but any white wine will suffice)

1 cup (250 milliliters) olive oil

1 teaspoon pure vanilla extract

½ teaspoon fine sea salt

2¼ teaspoons baking powder

RED WINE BUTTERCREAM FROSTING

1 cup (2 sticks/230 grams) butter, at room temperature

2½ cups (315 grams) confectioners' sugar

¼ teaspoon fine sea salt

½ teaspoon pure vanilla extract

2 to 4 tablespoons red wine (I prefer a bold red like Puglia's primitivo to give the frosting a deep, saturated color)

BOOZY MASCARPONE FILLING

1 cup (250 grams) cold mascarpone cheese (straight from the refrigerator)

¼ cup (30 grams) confectioners' sugar

2 tablespoons (30 milliliters) kirsch (or substitute any fruit liqueur)

½ teaspoon pure vanilla extract

(recipe continues)

1. Make the cake: Preheat the oven to 350°F (180°C). Butter two 9-inch (23-centimeter) cake pans, then lightly sift flour over them and tap out any excess (this prevents the cakes from sticking to the sides).

2. Mix the eggs and granulated sugar in the bowl of a stand mixer using the whisk attachment or in a large bowl using a handheld mixer on medium-high for 1 minute. Reduce the mixer speed and add the wine, olive oil, and vanilla. Mix until well incorporated. With the mixer running, add the flour, salt, and baking powder and mix just until the batter is smooth and combined.

3. Divide the batter between the prepared pans and bake for 30 to 35 minutes, until a toothpick inserted into the middle of each cake comes out clean. Let cool in their pans on wire racks for 10 minutes. Run a butter knife around the edges of each cake to release them from the pans and flip them out onto the wire racks. Let cool completely.

4. While the cakes cool, make the frosting: Beat the butter, confectioners' sugar, and salt in the bowl of a stand mixer using the whisk attachment or in a large bowl using a handheld mixer on high speed until smooth. Add the vanilla and briefly mix to combine. Add the wine, a tablespoon at a time, and mix until the frosting is smooth and spreadable. (The difference between adding 2 and 4 tablespoons of wine here will be in the look and the flavor. If you want a deeper color, add the extra tablespoons of red wine.) Cover and refrigerate the frosting while you make the filling.

5. Make the filling: Beat the mascarpone and confectioners' sugar in a large bowl using a handheld mixer or stand mixer on medium speed until smooth. (This combines the ingredients but also lightens the consistency of the filling by incorporating air into the mascarpone.) Add the kirsch and vanilla and beat until smooth and thick. Set aside until you're ready to assemble the cake.

6. When the cakes have cooled, trim the domed tops off each layer so the surface is flat. (I always snack on the trimmings . . . perks of being the baker!) Set one layer on a cake stand or plate and spread the mascarpone filling in an even layer over the top, then place the second layer on top of it. Spread the frosting over the top and sides of the cake, covering it completely.

7. Eat immediately or keep the cake in the refrigerator under a cake dome until you're ready to serve it (this keeps the frosting from melting and the filling fresh). When it's time to dig in—enjoy!

FILL A HORN WITH DUNG

"I felt the jolt of electricity, too!" Michelle told me as we bounded out of the building. "Seriously, I'm not even related to him, but I got all tingly!" After we found Nicola Tufaro's birth certificate and secured a copy with a stamp of authenticity from the comune, Michelle and I went to explore my ancestral town—a phrase I could now say with confidence! We walked up the steep hillside stone streets, straight out of a Fellini film, and passed clusters of elderly folks sitting outside on chairs, fanning themselves and passing the time talking.

Michelle and I wrapped up our fairy-tale morning with lunch sitting *fuori*—at a table outside, on the sidewalk under the cafe's awning. We both ordered a simple but perfectly al dente penne dish. *Why is pasta in Italy always so much better?* Then we got in the car and drove to L'Archetipo winery for a midafternoon appointment.

"Ciao. Benvenuti, signore," said Francesco Valentino Dibenedetto (who goes by Valentino). He was a few inches shy of six feet tall, wiry but muscular, and deeply tanned—the physique and color of a man who works the fields as much as

he tinkers in the cellar. He wore a simple brown T-shirt and shorts, and sported a hefty gray beard. His eyes were bright, alert, and intense; they pierced mine with a glance.

He went to school to become an agronomist (an expert in the science and technology of soil), and he spoke like one. Straight away, he launched into the importance of humus (no, not the chickpea dip). Organic matter on the ground—fallen leaves, for instance—plus rain makes humus; it's what happens in the soil when flora and fauna matter decompose and their "microbes create a complex system," he explained. "Real food for plants is humus. Nitrogen, phosphorus, and potassium are some of the words people throw around, but what plants should be eating is humus." Valentino told us he expanded the biodiversity of his vineyard with a bull horn stuffed with cow dung.

"Cow dung?" I asked Michelle, to make sure I understood correctly. She turned to him and clarified. She cleared her throat, "Yes, cow manure," she confirmed. "He fills horns of bulls with cow manure and puts them in the ground in September—usually September twenty-ninth, the day of Saint Michael's Feast." He takes them out on Easter. (The result

is nutrient-dense compost that is then mixed with water and sprayed across the property.)

"So you follow the calendar? I thought biodynamic agriculture followed the moon."

"Calendario!" he said, his arms flying up in the air. *"Non vero tempo."* The monthly calendar is fake time, he explained. "Christopher Columbus conquered with the sword and the calendar." Valentino follows the cycles of the moon but uses some calendar benchmarks to keep track of it all.

He told me he farmed organically for twenty-five years, but he could still see his plants getting sick, so he decided to move to a fully biodynamic system. The diversity issue is also why he chooses to use exclusively natural yeasts, those found on the grape skins, for fermentation; he said these are "yeasts developed in our climate and meant for our ecosystem," rather than industrially made yeasts, which are based on a globalized taste of wine and flatten the variety of flavors and smells possible in nature.

He created his own term, *sinergica*, and registered it ("Other producers can use it if they meet the requirements") to indicate what his website explains as "a synergy that springs from the achievement of balance between all the ecosystem links." This is the essence of biodynamic farming and winemaking; it applies Rudolf Steiner's spiritual-scientific approach to agriculture, known as "anthroposophy," and Masanobu Fukuoka's "do-nothing farming."

"Humus, synergy—it all goes back to history, but it's not the history we learn in school. Just calling something 'bio' [organic] is a trick, but there is a voluntary ignorance among many consumers." He was on a roll, and I was swept up along with him; poor Michelle was translating at hyper speed. She looked at me and said, "He'll continue for another hour if we don't redirect him." *That Pugliese passion, man.*

I asked if we could see his vineyard— sì, *certo*—and he picked up a shovel as he walked us under a canopy of vines. He dug into the earth and lifted the dark brown soil out to show us how healthy it was. As if on cue, a worm wriggled out, doing a happy humus dance. Valentino had made his point.

THAT EVENING IN LECCE, DOMENICO picked up a couple of boxes of pizza from his favorite neighborhood pizzeria. We sat at their kitchen table and Michelle and I recounted the day's adventures. "I got shivers," Michelle repeated to him, about finding my bisnonno's birth certificate. I told him I tried susumaniello—the native Pugliese red grape he had recommended. (L'Archetipo has a bubbly rosé cleverly called Susumante, a play on the grape susumaniello and the term *spumante*, meaning "bubbly.")

To accompany our pizza, we opened a bottle of wine we had gotten from the other winery Michelle and I went to: Natalino Del Prete's Anne, a 100 percent negroamaro wine (named for his wife).

When we visited Natalino's eponymous winery, he walked us around his vineyard, telling us his grandfather and father (who must have been of similar age to my bisnonno Nicola Tufaro, I couldn't help but think) had also produced wine. He said he had been making it the same way they did "since I was born!" He must have been in his seventies and had been making natural wine since long before it was fashionable. "I don't like *anything* with chemicals in it, including my wine." He *only* grew grape varieties indigenous to his land, so we expected a lot from this negroamaro. We sipped; it was like a mouthful of dark berries, with a bit of black pepper. It'd be perfect with our pizzas.

Domenico cut the pizza into slices with a pair of scissors. "It's better straight from the oven," he said, as if to excuse any imperfections that might have occurred during the two-block trip home to the apartment. There was no harm done to the prized pizza, from what I could tell—its bottom crust kept its structure as a basin for the sweet, salty tomato sauce, chunks of mozzarella, and various toppings—but he wanted to make sure I knew its perfection had been meddled with in transit. Italians are very proud of their pizza.

We were three glasses of wine in when the conversation returned to pizza.

"The difference between the pizza you find here and the pizza of Naples," Domenico began, "is that the dough here isn't as fluffy." I took another bite and agreed, remembering the pizza I had eaten on a visit to Naples one year. That pizza's crust was the carb version of a ball of burrata cheese: pillowy and pliable as I lustfully ripped it with my teeth.

This subtle difference in pizza styles, he said, "isn't like the debate between New York–style pizza and Chicago-style pizza. Chicago-style isn't pizza."

"Why not?" I asked, knowing full well I was welcoming an avalanche.

"Pizza is pizza!" he said. "And that's not pizza. It's like when Michelle asks me to get almond milk at the grocery store. It's not milk! Why does she call it milk?"

"What else should I call it?" Michelle retorted. "Everyone knows what we're talking about when we say almond milk. Should I call it almond water?"

"No, water is water."

"Should I call it white almond liquid?"

"I don't know what you call it—*non rompere le palle* [don't break my balls]—

but it's not milk. Milk comes from an animal. Milk is milk. Pizza is pizza. Wine is wine."

Sound like a familiar trio? The fermentation of cheese, bread, and wine are all seemingly so simple, but in reality none of them are quite *that* straightforward. Up to this point I had been a passively amused observer, with no skin in the game. (I drink nondairy milk on the regular; I don't care what it's called as long as it's an option.) "Actually," I hopped into the debate, "one of the things I'm learning is that it's not that simple with wine."

He looked at me with an inquisitive eyebrow raise. Michelle added, "True, it's a lot of what Valentino was talking about today, and why he doesn't put additives in his wines."

"Domenico, what would you say is in wine?" I asked.

ALBARELLO

ARCH

CANOPY

"Grapes," he responded.

"Just grapes?"

"*Sì. Uva e basta.*"

"Did you know there are seventy-two legal additives for wine? But there's no ingredients list, so you don't know what you're drinking most of the time."

Michelle and I unraveled the balled-up threads of knowledge we had shoved in our brains from the three hours we spent with Valentino, and Domenico listened with rapt attention.

He responded, "Then the stuff with all the additives is not wine. That is false advertising. Wine is wine."

MY LECCE SOJOURN CAME TO A CLOSE; the days I spent in southern Puglia were more fulfilling than I could have hoped. I left with the certainty of my family's past, which felt at once exhilarating and like a profound privilege—one I knew was unreachable for many people from various circumstances and for many reasons. I felt grateful, and it extended to my appreciation of the pseudo-family I had found in Michelle and Domenico during those days.

Before departing that Saturday, my hosts took me to their local pasticciotto kiosk to indulge in the legendary custard-filled pastry specific to Salento, the geographic area of southern Puglia in which Lecce rests. Everyone at the shop knew my hosts by name and enthusiastically met me, their American friend writing a book about wine in Italy. They welcomed me like a long-lost family member—without realizing that's *exactly* how I felt.

WINE IS WINE IS WINE IS WINE IS

THE CLUE TO EVERYTHING

"To have seen Italy without having seen Sicily is not to have seen Italy at all, for Sicily is the clue to everything," wrote Johann Wolfgang von Goethe, a titan of German literature in the eighteenth and early-nineteenth centuries. It wasn't just Goethe; many people and signs pointed in the direction of Sicilia (pronounced *See-cheel-yah*), so from Maria and Nicola's dining room table, I booked the accommodations, and while I was in Puglia I assembled the logistics of my winery visits. *Can I pull this off?*

For hundreds of years—from the twelfth century to the nineteenth— the island was independently ruled as the kingdom of Sicily, before joining with its landmass to the north in relatively recent history, 1860, to unify with the kingdom of Italy. Prior to the twelfth century, it was ruled by Arab Muslims, colonized by the Phoenicians, populated by Greek settlers, captured by the Roman Empire, followed by an occupation by the Byzantine Greeks, the Germanic Vandals, the Spanish, and the Normans (of French and Viking descent). As the island changed hands continually—at times an important player in robust civilizations, and at others, a forgotten landmass in the Mediterranean—its fate was often out of its control.

There was a particularly rough patch between 1900 and 1910, when more than two million Italians immigrated to the United States of America, the overwhelming majority of them from the island of Sicily or from southern Italy (like my ancestors). As a result, the fifth-largest ethnic group in the United States today is Americans with Italian heritage. There are millions of Americans who have done a dig into their ancestry similar to mine, with a parallel story.

Those immigrants left behind a homeland that was "among the poorest places in Europe, where landless peasants tried to scratch a living from poor soil, continually exploited by landowners under a system still virtually feudal" and a life where "malnutrition and disease were rife; so was violence," writes Charles Wills in *Destination America*. The situation was dire, and when they first arrived in

At the antiques market in Catania, Sicily, I bought Pane e Vino—Bread and Wine—*for obvious reasons.*

America, they were maligned. Life was not easy, no matter where they turned. (I think back to my naïveté as a university student, when I visited Italy for the first time and thought, *Why would my ancestors leave this?* I was clueless.)

I wanted to know Sicily as it exists now, and I had no idea what to expect. So I landed curious as ever in Catania, the second most populous Sicilian city (after Palermo), on the eastern coast, facing the Ionian Sea. With no appointments and nothing to do for half a day, I explored.

My first experience interacting with Sicilians was at the antiques market in Catania, and they won me over faster than simmering garlic in olive oil strikes your salivary glands. I eyed a tabletop container that looked like it might have been used for wine, and when I asked the vendor about it in Italian, he was ecstatic about my kindergarten language skills—

meraviglióso! "Most tourists come and look, but they can't say a word! Where are you from?" he said in Italian, while he shook my hand and cupped his other hand over top, a warm, double-palmed greeting. We continued to talk through several of the other items he had on his table.

I had such a pleasant time at the antiques market—eyeing a big Thonet-style rocking chair I wished I could tuck in my carry-on luggage, bulbous green glass demijohns, and stacks of tattered old novels.

I grabbed some freshly fried *arancini* filled with roasted eggplant and strolled past an amphitheater built in the second century CE. I came across an open-air street market with tented tables selling produce, which rippled down the streets as far as I could see.

As I joined the current of customers among the stalls, which flanked either

An outdoor food market in Catania

side of the path, my head turned all around like an owl's as a man hawked his eggplants to my left—*Melanzane, melanzane! Melanzane, eccole qui!*—and to my right a woman bought a bunch of basil, the scent of which wafted toward me. The hot weather, resting in the mid-nineties (degrees Fahrenheit), didn't seem to stop anyone from venturing out for their shopping at the *mercato*. This city came alive at these markets, and I found myself falling hard for Sicily, quickly.

I bought some cherries, then found a pizzeria. I sat outside as the sun set, eating a mammoth round of pizza and sipping the restaurant's house red—nero d'Avola, its rich tannins gripping the melty mozzarella as I ate every last bite, wishing Connor were with me to split the pizza and languidly delight in the evening. It had been almost a month since I left London;

I felt fiercely alive with independence and exhilarated by Catania, but I wanted to share the adventure with him. As I walked to my accommodations, I reached for a cherry from my bag and placed it on my tongue, closing my mouth around it and applying gentle pressure until it burst. I sucked its sweet juices, reminiscent of the nero d'Avola that stained my lips, until the pit was like a dry bone in my mouth.

THE FOLLOWING MORNING, AROUND THE time the temperature shot up faster than the sun could keep up with it, I met up with Gea Cali. She was from the area and had a passion for wine and a predilection for all things hospitality, and she had agreed to drive me to and from the winery of Arianna Occhipinti—the woman famous for redefining Sicily's wine scene.

As we left Catania, the cars zoomed

around us like a grown-up bumper car rink on speed. *Stronzo!*—*Jerk!*—Gea muttered behind the wheel as we fought our way through traffic. As we drove farther outside the city, though, the quiet vastness of rural Sicily was sweeping. When we got to Vittoria, the land morphed into farms with covered plots of tomato vines and olive and citrus trees. In terms of grapes, the region is now known for its indigenous reds—the light-bodied frappato and the fruity, powerful nero d'Avola (also called calabrese).

"Have you ever visited Agricola Azienda Arianna Occhipinti?" I asked Gea as we drove there. She said she hadn't, but she'd been wanting to, especially since her friend Gian Marco Iannello, previously a hotshot sommelier in Noto, had recently started working with Arianna. "Gian Marco . . . that's who I've been emailing with!" I said.

When we pulled up to the winery, Gian Marco was waiting for us and welcomed us with a quick kiss on both cheeks, a puckered *muah, muah*. He ran his hand coolly through his curly hair and explained that Arianna was presently occupied but would stop by shortly. He took us to a seating area outside, under shade, and introduced us to a man and woman who were also waiting to meet Arianna—a Belgian couple who were in Sicily visiting their good friend, winemaker Frank Cornelissen, a cult figure who was one of the first foreigners to move to Mount Etna and make a big name for the wines of Etna internationally. (His Susucaru Rosato gained fame after

chef-turned-rapper Action Bronson said it was the wine he'd been "waiting for" his whole life.) We sat together making small talk while we waited for Arianna, suspense building.

Arianna, a woman the *New York Times* called "Vittoria's star winemaker," would of course be too busy to spend hours with all the people who wanted to meet her. She'd been a wine celebrity for nearly a decade. Ever since her first vintage in 2004, when she was only twenty-one years old, working with four acres of land, "she has been embraced as a darling of the natural wine world," wrote Eric Asimov in the *Times*. By the years 2010 to 2013, she was considered a bona fide prodigy.

Just when enough time had elapsed that I started to wonder if I'd get the chance to meet her, she emerged with another woman, Francesca Padovani (one-half of the sister team behind Montalcino's Fonterenza winery). Arianna greeted the group as she leaned against the side of the building, an indication she wouldn't be hanging around for long. It felt like I was on the bleachers of the red carpet and she'd just stepped out of her limo; her presence was captivating. Without a spot of makeup and with her thick black hair pulled into a bun, she was a Sicilian beauty.

She exchanged pleasantries with the Belgians in fluent English, and when she turned to me, I introduced myself, then gushed, "I can't believe you started making wine when you were twenty-one." I collected myself, wanting to engage her beyond small talk. "Has the way you make wine changed?"

Gian Marco Iannello, Arianna Occhipinti, and Francesca Padovani

At that, she pulled out a seat across the table from me and sat down. "Step by step . . . little by little . . . I've grown," she said, her elbows on the table and arm motions punctuating her sentence.

Although she has always made natural wine, her winemaking techniques have evolved over the years. She follows biodynamic principles like the lunar calendar (though when I asked about planting a dung-filled horn somewhere on their sixty-four acres of vineyards, Gian Marco said with a chuckle, "We don't have time for that!").

I felt like I had an audience with the queen of Vittoria herself, but knew how some monarchies get overthrown; I asked if she worried about copycat winemakers.

"No one can reproduce this exactly," she replied, meaning the specific people working with the grapes on that exact soil. "Now that natural wine is getting trendy, this is important to understand."

"What do you think of natural wine being, as you say, 'trendy'?"

"Listen, I'm not making this wine to be 'natural.' It's *the* way to make wine . . . the A, B, C of winemaking."

Francesca, who also produces natural wine, pulled up a seat at the table. She had traveled from central Italy (Montalcino is in Siena) for the day. I wanted to ask Arianna about being such a notable female in this male-dominated arena, but I didn't want to be trite; I knew she'd had her share of journalists asking her about being a woman in wine. Francesca's attendance opened the door for me to direct my query to her.

I asked Francesca what had brought her to Vittoria for the day and she replied, "Women in natural wine are *amazing*, and it's important we stick together."

Elena Pantaleoni of La Stoppa winery in Emilia-Romagna and Elisabetta Foradori of Agricola Foradori in Trentino are some of the other women in this pack of rock-star female Italian winemakers Arianna has been so closely associated with. From everything I'd heard, the women in this unofficial club were exceptionally supportive of one another and even compare notes, like queen bees exchanging tips on how to build the best hive. "Do you still talk with those ladies often?" I asked.

"The group was important to help build my knowledge," Arianna said. "Now it's important because it's where I get my energy and inspiration. Francesca being here is a super present!" she said, and smiled at her friend. They reminded me of *The Sisterhood of the Traveling Pants*. *Sisterhood of the Natural Winemakers*?

Francesca nodded. "We are all linked, in a real way."

"Are you still fighting as women in the industry?" I asked. "Fighting for recognition, for respect?"

Arianna sighed. "Depends on the day."

"It's easier when we're together," Francesca said, and Arianna caught the end of her sentence and added, "It's easier than before. But we don't have to try to be men. We have our sensibility; we use that."

That sensibility—the sixth sense of artisans and craftspeople—reminded me of the instinct Debbie had in cheesemaking, as she intuited when the curd was ready to cut and reminded me to work quickly but with grace. Eventually Arianna and Francesca had to leave, and when I said farewell, I felt like I was holding my head a little higher than before. *Yeah, I'd be friends with them.*

FOR MUCH OF SICILY'S RECENT WINE history, it grew more grapes than anywhere else in the country, but the grapes were sold to producers on the mainland as mixing grapes. There was an important winery in Vittoria, Azienda Agricola COS (known as COS), that had made strides to push against that stereotype, and I knew I couldn't leave Vittoria without going there. Plus, I was dying to see their amphorae—ancient clay fermentation vessels.

When Gea and I arrived, there was a light, warm breeze coming from the Mediterranean Sea, and we were greeted by Biagio Distefano, one of the younger members of the staff, since the three founders (one of whom is Arianna's uncle) were no longer as hands-on as they had been in the early years. Biagio was a soft-spoken, whip-smart guy—a local born the next village over who had lived in London for seven years working in the wine trade. I did not hide my anticipation and excitement at seeing the amphorae—the main attraction.

COS was born in 1980, but it wasn't until 2000 that the founders discovered amphorae, from a visit to Josko Gravner up in Friuli after that year's Vinitaly. Gravner—a moon-following vintner—was using traditional Georgian *qvevri* (a type of clay amphora) to ferment his wine. ("A qvevri is an amphora, but an amphora is not necessarily a qvevri," Biagio said for clarification. Qvevri are thought to be the *original* amphorae.) They took the idea to Sicily and began using the vessels for some of their wines the following harvest. It became a mainstay of their production.

I wasn't sure what to expect from these curvy clay containers, but when Biagio walked us through a shed door to face about a hundred terra-cotta vessels (400 liters each), I was shocked when my eyes shifted down to the ground. The amphorae were all buried, with just the top five inches (10 centimeters) sticking up. I was accustomed to seeing photos of amphorae in plain air, so I had forgotten they're buried as a means of temperature control during fermentation. The top holes of the vessels stay open to the elements, like kids holding their mouths open to the sky, trying to catch a snowflake.

After the grapes are crushed and put in the amphorae, the team covers the openings at the top with cotton and seals them with a rubber band. Every day, they're uncovered and the cap is pushed down—just as I'd done at Comelli Winery. After fermentation, the contents are removed, pressed, and placed back in the amphorae to age for seven months. Two of COS's eleven wines ferment in amphorae (Pithos Bianco, a white wine made of 100 percent grecanico grapes, and Pithos Rosso, a blend of nero d'Avola and frappato).

We walked out of the room with all the amphorae and Biagio took us to the more traditional cellar, with stainless-steel tanks and a few barrels, where the rest of their wines were made.

In the cellar, he measured the pH of the liquids—it was like a flashback to the dairies I'd visited, where the cheesemakers dutifully measured the pH at each key step. "Wine is always acidic," he said and looked as his meter. "Three point four, I'm happy." (The pH scale tells you whether something is acidic or alkaline: 7 is neutral; a lower number means it's more acidic, and a higher number means it's more alkaline.) He showed me the reading. "This lower pH means wine is stable; it keeps wine having less bacteria. Are you ready to taste some?" *Absolutely.*

We sipped a delightfully salty wine made of 100 percent zibibbo (same thing as moscato) grapes, and an orange (aka skin-contact) wine called Rami, made of 50 percent grecanico grapes and 50 percent inzolia grapes. It tasted like a combination of the sea breeze I had felt outside and dried apricots, which its color resembled. I didn't know if I was making up that description, but it rolled out of my mouth.

"Yeah, that's it!" Biagio said. I might have been shyer had I known he used to be a sommelier at an upscale hotel restaurant when he lived in London. Luckily, he was my kind of sommelier: "The beauty of wine is nobody's right and nobody's wrong—that's what turns me away from wine critics."

"Ha! Yes. Wine should be approachable. What's your theory on food and wine pairings?"

"Today there is too much hype about pairings. It's more complicated than right and wrong, because it's very personal." It felt good every time I got that confirmation, whether it be from Elizabeth in Rome or Sofia in Bologna or Biagio in Vittoria.

He poured their Cerasuolo di Vittoria Classico DOCG. As the three of us sipped, it literally halted all conversation. It was juicy—bursting of intense black cherry and plum flavors—with a crispness blanched out by a full body.

"Wow" was all I could say. I understood why Cerasuolo di Vittoria was a wine the region felt immense pride in.

"Do you drink this every single chance you get?" I asked him. "Are your shelves filled with Cerasuolo di Vittoria?"

"Always drink a new wine. It's like watching a movie. Even if you like it, you want to watch a new movie."

Gea piped up, "I love this wine. I drink it whenever I can!"

We wrapped up our tasting and I told Biagio I was off to Etna the next day. He said, "Eduardo Torres Acosta is making the best wine in Sicily right now. He's in Etna; try to drink some of his wine while you're there." *Noted.*

Gea and I returned to Catania, where she threw an intimate dinner party (including Jennifer, the ebullient woman who had connected us), whipping together *pasta alla Norma*—a tubular pasta called *boccole* tossed with fried eggplant and tomato sauce—in a dark kitchen, no less, after a sudden rainstorm cut out the electricity! It didn't slow her down one bit. I was impressed.

The next morning, I got a pistachio gelato–stuffed brioche (*brioche con gelato* is a typical breakfast in Sicily's summer months—don't you love Italy?), and caught the bus to Mount Etna.

Arancini con Melanzane
(Fried Rice Balls with Eggplant)

MAKES 8 TO 10 BALLS

I still dream of the food I ate during the couple of days I spent in Catania. Pistachio everything (pistachio gelato, pistachio granita, pistachio pesto!); the ubiquitous eggplant, in caponata and pasta alla Norma; and, perhaps my favorite bite of all, the various arancini I ate, deep-fried and perfect with a glass of wine.

These fried, filled rice balls are often round, but are sometimes shaped with a point at the top and a big, round base, resembling a pear. They can be golf ball size, on the small side, or as big as a softball! Like many things in Italian cuisine, these variations are determined by region, preference, and how nonna did it. The arancini I had in Catania were approximately baseball size (one I had was pointed, the other rounded; this recipe makes the rounded version).

Arancini originated in tenth-century Sicily, when the island was under Arab rule, and if they've stuck around this long, you *know* they're good eating. An indulgence worth every bite.

Panko or bread crumbs will work for the coating. Use Arborio rice, the same rice you use to make risotto. Arancini are the perfect way to use up leftover risotto. If you're good at multitasking in the kitchen, cook the filling while stirring the risotto. (If that seems too stressful, finish the risotto, then cook the filling.)

RISOTTO
8 cups (2 liters) vegetable broth

2½ cups (500 grams) Arborio rice

2 tablespoons extra-virgin olive oil

½ medium white onion, finely chopped

¼ teaspoon fine sea salt, plus more to taste

3 tablespoons tomato paste

½ cup (125 milliliters) white wine (preferably one that's high in acidity, such as Sicilian carricante)

Juice of ½ lemon

½ cup (50 grams) freshly grated Parmigiano Reggiano cheese

FILLING
1 tablespoon extra-virgin olive oil

¼ medium white onion, finely chopped

½ teaspoon fine sea salt, plus more to taste

½ large eggplant (aubergine), cut into roughly ½-inch (1-centimeter) dice

½ cup (125 milliliters) red wine

½ (14-ounce/400-gram) can diced tomatoes, with their juices

3½ ounces (100 grams) mozzarella cheese, shredded or cut into ½-inch (1-centimeter) cubes

TO ASSEMBLE
Sunflower oil or other neutral oil (you will need between 1 and 3 quarts/liters of oil, depending on your wok or Dutch oven)

1 cup bread crumbs (to make your own, see page 319)

1 egg white

Fine sea salt for sprinkling

(recipe continues) **233**

1. Make the risotto: Pour the broth into a medium saucepan and bring it to a simmer. Then reduce the heat to medium-low to keep the broth hot.

2. Place a large, high-sided pan over medium-high heat and add the rice. Toast the rice, shaking the pan to move the grains around, for 30 seconds to 1 minute, until fragrant. Pour the rice into a bowl and set aside.

3. Return the pan to medium heat and pour in the olive oil. Add the onion, sprinkle with a pinch of salt, and sauté, stirring occasionally, for 2 to 3 minutes, until soft and translucent. Add the tomato paste and cook, stirring, for 1 to 2 minutes, until the onion begins to brown. Add the wine and stir to deglaze the pan, scraping up any bits stuck to the bottom. Return the rice to the pan and stir to combine.

4. Add a few ladles of the hot broth and cook, stirring continuously, until the rice has absorbed the liquid. Continue adding broth a ladle at a time, letting the rice soak up each addition before adding the next, until you've used all the broth, around 20 minutes. At this point, taste the risotto: the rice should be cooked, but al dente (with a little firmness to the bite). Add the lemon juice and cheese, season with salt, and stir. Taste and add more salt if needed. Transfer the risotto to a wide bowl or plate and let cool to room temperature (so it'll be easy to handle).

5. Make the filling: Set a medium pan over medium heat. Pour the olive oil into the pan and add the onion. Season with a pinch of salt and sauté for about 5 minutes, until the onion is translucent. Add the eggplant and stir. Season with another pinch of salt and cook, stirring occasionally, until the eggplant starts to brown, about 4 minutes. Add the wine and stir to deglaze the pan. Taste, then add a bit more salt if you think it needs it. Add the tomatoes and cook, stirring every couple of minutes, for 10 minutes, or until the liquid has evaporated. Remove from the heat and let cool.

6. Assemble the arancini: Fill a wok, Dutch oven, or large pot about halfway with sunflower oil (the oil should be deep enough that when you add a rice ball, it's completely submerged). Place over medium-high heat to get the oil hot for frying.

7. Place the bread crumbs and egg white in separate large shallow bowls.

8. With clean hands, grab a small handful (around ¼ cup/60 milliliters) of the cooled risotto and roll it into a ball. Make a large indentation in the middle and fill it with 1 to 2 tablespoons of the eggplant filling and some of the mozzarella. Place another handful of risotto over the filling and, using your palms, form the risotto into a ball that fully encloses the filling. Add rice where it seems thin or steal risotto from heftier parts of the ball to make sure there's an even layer around the filling. When you're happy with the shape, set the rice ball aside on a plate and repeat until you've used all the risotto.

9. Dip a rice ball in the bowl of egg white, using your fingers to coat it, seal the rice, and smooth out the shape. Let any excess egg drip off, then dip the ball in the bread crumbs and roll it around to coat evenly, then return it to the plate. Repeat to coat the rest of the rice balls.

10. To test if the oil is hot enough, nab a tiny piece of bread from your pantry and drop it into the oil. If it begins bubbling immediately, the oil is ready. Remove the tester bread and use a slotted spoon to gently put a few arancini into the hot oil, taking care never to touch the oil with your

fingers. Using the spoon, gently move the arancini in the oil so they don't rest on the bottom of the pot and become misshapen and so they fry evenly. Fry for 3 to 5 minutes (this will differ depending on how hot your oil is), until the arancini are browned on all sides. Remove them from the oil with the slotted spoon and place them on a paper towel–lined plate. Sprinkle them with salt immediately.

Allow the oil to get hot again if you've turned off the burner, and repeat to fry the rest of the arancini.

11. And finally, you can stuff your face. These are lovely to dip in an herby, garlicky fresh pesto sauce or a spicy arrabiata sauce. Enjoy! (No one will judge you for washing these down with some of that leftover carricante wine you've got on hand.)

LAND OF THE VINES

Greek mythology claims that Hades created an entrance to the underworld in Mount Etna, and that Zeus triumphed over the monster Typhon by throwing Mount Etna on top of him. At nearly 11,000 feet (3,350 meters) above sea level, it is the highest active volcano in Europe, with frequent eruptions leaving traces of lava on its slopes—no wonder it features prominently in the legends. I had the distinct feeling of approaching something not only grand, potentially deadly, and visually dominating, but quietly alive.

I took a bus to Randazzo, and one of the three sisters who ran the B&B where I had booked a room was kind enough to pick me up from the station and drive me the ten minutes to the accommodations, Parco Statella. This sister was named Manuela, and she was around my age; seeing her big smile and enthusiastic wave, I felt happy to be there, and grateful that I had made it to Etna without Typhon snatching me on the way.

A couple of hours later, after exploring the verdant grounds of the B&B and enjoying the cool, crisp air up on Etna (at the base of the mountain itself), I knocked on the lobby door to inquire about getting to town for dinner. Manuela said, "If it's okay with you, Eduardo can take you. He lives in one of the rooms here; he's driving into town anyway."

I thought Eduardo looked familiar and assumed it was simply because of his classic tall, dark, and handsome looks. But then we started talking . . .

Eduardo was from the Canary Islands of Spain, and he told me about how he had moved to Sicily in 2012 to intern at Azienda Agricola Arianna Occhipinti. "I was just there!" I blurted, to which he responded, "Arianna is my girlfriend." *Wait, this guy is with my new friend crush, the wine royalty of Vittoria?*

He explained that after his internship in Vittoria, he moved to Etna, where he spent several years working with Andrea Franchetti's Passopisciaro winery, a vanguard of viticulture on Etna. "I loved Etna immediately," he said, and in his downtime, he'd scouted out a few small parcels of land to rent and farm, the soils rich in volcanic ash.

Could this be Eduardo Torres Acosta? The same man Biagio at COS had said produces some of "the best wine in Sicily"?

Eduardo asked where I wanted to go and I, in turn, asked for his suggestions—my brain scrambled to figure out my next move on the chess board, determining which piece I was in the presence of. He paused to think. "Il Buongustaio dell'Etna. Great wines, great meat and cheese."

I moved my knight piece to test my theory, "Do they carry *your* wines?" I asked.

"*Sì, certo.*"

Hot damn, I'm in the car with Eduardo Torres Acosta. I had been on Mount Etna for all of thirty minutes and already I felt like there were larger forces at play.

I agreed that his recommendation would be an ideal place to go. (Getting to know a town by its local wine bar has rarely led me astray.) I couldn't wait to try his wine.

Eduardo's philosophy was nonintervention and fastidious care, working in adherence to generally accepted standards of "natural" winemaking; which is to say, he didn't spray or irrigate; relied on spontaneous fermentation of indigenous yeasts; added little, if any, sulfur; and hand-harvested the fruit. His modest quantities of "Eduardo Torres Acosta" wines had earned rave reviews.

Il Buongustaio dell'Etna was part wine bar and part shop, selling wines by the bottle off its shelves rather than by the glass, although you could stay and sit with your bottle (in which case they'll bring you a glass) and order some bites, too. After Eduardo dropped me off, I grabbed a bottle of his Versante Nord 2016, and the

Il Buongustaio dell'Etna

host sat me outside and across the narrow street at the only empty two-top.

There were three other round tables dotted near me, and two young gentlemen were at the closest table, snug next to mine, immersed in an animated conversation. One had long dark hair pulled into a bun, and he leaned back in his chair with his legs crossed at the calf. The other had lighter brown hair, recently shorn, close on the sides and a purposeful poof to its brushed-back height. I guessed they were in their late twenties.

I pulled out the book I was reading—a narrative about wine, duh—and pinched the stem of the glass between my fingers to give Eduardo's wine a sip. It lit up my taste buds and slid down my throat; it was bright and fruity, sturdy with tannins. It was a blend of 85 percent bold nerello mascalese (a grape native to Etna that has been compared to Piedmont's nebbiolo) and 15 percent other grapes, like nerello cappuccio, another of Etna's favorites.

By the time my snacks were brought out, I had found myself in a conversation with the two men next to me; they'd torn themselves away from their involved discussion to ask me how the 2016 vintage of Eduardo's wine was. It turns out they were both winemakers, too—they met in enology school and were reunited on Etna because Nicolò (with the long hair pulled into a bun) was in the process of interviewing for vignaiolo positions on the volcano. He was originally from Bologna but was intrigued by the prospect of winemaking in Sicily. The one with shorter hair, Alessandro, had been born and bred in Sicily and now worked as an assistant winemaker and viticulturist at Planeta Wine.

Etna's twilight zone continued to swirl around me: in my book—Robert V. Camuto's *Palmento*, all about Sicilian wine—I had *just read* about the importance of Planeta to Etna's wine scene. The patriarch of the Planeta family, Diego, believed in the potential of Etna long before it became a favorite among sommeliers worldwide (much like what the guys at COS did for Vittoria), making the Planetas "the most important wine-producing family in modern Sicily; no one has been more effective in showing the world that Sicily and its vines have something important to express." Planeta had grown to thousands of acres of vineyards but was still producing great-quality wines that represented Etna to much of the international wine-drinking community.

"There are two important grapes here," Alessandro told me, "Nerello mascalese—the red grape you're drinking there—and carricante, a grape that makes a special white wine. Carricante gets better with age; most whites don't do well with aging."

I told them about my journey to learn about Italian wine, to which Nicolò said, "Ah! Italy is super difficult about wine—because we have so much!" I knew what he meant—the diversity of Italy's grapes (and therefore its wines) was overwhelming. Even the differences between vines on the landmass of Sicily—between Vittoria and Etna—were considerable (and that's not to mention the wines made on the western part of the island).

Nicolò and Alessandro

Of course, my learning was about more than wine—it was about feeling connected to a place and to my roots, which I thought of as I considered Nicolò's name, and the fingers-crossed guess at my great-grandfather's Italian name that had helped me track down his birth certificate.

"What do you think about natural wines?" I asked, ever curious at the spectrum of responses that question would elicit.

"At the moment, it is *alla moda*, it's in fashion," Alessandro noted.

"Doing good natural wine is hard work," added Nicolò, "but it's become a marketing tool. And sometimes it's aggressive marketing—against conventional. Trust me, some people who do 'natural' do some not-very-ecological bullshit."

"It's a different style; there doesn't need to be a war between the styles," said Alessandro. I thought his boss at Planeta (a conventional winery) would be proud of his diplomacy.

"You need some standard," Nicolò said. "The most important thing, in my opinion, is that wine has to be balanced."

"If there's a defect in my wine, I have to fix it!" Alessandro nodded.

"What do you guys think about biodynamic?"

Nicolò pronounced, "I like biodynamic as an idea," to which Alessandro asked him, "Have you ever made biodynamic wines?"

"No."

"Me neither. They always look at the moon!" They laughed.

Then Nicolò summed up what I'd heard throughout my trip: "The only way to get good wine, to know what you're drinking, is to know the guy who produces your wine. Nothing is simple. Especially in the wine field."

Alessandro ordered a bottle of Planeta's carricante for us all to share as the sun tucked itself beneath the horizon. A procession of altar boys in white robes filed down the slender street, carrying a life-size Virgin Mary on their shoulders. A priest walked in front of them, holding a rosary in one hand and a microphone in the other. His voice projected from a speaker on the platform that held the effigy: *"Ave Maria . . ."*

Alessandro disappeared inside the wine shop, and when he returned, we learned he'd paid our entire bill. Nicolò and I looked at him. "Really?"

"Welcome to Etna, both of you!" he said. That's Sicilian hospitality for you.

The three of us went to a pizzeria for a proper dinner, and afterward Alessandro graciously dropped me off at the entrance of my B&B. I'd been on Lady Etna for less than twelve hours, and already she had bewitched me.

"ONE OF MY FAVORITE ITALIAN WINE professors says, 'Italy is an amusement park for wine geeks.' Italy was once called Oenotria—land of the vines."

Brittany Carlisi was an American who,

after some years in Rome, had relatively recently made Sicily her home—she was an Etna-wine evangelist. I connected with her to see what all the fuss was about regarding Etna's volcanic terroir and the wines it produced. Brittany knew straightaway where to take me first: Vini Scirto.

Giuseppe Scirto and Valeria Franco are the husband-and-wife team behind the label, one of the smallest producers on Etna. They met us at a café first thing that morning, and Brittany and I piled in the back seat of their beat-up old sedan to go to the vineyard, which used to belong to Giuseppe's grandparents.

He had one hand on the steering wheel, and the other held a cigarette. He took a drag, exhaled, and reminisced about la vendemmia as a kid: he was at his grandfather's side the whole day.

Giuseppe parked the car and the four of us emerged into the most beautiful backdrop of a vineyard I had ever seen. On the northern slope of the mountain itself, it felt like we were staring the volcano in the face, surrounded by lush vegetation, and not just the bright green leaves of the rows of grapevines: all the various plants around us—plum trees, peach trees—were rustling merrily in the slight breeze, bathing in the sun. Giuseppe reached up toward a peach tree and picked a fuzzy, juicy stone fruit from its branch. He handed it to me, and I bit in; its sweet syrup ran down my chin and I moaned, "Oh my gosh."

"If the fruit's this good, imagine the wine," Valeria said. We walked toward the vines and she added, "There is no more active terroir than Etna." The natural biodiversity and fertility of the land was awe-inspiring; it's what the vineyards on Mount Etna have become known for.

"People call Etna 'Mama,'" Brittany said. "Mount Etna is female—she's gentle."

The parallel to a mother went further: like any strict mom, Mount Etna didn't tolerate toxic visitors, and Etna has been one of the few terroirs resistant to phylloxera, a tiny insect that infests vineyards. "It can't survive on sandy volcanic soil," Brittany told me. "That's why these are ungrafted vines." (Grafting an American rootstock onto a European vine is how many vineyards evade phylloxera.)

It's also why the vines could be so old: Valeria pointed out a 150-year-old vine that was so gnarly it looked like the Salvador Dalí interpretation of a plant. "They're like a field of statues. Each is different from the next."

A few steps later, Brittany pointed ahead—"Ooh! This is where the *palmento* is"—clearly excited to show me whatever was behind the maroon doors of the shed. We entered, and I saw a large stone basin, with paths chiseled from higher platforms to the lower ones. "This is it!" Brittany said. I wasn't entirely sure what I was looking at, aside from something ancient and no longer in use. I remembered seeing similar ruins in an unused portion of Arianna Occhipinti's production facilities.

"What's a palmento, again?" I asked.

"It's how everyone in Sicily used to make wine," Brittany said, then launched into an explanation: "It's a three-level gravitational system. It's thought the first palmento was created by Pliny the Elder to make not just wine but also olive oil. He did everything according to phases of the moon—did you know NASA has proven that the moon makes a difference with this stuff?" I shook my head, wide-eyed at her enthusiasm.

"When the Romans came through, they added the lever press." She pointed up to the top tier. "The grapes would come through the windows up there. That's where the pressing began. A group of people would stomp the grapes and sing a song. Do you know why they sang?"

"Because they liked music?" I lamely guessed; I was enthralled by her love of the palmento.

"They sang because if one of them missed their part of the song, 'Get him outta here!' because the carbon dioxide fumes were getting to him, and he was

probably going to pass out." She put her arms around Valeria and Giuseppe to reenact the scene: they formed a circle, spinning around and stomping, singing "La la la!"

Brittany continued, "Those juices would pour down to the next part, the *fiore*, the flower, the most delicate part. Here, they'd take all the skins, stems, and seeds—the pomace—bring it into the center, where this huge wooden screw is, and wrap the pomace up with a rope. Two men, or a donkey, would turn this screw and it would press out that final extraction, which provided the structural elements of the wine. All the juices would flow down to the final basin."

"That's ingenious!" I said, thoroughly amused. "Why don't they still use it?"

"It's illegal now," Brittany said. *You know, sanitary standards.* Aside from that, Giuseppe said he and Valeria made wine the same way his grandpa did—natural.

"But I can't even use the word 'natural' anymore," Brittany said. "It's too divisive. People use it as an excuse for bad wine; that's why it pisses so many people off." It was a refrain I'd heard before.

We tasted their nerello mascalese red wine, A'Culonna.

"What's that mean?" I asked.

"It's named after a piazza in town where my grandfather would gather with the other elderly people from the village to talk," Giuseppe explained, "and he often brought them back here to drink wine." Everything about the operation of Vino

Scirto was connected to family history and in reverence to those roots. We toasted to Mama Etna.

IT WAS DURING OUR VISIT TO VALCERASA, a winery where agronomist Alice Bonaccorsi made one of the first Etna wines to be imported into the United States in the late nineties, when Brittany recollected the impact of her first harvest experience, right there at ValCerasa. With that, she reminded me of where my journey began, amid the vines in Friuli.

As we walked the rows, she remembered the "magic" of the experience. "By only growing indigenous varieties of grapes, mainly nerello mascalese, nerello cappuccio, and—the queen!—carricante, Alice knew that Etna's uniqueness made it spectacular."

In that moment, I determined to return to Friuli for the next harvest at Comelli Winery, in three months' time (which I did).

My inquiry into wine began partially because I sought some deeper feeling of "home" in Europe, but as I packed my bags on Mount Etna, UK-bound, I intensely missed Connor and—there was no other word for it—home.

For me, nothing means home more than bread—whether it was the scent of my mom's bread wafting from the oven during childhood or my adult routine of maintaining a sourdough starter. It was bread, of course, that would entice me to yet another adventure: this time, to France.

Here's your wine party with recipes from my Italy adventure; but you'll need some bread for scarpetta, to sop up any sauce left on the plate—turn the page to explore the perfect loaf.

HOW CAN A NATION BE CALLED GREAT IF ITS BREAD TASTES LIKE KLEENEX?

—JULIA CHILD

PART THREE

BREAD // FRANCE

Proofing baskets (also called bannetons) for dough

AN AUDIENCE WITH BREAD ROYALTY

It was early morning, and the sparrows in the bush outside of my London bedroom window chattered noisily, lifting me into awareness. My first conscious thought was, *It's time to bake bread*, and like a gluten zombie, I moved the covers off my body and got out of bed. This had become my norm. Another day, another loaf.

How did I become this person? I was never a "sourdough bro" type, nor did I have much of a desire to perfect the art of the flawless loaf; I've been spoiled by artisan bakeries in both Brooklyn and London, which precluded the need to buy subpar bread. *Leave it to the pros*, was my thinking.

But something had changed. I can tell you with certainty that making bread has transformed our home. Connor agrees—he's the one who made the observation in the first place. The joy of giving birth to a bundle of fresh bread is a worthy pursuit, and a joy I can't help but encourage others to try.

When I moved to Europe, I loved bread—I valued the good stuff, but I didn't understand how it got that way. My first attempt at maintaining a sourdough starter, when I was still in New York, became a forlorn side project, and then a dead one. I accepted my relationship with bread baking as one in which I admired the people who did it and delighted in the results of their craft. I might have stayed that way forever if I had not, on a crisp spring morning in London, met French bread royalty.

MY PALMS WERE CLAMMY AS I PEERED AT the clock: noon. My lunch meeting was in an hour. I looked in the mirror to straighten my shirt under my sweater and left for my audience with the reigning queen of French bread, Apollonia Poilâne.

I had spent the entire morning immersing myself in information about her: I read every article I could find in the *New Yorker*, *Gentlewoman*, the *Financial Times*, and *Monocle*, I watched her various French television appearances online. In the days prior, I'd filled my podcast stream with the British, French, and American shows she'd been interviewed on, listening to her transition effortlessly from French to English and vice versa.

As a journalist, it's in my bones to do thorough research before an interview. But in this case, my exploration *began* as rote research, shape-shifted to fascination, and finally turned into downright awe. There was something about Apollonia's story that seemed otherworldly. It was as though I'd listened to the entire Destiny's Child canon, watched *Lemonade* and *Homecoming* back to back, and then had a lunch date planned with Beyoncé. *What will she be like?*

Apollonia runs Poilâne (pronounced *pwah-lahn*), one of the most famous and beloved bread companies *in the world*, let alone in France. Her grandfather, Pierre Poilâne, had founded the bakery in Paris before World War II, and what distinguished his bread was that he kept the traditional craft of breadmaking the focus of his practice. He used natural fermentation, i.e., sourdough starter (*levain* in French), to make big brown crusty sourdough *miche*, round loaves that reminded the French what good ol' bread was. Among the mechanized industrial slabs quickly filling the shelves in boulangeries all around the city, his bread—which took more time to leaven (as fermentation necessitates)—stood out.

When Pierre's son Lionel—Apollonia's father—took over the company in 1970, he continued making the same bread, but added his undeniable charisma and knack for business. He boosted their celebrity acclaim by making it known that people like Robert DeNiro were fans.

(The actor has had Poilâne bread flown to LA straight from the bakery's wood-fired oven in Paris.) Lionel was as much a bread philosopher as he was a baker.

"There is no question that Lionel Poilâne makes the most famous bread in France, perhaps the world," the Francophile American writer Patricia Wells notes in her 1987 tome *The Food Lover's Guide to Paris*. She referred to Lionel as *le roi du pain*—"The king of bread." To merit that title in France, a place renowned for its outstanding bread, offers more than culinary stardom. If bread can be considered a metonym for France, and Lionel was bread's savior, then his importance to French culture arguably *exceeded* claims to the monarchy.

Apollonia ascended from bread princess to bread queen sooner than anyone could have imagined. In 2002, Lionel and his wife, Iréna, died in a helicopter crash, and Apollonia, then eighteen years old, took the helm of the bakery. She didn't skip a beat as she stepped into those giant shoes.

That's not all she did, though. She had also been accepted to Harvard and, unbelievably, went to college while holding the reins as Poilâne's CEO. Compared with what I did in my downtime as a college freshman—sitting on a bean bag and singing along to the *Rent* soundtrack on repeat—she was Wonder Woman.

Since those early years in her leadership role, she has kept the spirit of Poilâne's bread—*pain Poilâne*—alive and well while growing the business and navigating the ever-shifting culinary

landscape. She doesn't pay much mind to industry trends; she's far more interested in continuing a legacy.

As I walked briskly from the tube in West London to meet Apollonia at one of her café shops, Comptoir Poilâne (one of a handful of Poilâne outposts across the English Channel), I had a flashback to when I had first sought out a loaf of Poilâne bread as a culinary school student in Paris, half a decade prior. Surprised to find that Poilâne didn't even bother with baguettes in their repertoire, I bought their signature sourdough miche.

It was a revelation—the dark, thick crust gave way to a soft, delicately sour-tasting crumb, and it had smaller holes of fermentation than some of the splashier gaping sourdough holes I had come to expect from the artisan bakers in my previous Brooklyn neighborhood.

The crumb of a bread is the term for the interior of the loaf—everything inside the crust (including the pattern and size of the holes). It's known in French as *la mie*, and it is one of the more obvious variables among sourdough breads, with some styles showcasing a consistent pattern and others revealing irregular, assorted sizes of holes sprinkled throughout.

When I arrived to meet with Apollonia, I spotted her at a table in the midst of another meeting. In a matter of moments, she saw me, looked at her watch, and graciously stood to welcome me. "I'll be with you in a couple of minutes," she promised, and led me to a seat near the window. She was more petite than

I expected, but she had an undeniable stature. I sat and my heart rate calmed, returning to a normal pitter-patter thanks to her prompt hospitality.

When she pulled out a chair to join me, our conversation turned immediately to the crux of the matter, and the reason I had reached out to her: bread. "People always say to me things like, 'Oh, *this* is bread, *that* is not bread,' but the main part of the conversation is, *what* do we call bread?" Her accent was American (her mom was from the United States), but her interest in bread was distinctly French. "For me, it's that crossroad between cereal grains, flours, and fermentation," she continued. "That's my consideration of my business and of my craft."

I reflected on the word *craft*, and how it had become a marker of not just the product itself, but of the consumers who seek it out and the artisans drawn to make it. She continued, "Anyone can make bread, but Poilâne has been around for over eighty years, and if there's something that three generations have cultivated, it's a passion and culture for bread. My grandfather, my father, and I have a *passion* for our craft. We look at it for not just the beauty of the product but also the greater symbolism of bread bringing people together. Because you don't grow grain just for yourself."

"That reminds me," I followed up, triggered by a memory of one of the articles I'd read about her, "of you talking about the literal definition of the French word *copain* [friend], which is the word *pain* [bread] with the prefix of togetherness, *co-*."

"Right, someone you share bread with—*that's* your friend."

"It seems to me," I pivoted, "that you want to maintain the tradition of your family, but you're curious about how it fits into life *right now*. You're not trying to stay in the past." I thought with a company so rooted in its history, it would be tempting to constantly refer to the way things used to be.

"I mean, we live in today's world. What are we going to craft for tomorrow? There's a good parallel with breadmaking . . . tomorrow's batch is made of some of yesterday's dough." She was referring to the necessary "backslopping" of sourdough starter, in which a bit of the prior batch is used to start the next one. "You're currently working to make tomorrow's bread. With baking, you have a general sense of where you're going, but you're constantly adapting what you're doing to the moments, the seasons, environment, the day's weather forecast."

An avocado-Vegemite tartine—on that familiar tight-crumbed sourdough bread—landed on our table, and I took a bite. The bread had a sour flavor with hints of molasses; it was more than a vehicle for its toppings. I gulped down the food and asked, "When did you know you wanted to take over the business?" I was thinking of her decision to accept that responsibility and run things from Harvard.

"When did I *not* know?" she replied, with a big smile. "As a child, I said, 'I want to bake in the morning and be an architect in the afternoon.' My mom was an architect. I said this quite young, and I know it was something about a reverence for my parents, but ultimately, this was something I wanted."

"It was always there. That's rare, I think," I said, amazed by her certainty.

"Oh yeah," she acknowledged. "I remember seeing my friends graduating college and looking for their sense of direction . . . I've always known where I wanted to go."

I was one of those directionless graduates. I had no idea what I wanted to do, or rather, I wanted to do *everything.*

"You've got to stop by the bakery on rue du Cherche-Midi," she said. "Next time you're in Paris, let me know."

Noted.

FIVE YEARS EARLIER, I'D LIVED IN PARIS while attending culinary school, and my existence was intertwined with bread. Good bread was the most satisfying thing I could eat after time on my feet in the practice kitchen. With cheese from *le marché*, I didn't need anything else (except maybe a glass of wine).

Of course, I occasionally loved getting a croissant or *pain au chocolat*, but those were treats for me; the *viennoiseries*—sweetened yeast-leavened doughs, often laminated (made of butter rolled in thin layers between dough, like puff pastry)—didn't satisfy my carnal hunger like the crunch of a baguette crust giving way to a soft inner crumb, or a special trip to Poilâne for their sourdough miche. All around Paris I saw people walking

I get weak in the knees for Parisian rooftops.

the narrow sidewalks with the end of a baguette peeking out of their bag or held in hand, usually with a chunk already snatched from the tip. The elbow—the end of the baguette (*le croûton* or *le quignon* in French)—is always a special treat, and a basket of bread was a mainstay on every table. It reminded me of my mom's bread, a linchpin of our meals, and I felt at home.

TWO MONTHS AFTER I FIRST MET Apollonia in London, I was in Paris and the sun was shining. The fact that I could navigate the city without checking a map, relying on my years-prior memories of living there, gave me the feeling of soaring around it. I crossed the Seine to the Left Bank, stopped at Fromagerie Quatrehomme for some cheese to enjoy later, and made my way to rue du Cherche-Midi—the original Poilâne location, a

seventeenth-century convent that had been churning out loaves of bread since 1932.

I was ecstatic to have the opportunity to see Poilâne's famous *fournil*, the area of dough preparation, and their wood-fired oven, which is one of their hallmarks. Descending the stairs to their basement felt like entering an ancient burrow, like a rabbit warren dug centuries ago—I was engulfed in history.

I spotted a young man dressed in white, flipping loaves of dough onto a long wooden paddle. He deftly picked up a razor blade attached to a stick of wood and waved his hand over the boule like a wizard. After he removed his arm, he revealed an enormous, cursive P etched into the dough. *La grigne*. The bakery's stamp.

Working with haste, he inserted the

Poilâne bakery's famous fournil on rue du Cherche-Midi

A wedge of Poilâne's sourdough miche loaf

paddle (also called a peel, one of the most ancient baking tools that exists) into the small opening of the oven and then, with a quick jerk, plopped the dough onto the hot oven floor and pulled the peel out. Without missing a beat, he grabbed a wooden basket that held another round of dough and flipped it over onto the paddle, releasing the blubber-esque boule onto its smooth wooden surface to repeat the process yet again. The dough would soon be transformed into Poilâne's signature deep brown loaf with a nutty, caramelized crust, a 4-pound wheel of sourdough bread about the size of a barstool cushion—their famous miche, a country bread like no other.

Apollonia jauntily hopped down the stairs and welcomed me with a kiss on both cheeks. She motioned to a rack of baking sheets and asked, "Have you tried a *punition*?" While Poilâne might

not make baguettes, they do make small, crisp, golden shortbread cookies called "punishments," cheekily referred to as such because Pierre Poilâne's grandmother would pretend she was dealing out punishments when she gave them to her grandchildren. These sweet *sablés* are adored by children and are the perfect pairing with an adult's cup of coffee. Food bloggers like Clotilde Dusoulier of *Chocolate & Zucchini* and Deb Perelman of *Smitten Kitchen* have become enamored of this treat, too, so you can find recipes online to re-create them.

Apollonia encouraged me to pluck a punition off the rack, and its sweet, buttery crumb practically melted on my tongue. Then she turned to the wall behind her and pointed to a thick tin tube attached to the ceiling. "Did you see where the flour comes down?" She lifted the tube's waist-level opening gate to reveal that it was full of *la farine* (flour), directly dispensed from upstairs.

It was only then that I realized the tube was over a large mixing bowl and noticed the smaller bowl of chunky salt crystals next to it. Everything was right there. The sturdy simplicity of the bunker was echoed by the chastity of the ingredients used to make the bread—no weird packets of powder, no conveyer belts.

When Poilâne first opened, part of its success was its being an antidote to the industrial machinery and ingredients that were becoming prevalent in the 1930s. The Poilâne prescription insisted on using levain, rather than industrially made yeast, and allowing long fermentation to do its thing without shortcuts. For the Poilâne enterprise, *how* the bread was made was as important as how it looked, or the company's profits. "Making bread strikes a mysteriously prehistoric chord somewhere inside us," Lionel Poilâne said in his book *Guide de l'amateur de pain.*

It certainly struck a chord in me, and I left their fournil with a loaf under my arm and a resolution to dig even deeper into the history and science of bread.

BEFORE WE TALK ABOUT BREAD, WE NEED to backtrack further than flour, to something Apollonia brought up as a key concern of her craft: cereal grains. When you see the word *cereal*, you might think of Cheerios. Or when you hear "cereal," you may be word-swapping: I remember a conversation I had with my friend Dana Chivvis, during which she told me she

was on a team of three people working on a new podcast called *Serial* (yes, *that* podcast), but I heard her say she was working on a podcast called *Cereal. Cool*, I thought, *a podcast about breakfast foods!*

Cereals, as we talk about them in relation to bread, are essentially types of grass cultivated for their edible grain, which can be milled into flour. Examples of cereal include wheat, rye, spelt, barley, einkorn, rice, maize (corn), oats, and millet. Learning about grains not only influenced my technique (the grain dictates how strong the gluten is, how much the baker should handle the dough, and so on), but—just as important—helped me connect this food product to the greater agricultural system it comes from.

A grain of wheat (which is a seed) is called a kernel and is covered by a dry, inedible outer husk. Get through the husk, and the kernel itself has a hard, protective outer coat called the bran—nature's way of keeping out things like insects. Inside the bran, there's the endosperm and the germ. The germ is the embryo of the seed, which can be sprouted into a new plant; the endosperm is a starchy layer that essentially acts as food for the germ. To make refined (white) flour, the grain is ground and sifted to remove everything except the endosperm; the broken-up bits of germ can be sold as wheat germ.

In my research, I found a book from 1895, *A Text-Book of the Science and Art of Bread-Making*, in which the author called the non-endosperm portions of the grain "offal" (yes, offal, like chicken feet and bull testicles): "During the process of milling,

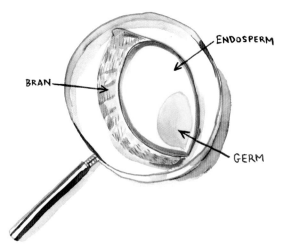

BRAN

ENDOSPERM

GERM

the grain is divided into flour and what is technically known as offal." Obviously, we no longer consider whole wheat bread an offal experience.

When a product is labeled "whole wheat," it includes the whole kernel, and the bits of germ and bran haven't been sifted out. ("Whole grain" is similar, but can indicate other non-wheat grains were involved; "multigrain" does not necessarily mean the entire kernel of each grain was incorporated, only that there is more than one grain in the product.)

The milling process grinds the wheat kernels and separates the endosperm, bran, and germ. Once the seed has been processed and its elements sifted, the nutritional quality of the grain is diminished, because although ground endosperm contains oils and proteins, the vitamins and minerals contained within the bran and germ have been stripped away. That's one reason why when you buy flour, there's sometimes more in it

than just the milled grain. In the standard 5-pound bag you pick up from the grocery store, there are often added "enriching" or "fortifying" ingredients (thiamin, riboflavin, niacin, folic acid, iron) meant to improve the nutritional quality of the flour. Enriching flour restores the micronutrients stripped out with the germ and bran, whereas fortifying flour introduces new micronutrients to it. The World Health Organization (WHO) recommends on its website, "Wheat flour fortification should be considered when industrially produced flour is regularly consumed by large population groups in a country."

There are other common additives, which are more prevalent in the mass-manufacturing of bread: ascorbic acid and glycerides are dough conditioners that help the dough rise by retaining carbon dioxide gas (a by-product of fermentation) and prevent bread from going stale quickly. Other additives, like potassium bromate—a powerful oxidizing agent that improves the rise and elasticity of dough—have been banned in some countries. (In the United States, some states allow potassium bromate and others don't. Thanks to laws like the Pure Food and Drug Act, we can be confident these additives aren't going to harm us, but it's up to us to decide if we *want* them in our bread.)

The French responded to the additives that had become commonplace (a result of the industrialization of bread) with the 1993 Décret Pain—Bread Decree—which defined categories of bread. I'll give you an example of how the decree plays out in daily French life:

When I lived in Paris, I learned from my French culinary school classmates about the hierarchy of French baguettes: baguettes were no more than one euro, but it's worth the extra thirty to forty cents to order a *baguette tradition* rather than a regular baguette (*baguette ordinaire*). No one will pay above a euro for a regular baguette, so bakeries used the cheapest ingredients to make them, but when you asked for a "tradition" (pronounced *tra-di-SYON*), you could expect something of higher quality, thanks to the decree, which states that a baguette tradition can

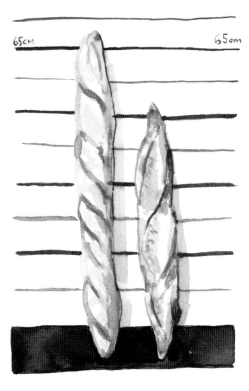

65CM   65cm

only have four ingredients (flour, water, a leavening agent—starter or added yeast—and salt); the flour itself can't have any additives, the dough must be fermented with baker's yeast, and it can't be frozen at any point in its production. (That same law says that for a bakery to call itself a boulangerie, the bread needs to be baked on site.)

In Paris, you can spot the baguettes traditions the moment you walk into a boulangerie: they have irregularly shaped pointy edges, showcasing how they were hand-shaped rather than machine-shaped.

The fact that France *has* something called a "Bread Decree" is the first clue to bread's deeply engrained cultural significance. The law was seen as an effort to save French bread from industrialization and to protect this cultural icon; it gave hope to bread lovers across the country.

Now, a few decades after the regulations were put in place, its success is contested—with artisan boulangeries shutting down at alarming rates as buyers opt for the convenience and affordability of plastic-wrapped loaves from supermarket shelves (the lowest category that can still legally pass as bread). Have the French changed their mind on what bread is, or should be?

"Beliefs are not static, and our ideas of what is healthy and what is not change over time," writes Sarah Lohman in *Eight Flavors: The Untold Story of American Cuisine*. She made this observation as she discussed monosodium glutamate (MSG) and how it's been both celebrated and vilified over time in the USA. (She references a meat tenderizer from the 1940s with a flashy label on the front advertising that it included MSG as a selling point.) I was so intrigued by her argument—and thought I saw some pertinent parallels with not just bread, but wine and cheese, too—that I called her up.

"There's a genuine ignorance of science when it comes to food," she said. "With bread, I think we're finally coming back around to it. When you stop eating bread and then come back to it, you're like, 'This is the best thing!' We don't give our bodies enough credit. If you eat a lot of dairy, you're going to fart; if you eat a lot of bread, you're going to feel bloated— this is naturally how our bodies function. It's okay if you don't eat much gluten. Just don't be ignorant about it."

Was the gluten-free trend the reason for the shuttering of so many

boulangeries in France? Or was it because there was a new accepted norm, a substandard benchmark, for what was admissible as bread?

Sarah, a food historian, brought up the USA's Pure Food and Drug Act of 1906 (which was passed, in part, in reaction to *The Jungle*, Upton Sinclair's exposé of the meat industry, and led to the creation of the FDA). This law was passed with the express purpose of protecting the consumer; before it was enacted, mislabeled and adulterated products were sold abundantly, with no consequence to the companies when their products made people ill. Similarly, the Bread Decree was supposed to protect citizens from naively buying bread that didn't pass the sniff test of what traditional French bread *should* be.

But before I talk about bread *in France*, let's get on the same page about sourdough. Bready or not . . .

SIMPLY NOT SO SIMPLE

Bread, at its most basic, is water and flour. Yeast is necessary to make the bread expand like a balloon, but when that comes in the form of a sourdough starter, it is born out of the water and flour. The hidden ingredient, which should not be overlooked, is time (as with all things fermented). Given time, water and flour develop the cultures that make an otherwise inert dough completely come alive. This is the simplicity of fermentation: when yeasts and microbes naturally found in the flour (and the surrounding environment) are fed and nurtured, they become potent. If a sourdough starter isn't used, bread can instead be made with store-bought yeast in the form of powder, paste, or granules. Salt is often added, and although it's not entirely necessary, it does play an important part in flavor and appearance (it gives the crust a saturated, sometimes even reddish, hue). Salt also acts as a preservative and makes the gluten stronger.

You can make a sourdough starter—referred to as such because a small portion of it is used to "start" the fermentation of your bread dough—yourself at home. You just need flour, water, and time.

To give birth to your own sourdough starter (also called a "mother" not just because it "births" many loaves of dough, but because it can reproduce the desired effects over and over again) is as simple as mixing equal parts flour and water and giving that mixture fresh flour and water day after day until you see the telltale signs of life. A living, bubbling creature should emerge within seven days. (See page 270 for instructions on making your own starter.)

Those bubbles are the result of fermentation: carbon dioxide (CO_2) is produced by the wild yeasts (*Saccharomyces exiguous*, *Candida humilis*, and others) and bacteria (mostly *Lactobacilli*; your loaf keeps better longer thanks to these bacteria) in the starter. The CO_2, emerging as tiny pockets of air trapped inside the dough, causes it to rise. (When using added yeast, the yeast strain *Saccharomyces cerevisiae* plays a similar role.)

Flour and starter in a large mixing container at Le Bricheton in Paris

When yeast cells are at a warm temperature, the air pockets grow more quickly, which is why adding warm water and keeping the dough in a warm place facilitate growth. Think of a hot-air balloon—the balloon rises due to the expansion of the hot air from the gas burner below. When yeast is warmed, it produces more carbon dioxide, causing the dough to rise. (But beware: If the water you add is too hot—140°F/60°C or above—it'll kill the yeast.) This process is visible during the handful of hours after feeding a starter, and also during the bulk fermentation phase of making a loaf, when (as its name suggests) the fermentation of the dough yields a "bulking up," a growth in size.

The interplay between heat and humidity is a main principle in understanding your starter and your bread dough: *more humidity and/or heat = quicker fermentation; drier and/or colder air = slower fermentation*. This is why your starter will behave differently in July than it will in December. If you're thinking, *Great, then I'll just keep my dough really warm*, let me stop you right there. Time is your friend. Don't rush fermentation; it's what gives your loaf flavor!

Fermentation happens like a bell curve in which microbial activity increases up to a peak point, then decreases. The optimal time to use your starter, to incorporate it into a dough, is when the fermentation bubbles are vigorous—evident signs of kinetic activity. An actively bubbling starter is often referred to as a mature, active, or ripe starter. (The bubbling I'm talking about isn't like boiling water; it's like an extremely slow-motion version of that. When you look at an active starter, you can watch the carbon dioxide bubbles pop at the surface . . . but it's on sloth time, with one or two subdued "pops" per minute.)

I'm still using the sourdough starter I began when the idea for this book was first

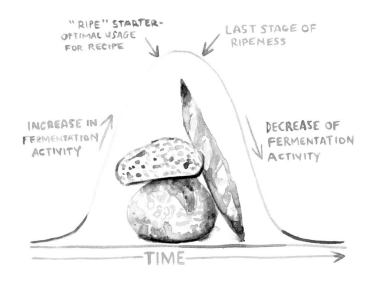

"RIPE" STARTER-
OPTIMAL USAGE
FOR RECIPE

LAST STAGE OF
RIPENESS

INCREASE IN
FERMENTATION
ACTIVITY

DECREASE OF
FERMENTATION
ACTIVITY

TIME

forming in my mind. You could also ask anyone you know who makes sourdough bread for some of their starter, rather than making it from scratch; some starter needs to be discarded each time it's refreshed, so bakers are usually happy to share.

Sourdough discard is the name for the portion of starter that you "get rid of"/don't use when you do a feeding. (You only use a portion of the starter because it needs a higher percentage of new flour and water to feed on.) I hesitate to say "get rid of" the sourdough discard because that presumes tossing it in the trash, which I don't recommend (waste not, want not, right?).

Get crafty with the discard! Try incorporating it into pancakes, banana bread, waffles, galettes, and other treats, like brownies (my friend Izy Hossack has a popular sourdough brownie recipe on her blog, *Top with Cinnamon*).

You should feed your starter daily to keep it healthy, but if you're only going to make one loaf a week, here's what I'd recommend: keep your starter in the fridge between bakes, which slows down fermentation and prevents you from going through bags of flour just to keep it alive. Take it out of the fridge the day before you're going to start your dough and feed it, leaving it to ferment on the counter that day, then proceed to make your dough as you normally do the following day. That next day, after you've made your starter mix for the dough, feed a portion of dough that will become your new maintenance starter and let it sit (covered) at room temperature for a few hours before popping it in the fridge until next week's

bake. (If you're going away for longer than a week, your starter can survive without feeding in the fridge for 6 to 8 weeks. Longer than that, and you should dehydrate it, as described on page 272.)

You'll often hear bakers talk about their starter like a pet, for good reason. "I fed my starter, but it's not acting normal." "Did I remember to feed my starter?" The main difference is that when you go on vacation, you can just pop your starter in the refrigerator to stall fermentation—no kennels or pet-sitters necessary.

ONCE YOUR STARTER IS READY, YOU'LL start delving into bread recipes. Something you'll come across in these is baker's math or baker's percentages. I was confused by this when I first saw it in a recipe, because I added up the percentages and the total was way more than 100. *What's this all about?*

Basically, it expresses ingredient quantities in relation to the total weight of flour in the recipe. All the flour called for in the recipe will always add up to 100 percent, and the other ingredient percentages only relate to the total flour, not to each other. (That's why adding them up doesn't equal 100.) Why bother with ratios? Because it makes scaling up or scaling down any recipe much easier.

Another reason baker's math is important is that you, the baker, are thinking about dough hydration—you want the gluten particles in the flour to absorb water, swell up, and stick together. This creates a network that retains carbon dioxide—those bubbles we rely

Starter discard inspiration: a sweet potato, spinach, and goat cheese galette; the crust is made with sourdough starter discard.

on to make the dough rise. It's up to you (or the recipe) to decide *how* hydrated to make the dough. Dough hydration is the percentage of water in the recipe in relation to the total weight of the flour, and that includes the flour and water present in the sourdough starter. (Standard hydration is 70 to 80 percent.)

Let's look at how it works in a recipe, using the chart at the bottom of this page and my sourdough recipe on page 273.

If you're just starting out making bread, don't get too preoccupied about the percentages—you're probably working off a recipe anyway, so just follow the recipe. If you're like me, you'll need some practice with this before it makes sense. I just kept making bread—it's not the worst thing to have to practice.

Sourdough, which I found intimidating at first, has completely stolen my heart and become my uncontested favorite type of thing to bake. As I was getting the hang of sourdough, some of the loaves I made fell flat, and some of them were pillowy wonders. I

got flour on everything, including on dish rags, which gooed up everything else in the washing machine (to Connor's delight). Every morning as I brewed coffee, I refreshed my starter; a rhythm emerged in my routine.

What's more, my starter (named Skinny, for all the flat loaves I made before I got the hang of it) helped me notice things: the changes in the weather and even in my mood. When you repeat the same act every morning, you observe the subtle changes in yourself; Skinny became an unexpected tool of self-reflection.

I inhaled information about the various sourdough methods, and the experts each seemed to have their own philosophy. Some were science-forward, while others led with intuition. I referenced Sarah Owens's *Sourdough* cookbook and Irish baker Jordan Bourke's *Healthy Baking*, but also websites like Maurizio Leo's The Perfect Loaf, and I dove into cult favorites like Jeffrey Hamelman's *Bread* and Chad Robertson's *Tartine Bread*.

INGREDIENT	QUANTITY	BAKER'S PERCENTAGE
Total flour *which includes . . .*	550 grams	100%
Strong white bread flour	475 grams (the 25 grams in the starter mix, and the 450 grams in the dough mix)	86%
Whole wheat flour	75 grams (the 25 grams in the starter mix, and the 50 grams in the dough mix)	14%
Water	400 grams	72%
Salt	10 grams	1.8%

To borrow from Robertson, a cult figure among bread-heads and the man behind Tartine Bakery in San Francisco, "Traditional, intuitive bread making does not lend itself naturally to a written recipe." With that in mind, Robertson (and others who have dedicated their lives to this craft) have put together thorough guides for making sourdough. A fully comprehensive sourdough manual asks for more space and dedication than I have budgeted for in this book; my role here, as I see it, is to stoke your interest and arm you with the basics. I've included my go-to sourdough bread formulas to start you on the sourdough-bread-making path. It was a progression for me to get to the point where I could consistently make a fantastic loaf. Trust me, if I can do it, you can, too. The best way to begin is to do just that: *begin*. Begin with a yeasted dough (not sourdough) first if you're more comfortable with that—I've also included a recipe for a loaf that uses added yeast, Susie Q's Sour Cream Challah (page 287), which is near and dear to my heart and was my gateway loaf to the wide world of baking bread.

Roberston says in the introduction to his magnum opus, "Keep in mind that you'll need time and experience baking yourself to understand how things work." The only way to do it is to put your hands in the dough and start, learning by observation and trial and error.

"Bread is such an act-and-react thing," said my friend Michael Harlan Turkell, host of the radio show *Modernist BreadCrumbs*. "No food is as affected as bread by the weather, humidity, temperance of the yeast, temperature of the water, liveliness of the grain. I love the chaos of it."

Whether you consider yourself a chaos chaser or not, I guarantee you can master sourdough bread. During the COVID-19 crisis I held the hands (metaphorically, at an appropriate socially distanced length) of countless friends, family members, and complete strangers as they became sourdough bakers, and I'm here to do the same for you. Let's dive right into the deep end!

For baking, weight measurements are the way to go for precision and accuracy, rather than cup (volume) measurements, so get yourself a kitchen scale if you don't already have one. (You'll use it for many things other than bread baking! Every baking recipe is more accurate by weight.)

I talk about these terms at more length throughout these chapters, but for easy reference:

AUTOLYSE: The flour and water quantities in the dough, combined. This step in a recipe increases the dough's ability to be stretched, meaning the gluten bonds in the flour will extend to accommodate the CO_2 bubbles that form in the dough—which means a successful rise. (It was introduced by chemist and baker Raymond Calvel in the 1970s.)

BULK FERMENTATION: The first rise of the dough (primary fermentation); it occurs after all the ingredients for the dough (including the starter) have been combined, and after the series of stretch-and-folds. It is a critical fermentation period, as the yeast and bacteria in the starter feed off their new environment, generating flavor and leavening the dough (with the creation of CO_2). During this time, the dough will bulk up in size considerably.

PROOF: The final period of dough rising (secondary fermentation). Different bakers and recipes call for different styles of proofing. Sometimes it's longer and necessitates cooler temperatures (my Go-To Sourdough Recipe on page 273 calls for placing the dough in the fridge overnight to proof); other times it calls for room-temperature proofing (such as for the Honey and Olive Oil Loaf with Einkorn on page 343).

STARTER: The flour-and-water combination that contains the live culture of wild yeast and bacteria necessary for fermentation to occur. It begins as a *pre-ferment* (a mixture of flour, water, and a leavening agent, left to ferment). There are many terms for a sourdough starter (including *levain*, *leaven*, and *mother*, to name a few). In this book, I use the term *maintenance starter* to indicate the culture of bacteria and yeast that you can continue indefinitely with proper feeding. You never use all of your maintenance starter in a recipe; rather, you take a portion of your maintenance starter and feed it to create a "dough starter"—the offshoot culture of bacteria and yeast you'll add as a leavening agent to the dough mix. When a starter is at its peak point of fermentation, it is referred to as a *mature*, *ripe*, or *active* starter.

STRETCH-AND-FOLDS: This refers to a series of actions done to strengthen the gluten bonds in the flour for doughs that use sourdough as the leavening agent. This is sourdough's version of kneading. It is essentially what it sounds like: the dough is stretched and folded over itself. Stretch-and-folds occur multiple times, at intervals, after the dough is mixed and just before bulk fermentation. As the dough undergoes this process, you will notice it contracting with each successive series—this is a normal effect of the gluten strengthening. In addition to gluten development, this process also helps keep a consistent temperature throughout the whole mass of dough, and redistributes gases and microbes.

First series of stretch-and-folds   *Second series of stretch-and-folds*   *Third series of stretch-and-folds*

How to Make a Sourdough Starter

When you're making your starter, patience and consistency are key. Even if you think you've failed, stick to the plan and you'll see it work within a week. Remember, time is an important ingredient, and just because you don't see anything happening right away doesn't mean you've failed. Once your starter responds consistently to feeding, with rising and falling and pockets of carbon dioxide visible, then it's ready to be used to make bread.

I call for all-purpose flour here because most of you probably already have it in your pantry, but you can absolutely use bread flour or other grain-based flours (spelt, rye, einkorn, and so on).

Home baker's active starter

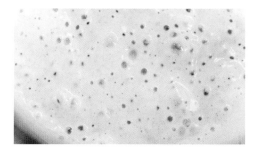

The bubbles are evidence of fermentation.

60 grams all-purpose (plain) flour each day for up to a week

60 grams room-temperature water (ideally filtered water) each day for up to a week

1. **DAY 1** Combine the flour and water in a bowl and mix well. Put the mixture in a medium glass or ceramic container (smaller than a mixing bowl but bigger than a jam jar). Cover with a lid (or plate, or shower cap, or anything that covers it enough to prevent drying out but isn't completely airtight) and let sit in a warm area of your kitchen, away from too much natural light, for 1 day.
2. **DAY 2** Feed your starter: Add another 60 grams of flour and 60 grams of water and mix well. Cover and let sit in a warm area of your kitchen for 1 day.

3. **DAY 3** This is when you will start to discard some of the mixture. Remove up to half of it. (I hesitate to call it "sourdough discard," since it's not technically sourdough yet . . . but—same as my advice for sourdough discard—when you remove it, I recommend trying to incorporate it into other baked goods rather than throwing it out.) Add 60 grams of water and 60 grams of flour to the portion remaining in the container and mix well. Cover and let sit in a warm area of your kitchen for 1 day.
4. **DAYS 4 TO 7** Repeat step 3.
5. By day 7, you should have a starter! This is your *maintenance starter*. Depending on your environment and the type of flour you use, it may come together by day 4, or it may take every bit of those 7 days to show signs of

being ready. Indications that your starter is ready: it will be bubbly on top and will smell slightly and pleasantly acidic. (If you don't see any of these signs after a week, refer to my troubleshooting notes below.)

Note: While your starter will be usable after this first week, it will become even stronger and vigorously bubbly as you continue to feed it. Your loaves will also improve along with your starter's robustness.

TROUBLESHOOTING

Try to use water that is filtered, because water that's high in chlorine or chloromine (disinfectants often found in tap water) hampers fermentation. The temperature of the water when it's added to the starter mixture should be between 82° and 91°F (28° and 33°C), because if it's too cold, it inhibits fermentation, and if it's too hot, it could kill any yeast you're trying to feed.

The temperature of the room where your starter sits should be no cooler than 68°F (20°C) and ideally around 80°F (26°C) for the microbes to really get working. If your home is on the cool side of that spectrum, you can encourage the process by using a home dough proofer or yogurt maker, if you have either, or place the starter in the oven (turned off) with the oven light on as a makeshift proofing drawer.

A few days in, you may notice that the starter has separated, with liquid pooling at the top. That's not ideal but it's not a deal-breaker—give it a good stir, reincorporating any liquid, and just keep feeding it on schedule. In no time, you'll see it recombine and begin to form pocketed bubbles, indicating that it's ready for use.

If on the seventh day it's still separating, that might mean the acidity balance is out of whack. To help it find equilibrium, increase the amount you discard when you next feed it: put 20 grams of your in-process starter in a bowl (discard the rest) and mix it with 60 grams of all-purpose flour and 60 grams room-temperature water. Alternatively, start again with a clean slate. You can do this!

MAINTAINING YOUR STARTER

To keep your starter going long-term, continue the same feeding-and-discarding routine you've done to create the starter. I keep a small "sourdough discard" jar in the fridge, where I collect all the leftover starter, and I use it to make any number of baked goods (for some ideas, refer to page 264). Once your starter is active, you can use different kinds of grain-based flours to feed it without a problem.

MINIMIZING STARTER WASTE

A note on flour quantity—if you'll be making multiple loaves at a time, continuing to feed the starter with 60 grams of flour and 60 grams of water gives you enough starter to create more than one starter mix per day. However, if you'll only be baking one loaf, you don't need to use as much flour (and therefore water). You can decrease the quantities. My standard starter feeding measurement is 40 grams of flour, 40 grams of water, and 10 grams of starter. This quantity gives me enough to make a starter mix for the day's dough and some leftover to feed my maintenance starter.

PAUSING YOUR STARTER

If you're not going to make bread for a week or so, there's no need to feed your starter every day. Ditto if you're only making two loaves a week. You can use the refrigerator to stall the starter—the important thing is to take it out of the fridge and feed it the day before you'll be putting together your dough. Your routine can go like this:

A couple of hours after the feeding, put your starter in the fridge (in a jar with a sealed lid) until the day before you make your next loaf of bread (take it out and feed it once a week if you're making bread less frequently than that).

To resume use, let the starter come to room temperature, then feed it. The next morning, take the amount of starter called for in your recipe and feed your main starter—putting it back in the fridge shortly thereafter if you intend to pause it again, or leaving it covered on your countertop if you plan on using it again the following day.

You can also freeze your starter for up to two weeks. Right after you've fed it, put the starter in a plastic bag or ice cube tray and freeze it. Thaw it at room temperature the day before you need it and feed it as soon as it has thawed.

For a longer-term pause, you can dehydrate your starter. (I've done this to travel with it.) Feed your starter as you normally do and then let it sit, *un*covered,

on the counter overnight. The top layer of the starter will dry out as the starter reaches ripeness, and the next morning you can simply peel off that dry, rounded dome of starter. (The wet starter under that is your sourdough discard. If you want to continue making dehydrated starter—to separate portions for gifts, for example—you'll need to feed the maintenance starter and repeat this process. You can't continue dehydrating the top portion because it will no longer contain the active microbes.)

Let the dry, rounded dome of starter rest in the open air to dry out fully. Wrap it in a reusable beeswax wrap or plastic bag. Keep it in a safe place. When you're ready to use it (however many months down the line!), all you need to do is break it up into little pieces, add enough water to just cover it, and let it rehydrate. Once rehydrated, feed it[*]—and you're off to the races!

---

[*] *Equal parts flour and water; how much flour and water will depend on how much starter you dehydrated, but my average feeding ratio is 40 grams flour and 40 grams water at this point.*

My Go-To Sourdough Bread

As the name suggests, this is my go-to loaf: it's always a crowd-pleaser and serves as a base for many variations (see pages 310 to 312).

This is a recipe adapted from multiple baking guides I've used and bakers I've learned from, incorporating my favorite aspects of the many styles I've found throughout my sourdough journey. My version yields one rounded boule (French for "ball"), a country-style loaf with a thick, crunchy exterior and a soft interior with modest but substantial fermentation holes and some brown flecks sprinkled throughout.

The recipe begins with mixing a robust sourdough starter using your maintenance starter; this first step ensures you use your starter at its ideal ripeness, setting you up to make a successful loaf.

For the baking vessel, I use a lidded Dutch oven—a shallow version with shorter sides—which I preheat in the oven before I load the dough into it. The lid traps the steam released by the dough as it bakes. This makes an enormous difference (I talk more about the importance of steam in baking on page 351). You can also use a regular (i.e., not shallow) Dutch oven; the high walls just make it a little trickier to insert the dough and remove the loaf, because the pot will be incredibly hot—using parchment paper to hoist the boule in and out will be your saving grace there. A cast-iron combo cooker is also a fantastic alternative. If you don't have any of those options, you won't get that thick, crunchy crust—but you can absolutely still make this bread! Don't let the tools (or lack thereof) prevent you from trying this. If you get hooked (as I suspect you will—I did), you can slowly add the tools you're missing to your kitchen kit.

Because of the level of hydration in this loaf, the dough can stick to your hands as though Spider-Man's web is attacking you; it takes practice to learn how to handle and shape it. You could learn from and bake with half a dozen French boulangers (like I did) and still struggle with this (like I did). But I got the hang of it, and you can, too.

The specific kind of flour you're using—not just the grain but also how it's milled—will yield slighty different results. Humidity will also affect how your flour reacts to the water in the dough. Once you know what you're working with regarding your environment, all you need is practice. When the dough goes into the basket for its final rise, it should have a nice taut skin, which will trap carbon dioxide and make the dough blow up like a balloon.

I'm providing a timeline for the steps in this recipe for clarity and ease, but feel free to tweak the start time (and adjust the following steps accordingly) based on what's best for your schedule.

(recipe continues)

Some of my homemade sourdough loaves. I used the pattern of the banneton to create the spiral design.

Shaping dough at Le Bricheton in Paris

EQUIPMENT

Kitchen scale

Cotton or linen kitchen towels (not terry cloth) to cover the dough in its bowl

Large bowl

Bench scraper to help preshape the dough and to clean your work surface

Linen cloth to line the final proofing bowl

Banneton as your final proofing bowl (or a large bowl), 10 inches (25 cm) in diameter

Shallow Dutch oven with lid (I use a Le Creuset "shallow casserole"), 12 inches (30 centimeters) in diameter (see headnote on page 273 for alternatives)

Parchment paper

Blade for scoring (known as a *lame*)

TO REFRESH YOUR STARTER

20 grams whole wheat flour

20 grams white bread flour

20 grams maintenance starter (see page 270)

35 grams room-temperature water

FOR THE DOUGH MIX

50 grams whole wheat flour

450 grams white bread flour

400 grams warm water (between 82° and 91°F/28° and 33°C)

10 grams fine sea salt

FOR PROOFING

Rice flour, bread flour, or all-purpose flour

(recipe continues)

1. **DAY 1, 7:30 A.M.** Refresh your starter: Combine the whole wheat flour, white bread flour, maintenance starter, and water in a small bowl. Cover with a small plate and let sit in a warm area of your kitchen for 6 hours, until it has doubled in size, is bubbly, and smells pleasantly acidic. But before those 6 hours are up (3 hours after refreshing the starter), you'll move onto step 2.

2. **10:30 A.M.** Autolyse (see page 268): Combine the whole wheat flour, white bread flour, and water in a large bowl. Mix until there is no dry flour visible. Cover with a clean kitchen towel and let the dough sit for 3 hours, until your starter is ready.

3. **1:30 P.M.** Mix the dough: Pour the salt onto the dough and add 75 grams of the refreshed starter (this should be approximately the full amount of refreshed starter, but you may have a bit more than you need for the dough. For tips on what to do with discard starter, see page 264). Wet your hands so they don't stick to the dough, then mix to incorporate the salt and starter. I do this by lifting the dough up and over itself, slapping it on the bowl, and pressing down with my palm (and repeating) until all the ingredients are well combined. Cover with a clean kitchen towel and let sit for 30 minutes.

4. **2:00 P.M.** Start a series of stretch-and-fold turns in the bowl. Wet your hands, then grab a handful of dough on its north side and pull it up, stretching it but making sure not to stretch it so far that you tear it, then fold it back over onto itself (toward the south side of the bowl). Now rotate the bowl a quarter turn and repeat; stretch and fold the dough four times total (north, east, south, west). Wet your hands again whenever the dough starts to stick to them. Cover the bowl with a clean kitchen towel and let the dough rest for 30 minutes.

5. **2:30 P.M.** Repeat the stretch-and-fold process, cover the bowl with a clean kitchen towel, and let the dough rest for 30 minutes. You'll notice the dough becomes less elastic as you continue to stretch and fold it over onto itself. This is normal; as its extensibility increases, so does its contraction. You can jiggle it a bit and allow gravity to help you with the stretches in subsequent turns. Stretching the dough well in this step is important; otherwise, your crumb (interior of the loaf) may be denser than you'd like.

6. **3:00 P.M.** Repeat the stretch-and-fold process and cover the bowl with a clean kitchen towel. Let the dough sit on your counter (ideally in a warm spot) for 3 hours for bulk fermentation (see page 268). At the end of bulk fermentation, your dough should have grown significantly in size, but not doubled, and you might see some subtle fermentation bubbles on top. If you press gently on the dough with your fingertip, it will slowly rebound, leaving a slight indentation.

7. **6:00 P.M.** Lightly dust your work surface with flour. Tip the dough onto the work surface, easing it out of the bowl without knocking out much air. Using a bench scraper and a floured hand, form the blob of dough into a taut round. Let it rest on the work surface for 20 minutes.

8. Next I liberally dust a banneton (proofing basket), which can either be lined with a linen cloth or not (see Note on page 277), or a cloth-covered bowl with flour (rice flour is best for this as it's less absorbent than wheat flour), then shake out any excess. This ensures your dough doesn't stick to the banneton or cloth, allowing you to remove it easily. Set aside.

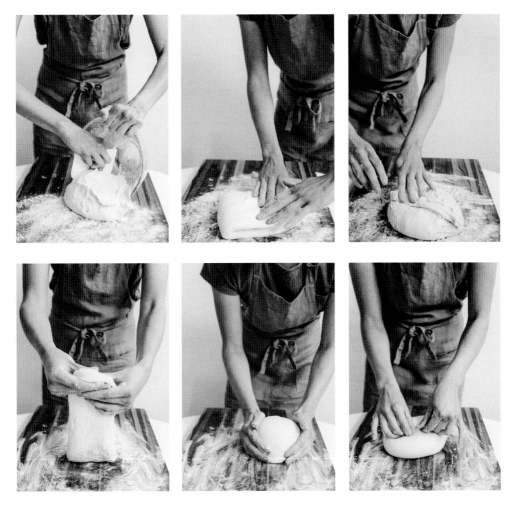

Shaping the dough after bulk fermentation

Note: To use the design of a pattern from your banneton (like the spiral pattern shown on page 274), use the banneton without its cloth lining, but still dust liberally with rice flour to prevent the dough from sticking to its ridges.

9. **6:20 P.M.** With floured hands, stretch the left side of the dough out and back over the center. Repeat on the right side, folding the dough over the flap you've just placed. Stretch the dough from the north side out, over the top, and bring it under the dough itself so the smooth side that was facing the counter is now facing up.

10. Using both palms (reflouring your hands and working quickly to prevent sticking), cup the dough on either side, then spin it while pulling gently down toward the countertop. This will create a taut skin on

(recipe continues)   277

the top of the dough. Lift your shaped boule and place it in the banneton or cloth-lined bowl with the nicely taut side facedown. Sprinkle rice flour on top of the dough.

11. Cover the banneton or bowl with a clean kitchen towel, tucking the long ends under the bottom of the bowl, and proof in the refrigerator for around 15 hours (overnight).

12. **DAY 2, 8:30 A.M.** One hour before you're ready to bake, preheat the oven to 485°F (250°C). Place a Dutch oven (or other pan as described earlier) in the oven to preheat. Line a sheet pan with parchment paper.

13. **9:30 A.M.** Remove the dough from the refrigerator. Set the prepared pan, parchment-side down, over the banneton or bowl holding the proofed dough and invert them together, gently transferring the dough onto the parchment.

14. Taking care not to burn yourself, remove the heated Dutch oven from the oven.

15. Using a blade for scoring or a very sharp knife, score the top of the dough with several confident, swift cuts (you could make a box design or several parallel angled slashes). Using the parchment to lift the dough, transfer it and the parchment into the Dutch oven and cover with the lid.

16. Bake the bread for 30 minutes, then reduce the oven temperature to 430°F (220°C), remove the lid, and bake for 15 minutes more, or until the crust is richly browned (if you're unsure whether the bread is done, stick a thermometer into it: it should register at least 208°F/98°C). Carefully remove the pan from the oven and transfer the baked loaf to a wire rack. Let cool completely before slicing or storing. (Cutting into it while it is still warm will interrupt the last stage of the baking process, resulting in a gummy interior crumb.)

HOW TO STORE YOUR BREAD

One of the huge perks of sourdough bread is that it naturally lasts longer than commercially yeasted bread (which will grow mold and become stale sooner), largely thanks to the acidity of the *Lactobacilli*, which discourages the growth of decaying bacteria and mold. As with cheese and wine, fermentation is a tool for preservation here. Still, you'll want to keep your bread as fresh as possible until it's all eaten. Store it wrapped in a cotton cloth or in a cotton bread bag or a paper bag; this allows the bread to breathe. In most climates, a plastic bag is *not* a good option because there's enough humidity to cause the bread to "sweat" (the same reason you should avoid wrapping cheese in plastic wrap).

For tips on using stale bread and freezing bread, see "Leftover Bread" on page 319.

WHERE'S THE BREAD?

France is the country where bread shortages helped trigger a revolution! A shortage of bread, piled upon other grievances with the monarchy, led to the French Revolution. Marie Antoinette's famous (supposed) announcement "Let them eat cake!"* was a response to the *lack of bread* available to French commoners. Bread was of the utmost importance; it still is a big deal in France. To understand French bread is to understand its role in French culture.

"Where's the bread?" my French hairdresser sang as he told me a story of his father visiting him in England. "It's *always* 'Where's the bread?' My dad even asked for it at a fish and chips shop! Which is to an English person, of course, ridiculous."

Paris resident and blogger David Lebovitz wrote, "Even at Asian and Indian restaurants, you'll see locals searching around for a breadbasket." The Frenchman who introduced me to the wonders of Comté cheese in the Jura, Jean-Louis, told me he was shocked when he moved to America and discovered people were *not* eating bread at breakfast, lunch, and dinner. "Most people only ate bread when it was sliced, either toasted or in sandwiches!" he exclaimed, as though it was a crime to reduce bread to such secondary status.

Despite these anecdotes, there's been a steep decline in the number of French people who are buying and eating bread. The year I resolved to learn about bread in France, the *New York Times* published an article titled "French Baguettes from a Vending Machine? 'What a Tragedy.'" The writer cited that bakeries in rural areas were disappearing at a rate of 4 percent or higher within a single year, although he added Paris was the exception. "In Paris, people walking home at the end of the day, munching on a bit of baguette, remains a part of the cityscape." *Some* stereotypes endure, but even still, the landscape is shifting.

---

* *"Let them eat cake" is a translation of "Qu'ils mangent de la brioche"—a reply that referenced a* viennoisserie, *a type of bread that takes inspiration from cake's ingredients list.*

Writer Lindsey Tramuta has been the conduit between many foreigners and Paris through her books *The New Paris* (and podcast of the same name) and *The New Parisienne*. American-born and French-wed, she's lived in Paris for over a decade. She's part of a group of people who know and care about the food scene in Paris and have a vested interest in how it evolves.

Lindsey told me, "There's an awareness now [of good bread versus bad bread]. If a restaurant serves a rock-hard, stale baguette, I'm not going to eat that, and people are starting to realize they don't *have* to eat that. It's going to keep getting more and more interesting and bread will keep getting better, and because it's getting better, the rates of people buying bread will remain stable."

"It's wild that there's a need for bread stability *in France*!" I said.

She nodded. "The French government has even run marketing campaigns to encourage people to pick up bread again. One campaign was *'Coucou, tu as pris le pain?'* ['Hi there, did you pick up the bread?'] It was genius, because that's something French people say to each other. I've texted that to my husband. That's a real exchange!"

Even with bread consumption declining from its former epic proportions, the link between bread and France is substantial. Steven Laurence Kaplan has made a career writing books about the complicated relationship between the two. In *The Bakers of Paris and the Bread Question, 1700–1775*, he looks closely at

how bread was the main source of calories for the majority of people, and he says that to eighteenth-century Parisians, bad bread in markets was intolerable: "It signified either an act of social crime or a mark of social breakdown, two different levels of crisis."

He also describes the longtime fascination with white bread—which was usually only available to people of privilege—and the historical stereotype of bakers: the school dropouts, the misfits, "who could be seen in shop doorways looking wretched, haggard, and pale, like flour-drenched scarecrows."

In his book *Good Bread Is Back*, Kaplan outlines the nosedive of French bread and the correlation to industrialization, which coincided with World War II, an event that shook every country in Europe to its core. That collision—industrialization and the war—indelibly changed the landscape of French bread. After the war, he writes, "Bread was no longer a secondary but a 'tertiary' commodity, and it no longer commanded the same 'vigilance.' Instead of reacting by asserting their values and skills, most bakers took the easy way out: they managed to earn a living with increasingly risky methods, but they sold their artisanal heritage off cheaply."

To reduce the time-intensive aspects of baking—the long hours of the dough's fermentation and therefore the overnight work shifts required to supply fresh bread for morning customers—bakers turned to rapid kneading machines and added ingredients like ascorbic acid and fava bean flour. These shortcuts sacrificed the taste of the bread but cut costs and saved time. After the war, most people were happy to have their bakery up and running at all, and they were wooed by the pillowy white loaves that came as a result of those methods.

Additives in food are not an unfamiliar idea, as we've seen with wine; people have used supplements to enhance or improve foods from the earliest written records. Even prior to World War I, "improving powders" made the rounds at bakeries, and by the eighteenth century, alum (a colorless compound, a double sulfate of potassium and aluminum) was used to whiten flour. By 1995, a new norm was officially established for what constituted bread in France, as laws allowed around one hundred additives in bread. "It's no longer bread, it's a whole sandwich," *Les Nouvelles de la Boulangerie-Pâtisserie*, a bakers' association, wrote in response to these laws.

I don't mean to paint a bleak picture, but rather to offer context for my exploration. There *are* producers trying to resurrect this delicious cultural symbol. I

wanted to learn from *them*. But before I could try to bake in a Parisian boulangerie, I had to practice making bread at home.

I began by brushing the dust off the recipe notecards my mom had written showing how to make some of her treasured loaves. I made her challah—stoking nostalgia without fail each time—and my confidence grew as each golden loaf emerged from the oven.

Even as I improved, I felt the intimidation of sourdough peering over my shoulder, as if to say, "But you haven't mastered *me*, yet." Indeed, Kaplan writes of French bakers, "In the bread making business, even the most confident experts remained humble before the process of fermentation, for this operation was governed by an often haughty and capricious nature."

Sourdough bread—*pain au levain* in France—is an art form unto itself, and sourdough bakers represent a subculture of their own. They have Reddit subpages, guilds, and specialized accessories. They nerd out. For many of them, the *only* yeast is *wild* yeast.

I shot a video with one such man, Tom Scanlan, a professor at Ohio University who moonlights as a baker. In the video, we took viewers through a staccato-paced guide on how to make sourdough bread; it garnered fifty thousand views in no time. There was clearly an appetite for making homemade sourdough—an interest I shared with my viewers—but by the end of our shoot, my head was spinning. It was so daunting that it wasn't until years later, when I was drawn to explore bread in France, that I found the courage to attempt it again . . . and I got the encouragement I needed from a heroine of the sourdough movement in America, Sarah Owens.

"There are so many myths around sourdough! But it *is* accessible," she reassured me. Sarah doesn't rush when she speaks—her Southern roots are evident in her cadence, and her melodic affirmation made me feel at ease immediately.

"Doesn't fermentation work best in a warm environment?" I asked. "How's this gonna work in England?"

"Sourdough can be made anywhere— hot and humid or cold and damp," she explained. "It just means you have to follow a different schedule to work with the community of microbes in your starter culture."

When I asked Sarah her thoughts on why there had been such a resurgence of interest in making this kind of bread globally, she answered, "Stomach issues. That's what brought me to it, too. In general, our food systems have seen the sort of progression from being basic food staples, made with integrity, to being completely industrialized. We're suffering the effects of that, so we're returning to the past in order to look forward to the future."

Beyond the health concerns, she admitted she was addicted to "the never-ending chase" of bread baking. "You're never going to make the *perfect* loaf, never going to conquer the elusive medium of flour, microbes, and water.

That attracts people, myself included."

That day, after my call with Sarah, I began my sourdough starter by mixing equal parts flour and water. I went to a yoga class later in the afternoon and the teacher instructed, "Make your body supple, like bread." I took it as a sign I was on the right path.

WHEN I LIVED IN PARIS IN MY LATE twenties, my appetite for bread was immense. Alone in my small flat, I would smear salted butter on a chunk of bread and calm my confusion with its glutinous pull. It satiated my heart, which felt like it was dragging me in opposite directions. I was in Paris to attend culinary school, while my relationship with Connor, back in New York City, was at a tipping point. I could tell we were on a precipice with things either getting *really* serious or falling apart. One or the other.

Speaking of the other. There was another guy. A Dutch musician with an adorable accent and mean guitar skills. Shortly before Connor and I got together, I was with the Dutchman while he was in New York for a month recording a new album. It was the definition of puppy love. He wrote a song about me, for crying out loud.

So naturally, every time Connor and I had a disagreement, every time I had a flicker of doubt, my mind went to the "other." It's a story as old as time—

archetypes from novels centuries old coming to life in my waking hours. Except in the olden days, there was no social media, no WhatsApp, to keep us connected. In moving to Paris, I found myself in his time zone. It felt like a dare.

The truth about me is that I wish I could live fifty different existences. I want to follow every possible path of this life, and experience wherever they lead. I hate the idea of doors closing (metaphorically, of course); I want to do everything I can to keep options available, to keep those doors agape! I wish I could multiply myself like yeast cells reproducing by mitosis as they gobble up all the plentiful sugars and starches. If I *must* make up my mind, I want to know what's behind each door beforehand.

The fact that Amsterdam was a three-hour train ride from Paris made the temptation to "just explore" reconnecting with the Dutch guitarist *real*. Every day I felt like I was teetering on a cliff and just might jump.

Steven Kaplan once wrote, "Commonly associated with the human body as well as with the divine, bread is a hyphen between life and death, linking the here and now to the hereafter." While there are many questions in life, it is no secret why I craved bread in those months in Paris.

It was Paris, where I lived alone and spent most of my time in my culinary classes sweating over steaming pots of broth and dipping into radiating ovens, that offered me the space to find clarity. I used that time to let my feelings sort themselves out—an emotional fermentation.

Only then could I be confident in seeing all the ways in which Connor and I have, as the French say, *des atomes crochus. He's* the one.

REMADE ALL THE TIME

There is a remarkable connection between bread and love. Not metaphorical, but in a literal way that supersedes words. My mom, a proficient bread baker, has filled the house with the sweet scent of her loaves for as long as I can remember. In my experience of her bread, the immediately felt sensation is love. It's baked into the loaf as surely as the poppy seeds sprinkled on top. Her challah is intertwined with my life as a constant support—more so than any single material object I've possessed. It was present at celebrations and holiday meals, as it was at the kitchen table for awkward teenage conversations about sex and alcohol. It was ubiquitous when I was in Ohio recovering from the ski accident in my twenties, held in one hand as I read letters from Connor in the other hand. (Like a young Ernest Hemingway, he sent love letters from New York City nearly every day of those three months my brain healed. Can you blame me for falling madly in love with the man?) When Mom's bread is passed around and we each rip a piece off (*get that knife outta here*), I know I belong.

Mom's bread is intertwined with decades of family lore. My dad fell head over heels in love with her when she left a freshly baked loaf of bread on his office desk for him after their first date. Her long and accomplished career as an eye doctor is at risk of being a mere footnote (to me, anyway) in the shadow of her glorious bread. Year after year, she raises a record-

breaking sum of money for a local fund-raising event by auctioning off a monthly basket of an assortment of her homemade loaves. Watching my mom knead dough at the kitchen counter for my whole life, I probably ended up with more instinct by osmosis than if I had spent a day researching the art of kneading.

I made a video, "Ode to My Mom's Bread," and followed her in the kitchen as she worked, my camera buzzing around her like a fly. When we recorded the episode, she made her bread from memory, barely even bothering to measure ingredients, yet speaking the quantities aloud. "One teaspoon of salt," she said as she poured it from its container into her palm. I asked her to pause there, and peeked my head out from behind the camera. "Do you think that's *really* a teaspoon?" With her other hand, she pulled a teaspoon out of a drawer and proceeded to pour the contents of her palm into it. Her measurement was absolutely perfect, down to the last grain of salt. My mom's sour cream challah will go down in family lore as a representation of my mom's brilliance and warmth.

This is a great loaf to bake if you're keen to try making bread but still unsure about attempting sourdough.

Love doesn't just sit there, like a stone, it has to be made,
like bread; remade all the time, made new.
—URSULA K. LE GUIN

My mom in the early 2000s, making her challah

Susie Q's Sour Cream Challah

MAKES 2 LOAVES

When I started writing this book, I asked my mom where she initially got her challah recipe, and learned that "mom's loaf" has evolved over time. This current iteration, which she's made consistently for over a decade, was adapted from a dinner roll recipe from a 1990s issue of *Cooking Light*.

2 (¼-ounce/7-gram) packets active dry yeast (4½ teaspoons)

½ cup (125 milliliters) warm water (around 110°F/43°C)

½ cup (1 stick/115 grams) unsalted butter, at room temperature

½ cup (105 grams) sugar

1 cup (240 grams) sour cream

2 large eggs, whisked

5 cups (600 grams) unbleached all-purpose flour, plus more for dusting

1 teaspoon fine sea salt

1 tablespoon canola oil

1 egg white, beaten, for the egg wash

Poppy seeds, for garnish (optional)

1. Combine the yeast and warm water in a large bowl. Let stand for 5 minutes.

2. Cream the softened butter and sugar in a medium bowl using a whisk until smooth. Gradually stir in the sour cream until combined. Set aside.

3. Add the eggs to the yeast mixture and mix well. Add the sour cream mixture and stir until smooth. Add 1 cup (120 grams) of the flour and the salt. Gradually mix in the remaining 4 cups (480 grams) flour until you have a shaggy dough.

4. Sprinkle a work surface with flour. Tip the shaggy dough out onto the surface and sprinkle with a couple more pinches of flour.

Knead the dough with the palms of your hands (avoid poking it with your fingertips), adding flour as needed to prevent it from sticking to the work surface and your hands, until the dough is smooth, not sticky, and gently springs back when pressed with a fingertip (also called the "poke test"), about 5 minutes. (Another way to check that the dough has been kneaded long enough is by performing the "windowpane test": Cut off a chunk of the dough—around 50 grams—and stretch it gently between your fingers into a thin sheet. If it breaks too easily, it needs more kneading, but if you can stretch the dough thin enough to see your fingers through it when it's held up to the light, it's good to go.)

5. Pour the canola oil into a large bowl, then place the dough in the bowl and rotate to coat it with oil. Cover the bowl with a clean dish towel and place in a warm (75° to 80°F/24° to 27°C), draft-free area for about 90 minutes, until the dough has doubled in volume.

6. Remove the dish towel and punch down the dough. Turn the dough out onto your work surface and divide it into two equal portions. Cut each portion into thirds so you have 6 portions. Roll each of these portions

(recipe continues)

into a rope on a clean work surface (or just in the air, rolling the dough between your palms) about 15 inches (38 centimeters) long. Working with three ropes at a time, braid the ropes, pinching the ends to make sure they don't unravel during the second rise, to form two loaves.

7. Line two sheet pans with parchment paper or a silicone baking mat. Place each shaped braid on its own pan. Cover each with a clean dish towel and let rise in a warm, draft-free area for 30 to 45 minutes, until they bulk up in size a bit (but are not doubled).

8. Near the end of this proof, arrange two racks in the oven—one on the bottom notch and the other second from the top—and preheat the oven to 375°F (190°C).

9. Prepare an egg wash by whisking the egg white and 1 tablespoon of water in a small bowl until frothy. Uncover the dough and use a pastry brush to brush the loaves with the egg wash. Sprinkle with the poppy seeds (if using).

10. Bake for 35 to 40 minutes, until the loaves are a dark golden brown and sound hollow when you knock on the underside. Make sure to switch the sheet pans' positions on the oven racks and to rotate the loaves 180 degrees halfway through to ensure even baking.

11. Transfer the loaves from the sheet pans to wire racks and let cool thoroughly. Then *enjoy!*

LE PETIT GRAIN

"These guys love sourdough," my friend messaged me, and sent a link to a boulangerie called Le Petit Grain. Two men run it, she said, "both named Ed—Eduard and Edward," and they were gaining attention with their sourdough bread, made in the Belleville neighborhood on the east side of Paris.

Lucky for me, that friend was writer Lindsey Tramuta, and she knew the Eds personally. (I think of her as the unofficial mayor of Paris—she knows everyone.) She connected me with them via email, and I got a short response from "Ed" (I couldn't tell which one), telling me to give him a call on his cell phone. My mission was to apprentice, or *stage*, as the French say, in their bakery, so I wanted to come off as professional and capable—I wrote out a script in French of what I might say upon calling Ed.

My French was rusty. I'd have to work on that. I took a deep breath and dialed his number. After a few rings, it went to voice mail, and I panicked, leaving an improvised version of the script, which, as I tried to read it from the notepad in front

of me, I realized was barely legible chicken scratch. I hung up the phone.

That wasn't great.

Less than sixty seconds later, my phone rang. It was Ed.

"Allô?" I picked up the phone.

Turns out, this Ed was the British Ed, Edward Delling-Williams, and our conversation shifted to English. He grew up in Somerset, and after working in the kitchen of the famous London restaurant St. John, he moved to Paris to put his skills to use at the acclaimed restaurant Au Passage, famously hidden in an alley. He and Eduard, a coworker at Au Passage, teamed up to open a restaurant, Le Grand Bain, which led to opening their bakery, Le Petit Grain.

"We weren't happy with any of the bread we could get for the restaurant, so I started making my own," Ed told me. "About the time I realized I couldn't sustain making bread *and* be the head chef of the restaurant, the storefront down the street opened up. We decided to make great bread not just for our restaurant, but for anyone else who wants it, too."

Belleville, the neighborhood his restaurant and bakery are in, has historically been a rougher area, and although it's beginning to gentrify, it's still often coupled with the labels "edgy" or "fringe." It's Édith Piaf's Paris—a world away from the glitz of Saint-Germain-des-Prés or the glittering Eiffel Tower. (Piaf, the iconic French singer, was—as legend has it—born in a doorway on rue de Belleville, to a busker father and café singer mother.)

"I'd love to see what your team does," I said to Ed, "and get my hands dirty *with* your bakers—I was hoping . . . Can I help out in the bakery?"

We'd already established some of the basics—I went to culinary school, I was writing a book about bread in France, and I could speak conversational French. "Do you make bread?" was his response, for which I was prepared. "Yes, absolutely. My starter's name is Skinny." I was to show up in several weeks, for Friday morning's shift.

"Show up at four thirty a.m.," Ed requested. "The bread guys will be there, the pastry folks will get there a bit later."

I took the train to Paris from London the day before I was to be at the boulangerie, and that evening I ate at Ed and Ed's restaurant, Le Grand Bain. It was on a side street in Belleville that was blanketed with colorful graffiti. I sat at the bar and ordered a glass of natural red wine from the Aveyron region of France while I looked over the food menu. A basket of bread appeared in front of me, accompanied by a thick round of salted

butter. The hefty sourdough slices, baked that morning down the street at Le Petit Grain, lay snug in a sturdy cloth basket. I pulled out one of the pieces and studied it: a deep brown crust with a golden hue and large fermentation holes. I wanted to rest my cheek on it and take a nap. Even before I went in for a bite—without butter, first—my mouth started watering in anticipation. I sunk my teeth in and was delighted that it was delicately nutty and sour and had retained such moisture.

"*Mm . . .*" I let out. It was more than esculent—it was ecstasy-inducing. After a generous slather of the *beurre salé*, I felt so enchanted that I wondered if this

Chef Edward Delling-Williams at Le Grand Bain

The open kitchen of Le Grand Bain restaurant in Paris

constituted promiscuity. Alone at the bar, horns playing over the speakers and with the ambient chatter of a full restaurant, I was reminded why I was so taken with this city. Its romance pins you down in the most unexpected places.

The wild garlic soup with curry oil drizzled on top came with slices of Le Petit Grain's seeded loaf. I ordered a couple additional items off the menu and another glass of wine and spent the next two hours eating contentedly, sipping wine, and observing the restaurant as though I were a fly on the wall. It was the most enjoyable dinner I'd had in ages. I watched the narrow lane of the street outside go from bright dusk to lamplit, and I realized I'd be back on this road before the sun shone again—rue Dénoyez hosted both the restaurant and, a few storefronts down, the bakery.

I asked for the bill and went to get some sleep before my alarm went off at four.

WHEN I GOT TO THE BAKERY THE NEXT morning, several hours before sunrise, a petite woman named Marie Lemarchand was there with her hands in a pile of flour, her straight brown hair pulled up into a bun. She let me in with a perplexed look on her face, and when I reminded her Ed should have told her I'd be coming, she responded, *"Ah, oui,"* and turned back to her flour.

The first few hours of the day, she asked me only to measure ingredients, rearrange tools, or set out the freshly baked loaves in the front of the shop—the first loaves went out around six o'clock. When I placed them on the wooden shelves, I was instructed to cluster them

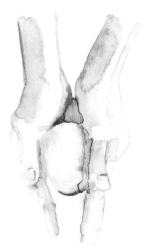

together as much as possible, as bread that cools slowly stays fresh longer.

She guarded the sourdough starter as though it were a precious jewel. I learned she was proficient in English when she beckoned me over to look at the starter and told me, "There's lactic fermentation, then acetic fermentation. If the starter gets too warm, then it starts doing acetic fermentation and the resulting loaf won't be as sweet, so we have to regulate its temperature."

Some fermented foods (like sauerkraut) contain more lactic acid fermentation, while others (like kombucha) are heavy on the acetic acid. Sourdough starter contains both lactic acid bacteria and acetic acid bacteria, and the balance of the two will affect how your loaf tastes. Lactic acid bacteria give a smooth, creamy tang of flavor, whereas acetic acid bacteria result in a more pungent, vinegary flavor. (Acetic acid bacteria and lactic acid bacteria are present in the making of wine and cheese, too, and are one of the many variables an artisan must try to balance.)

Marie was right to take such care of the sourdough starter and its good bacteria, because, as fermentation guru Sandor Katz says in *The Art of Fermentation*, "Much of the practice and technique of fermentation amounts to understanding the selective environment you want, and effectively creating and maintaining it."

What's more, identical microbes will respond differently when placed in different environments. "The bacteria start to change, integrating foreign elements into their genomes really quickly," Ben Wolfe, an expert on the ecology of microbes in food systems, told *Modern Farmer* magazine.

As the sun came up, Marie finally let me handle the delicate, fermenting dough she had mixed the day prior. "Can you shape these into boules?" she requested.

Even after the practice of making my own sourdough loaves at home, my hands were slow and clumsy compared to hers. After feeling underutilized for a couple of hours, I was now flustered and felt unequipped. In a flash, I transported back to the first weeks of culinary school, when I was regularly humbled. The same lesson seemed to apply to bread baking: in a professional capacity, food production is a different ballgame.

Around the same time, close to nine o'clock, Ulyccio, another baker, walked in to start his day. He joined the effort next to me, and Marie went to start another step.

a conclusive *"Uhp!"* (One of my favorite Frenchisms, *uhp* is frequently used as a sound that correlates with a finished action. In culinary school, the kitchen was absolutely littered with *uhp*s, as the pot hit the stove, as the chicken carcass was removed from the *faitout*, as the egg yolk dropped from its shell.)

I tried to emulate Ulyccio, but the dough stuck to the table every time. Eventually, Marie came over and wedged her little body between me and the massacred ball of dough. "See this texture, that's not good." I had overworked the dough in my attempt to fix my multiple mistakes, only making them worse. What should have been as smooth as a baby's bottom was as wrinkly as a pug.

"To be proficient, you need practice," Marie said. She was direct but not unkind. "During the year," she continued, "even I need to constantly be adjusting and tweaking. It's never 'easy.' The different temperature of different days affects the dough." She always had her antennae up, attuned to what the dough needed.

The three of us spent the next seven hours mixing flours and shaping dough. We scooped flour from the big brown bags under the counter. The bags had labels on them, like T150 ("Whole wheat," Marie said) and T65 ("More refined," i.e., white flour). There was one that said *petit épeautre*—einkorn (an ancient grain, and the oldest known cultivated wheat variety). *"Faites attention* when you're mixing that one," she said. "It's fragile. It's more difficult to work and there's less gluten than in normal wheat. But it is tasty."

She kept looking over at me, like a mother watching a clumsy toddler.

Ulyccio tried, in French and broken English, to give me tips on *façonnage*, shaping the dough. "Move quickly," he said, "and keep spinning it." He spun boules so quickly his hands blurred in my vision, then he'd plop a loaf in its basket with

At Le Petit Grain bakery with Ulyccio and Marie

Say what you will about the European stereotype of a lax work ethic; we never properly stopped for breakfast or lunch. There were no breaks. At around eight a.m., Marie handed me a chunk of bread and some olive oil for a snack as she ripped into the loaf herself. "Breakfast," she said, with chipmunk cheeks. It was nearly noon when I saw her cutting up an apple, which she slowly ate over the next thirty minutes—grabbing a wedge when she found time between scraping wet dough and eyeing the scale.

They weren't frantic working conditions, and I'm sure I could have stopped for a substantial break if I had wanted to, but I didn't feel the need. I was on this team, and I intended to pull my weight; I was angling to get a longer-term apprenticeship there.

I could see how, in the daily grind of this job, it could get stressful, swiftly. I remembered one baker in England telling me, "We work in a goldfish bowl. There's nowhere to hide."

That baker, a woman named Kimberley Bell, had created one of the best "goldfish bowls" in all of England. Her bakery and café in Nottingham, Small Food Bakery, has an open kitchen with transparency on all levels of the organization to match it. Her bakers travel with her to farms to see where the grains come from, and the bread they make is an antidote to the majority of bread made in the UK, which uses the Chorleywood

The bakers' work surface at Le Petit Grain

method, a chemical addition that allows for an extremely expedited rise. Kim is an undercover activist, sourcing from local farmers and creating a strong community from field to famished mouth.

"You can't un-know the politics of food," she told me. Instead of getting defeated by some of the systemic problems, she chose to lead with her business decisions. She shared stories of polymaths she'd met, people who were farmers and bakers and philosophers, and making a real difference with their work.

"You're interested in bread in France?" she asked rhetorically. "You should look into a man named Nicolas Supiot. He makes bread in a completely closed system—he mills his own wheat, then he bakes bread with it. I think he's pretty eccentric—he bakes barefoot! He calls himself a 'peasant baker,' and he's leading a movement."

AT LE PETIT GRAIN, MARIE SHOWED ME the small mill in the front room. "It's all about the chain of production," she said. "As a baker, you have to think about the grains that become flour." She told me about her aha moment with bread's production line: "I did a *stage* with Roland Feuillas in the South of France. He wants to put bread back where it comes from. It's supposed to be the root of life, but it's gone so far from that."

It was the first of many times I would hear of Feuillas and his work. He was a part of the group of self-defined *paysans boulangers*—peasant bakers—in the same wave of pioneers as Nicolas Supiot.

Marie, Ulyccio, and I made the seed loaf I had enjoyed the night prior with my wild garlic soup. I soaked the seeds in water first, so they wouldn't dry out as the loaf baked, then added them to the dough. When I went to shape the loaves, I was cognizant of the feel of the dough and how much flour to have on my hands and on the table so I could work the dough smoothly. I was getting the hang of it, and I finished the task without embarrassing myself (I think).

BREAD VS. FLATBREAD

The baker Ian Lowe, an American who lives in Tasmania and has a bakery called APiece [sic] of Bread, says bread is *all* semantics: "Are noodles bread? If not, why? Many rice noodles in Southeast Asian countries are made from a slurry that undergoes lactic acid fermentation to lower pH, providing shelf stability at ambient temperatures. How is this different than bread?" The categorization of noodles as bread may feel extreme, but let's peel that argument back.

Flatbreads are thought to be a type of bread, but they don't go through the leavening process most of us associate with bread.

Yet there's also leavened flatbreads, which are breads that are yeasted but not as risen into what we think of as bread. They fit somewhere in the middle. I'd put focaccia in this camp.

What about Ethiopian injera? It's a bubbly sourdough flatbread that incorporates wild yeasts but is still flat. Where does that go?

Then there's Irish soda bread, which rises more than my sourdough pancakes, for instance, but without yeast. It relies on the chemical reaction when baking soda meets the lactic acid in buttermilk, which creates the carbon dioxide necessary to rise. Other breads, like Native American fry bread, use baking powder to help the dough rise.

The Tassajara Bread Book—a seminal cookbook, the "baker's bible"—includes recipes for both "yeasted breads" and "non-yeasted breads" (classifying both as, indeed, bread), and other cookbooks use the term "quick bread" as a catchall term.

Author Michael Harlan Turkell told me, "The biggest point is the oven itself; is bread baked on the bottom floor, or walls/ceiling, like a *tonir*[*]?"

Almost every culture has a flatbread, and some of my favorites include Armenian *lavash*, Indian *naan*, and perhaps my most beloved, *khachapuri* (also called Georgian flatbread), which is sometimes made with yeast and sometimes with baking powder.

---

[*] *The Armenian term for a cylindrical stone or ceramic oven in which pieces of dough are stuck to its sides to cook.*

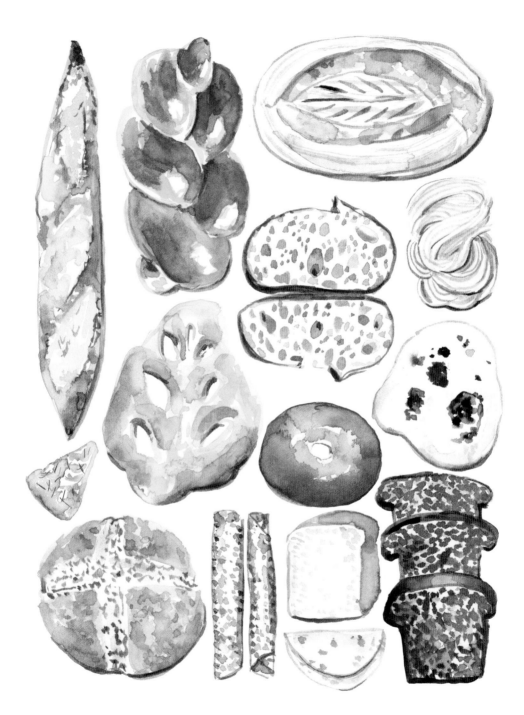

Ratatouille Khachapuri

MAKES 1 KHACHAPURI, TO SERVE 4

The first time I had *khachapuri* was at a Georgian restaurant in Paris. "There's one reason you *need* to try this restaurant: their khachapuri," my friend Natalie told me. This was before I lived in Paris for culinary school, and I was visiting her as a wide-eyed tourist. *Why is she taking me to a Georgian restaurant in France?* I wondered, but instead asked, "What's *catch-a-poori*?"

"It's the bready-cheesy-eggy dish you will be obsessed with." My friends know me so well.

Indeed, khachapuri further proves nearly every culture has a staple bread-and-cheese dish. (And egg! I'm getting Welsh rarebit vibes—see page 87.) There are different versions, from different regions of Georgia. Some variations enclose the cheese-egg mixture in a flat, stuffed circle, like a gratuitously thick, enclosed cheese quesadilla, but the style I riff on here is boat-shaped, with a cheese-filled crust, and topped with a single egg.

Typically, that cheese-egg combo in the crust bubbles away in the center of the dish, too, but since I think of Paris when I think of khachapuri, I make a French-inspired version: ratatouille khachapuri. The crust is still filled with the aforementioned cheese-egg combo, but the belly of the boat is filled with ratatouille, a Provençal vegetable stew.

When you're cooking each part of the ratatouille, before you curse me for not having you toss all the vegetables into the pan together, let me defend myself. Follow my instructions and cook each vegetable separately, because they have different cooking times, and season with salt and pepper each time you add a new vegetable to the pan. You'll end up with an exceptional ratatouille instead of a decent yet mushy one.

Georgians top just-baked khachapuri with butter, which is yet another reason this dish brings me back to Paris. Finishing a dish with a dollop of butter is very French to me, as *monter au beurre* was the culinary school direction to complete sauces, soups—just about everything.

DOUGH

1 cup (230 grams) full-fat plain yogurt

1 tablespoon neutral oil (preferably sunflower oil)

½ teaspoon fine sea salt

1 teaspoon unsalted butter, melted

2 cups (260 grams) all-purpose flour

½ teaspoon baking powder

RATATOUILLE FILLING

Extra-virgin olive oil, for sautéing

1 medium eggplant, cut into 1-inch (2-centimeter) cubes

Kosher salt and freshly ground black pepper

½ large zucchini, quartered lengthwise, then cut crosswise into ¼-inch-thick (1-centimeter) slices

1 yellow onion, thinly sliced

(recipe continues)   **299**

1 red or yellow bell pepper, cut into ½-inch (1-centimeter) cubes

1 garlic clove, peeled

1 beefsteak tomato, cut into ½-inch (1-centimeter) pieces

2 tablespoons chopped fresh parsley

CHEESE FILLING

2 cups (230 grams) shredded and/or crumbled cheese (a combination of equal parts shredded mozzarella, queso fresco, and feta cheese)

4 tablespoons (½ stick/60 grams) unsalted butter, melted

1 egg

TO FINISH

2 eggs

1 tablespoon unsalted butter

A few fresh basil leaves, chopped

1. Make the dough: Mix the yogurt, oil, salt, and melted butter in a small bowl. Mix the flour and baking powder in a large bowl, then gradually add the yogurt mixture, stirring as you pour. Form the dough into a ball, cover the bowl with a clean kitchen towel, and let sit in a warm place for 1 hour.

2. While the dough rests, start the ratatouille: Pour about 2 tablespoons of olive oil into a large skillet over medium heat and add the eggplant cubes. Season with salt and black pepper and stir. Cook, stirring occasionally, for 8 to 10 minutes, until the eggplant cubes are cooked through and slightly golden. Transfer the eggplant to a large plate to cool.

3. Add 1 tablespoon of olive oil and the zucchini to the pan, still over medium heat. Season with salt and black pepper and stir. Continue to stir occasionally as the zucchini cooks, 5 to 6 minutes, until softened and golden. Transfer the zucchini to the plate with the eggplant to cool.

4. Add 1 tablespoon of olive oil and the onion to the pan, still over medium heat. Season with salt and black pepper and stir. Cook until the onion is translucent, 3 to 5 minutes, then stir in the bell pepper, garlic, and a pinch each of salt and black pepper. Cook for 1 minute, then stir in the tomato. Taste and season with more salt, if desired. Add the parsley, give one last stir, and remove the pan from the heat. Let cool, then remove the garlic clove and transfer the mixture to a medium bowl. Add the zucchini and eggplant and gently toss to combine the vegetables.

5. Make the cheese filling: Mix the cheeses, melted butter, and egg in a bowl until well combined. Set aside.

6. Place the dough on a lightly floured work surface and knead for a few minutes, until it's a smooth ball. Cover with a clean kitchen towel and let sit for 10 minutes.

7. Preheat the oven to 450°F (230°C). Line a sheet pan with parchment paper.

8. Lightly flour the work surface and place the ball of dough in the center. Using a rolling pin, roll the dough into a 12-inch (30-centimeter) circle. Transfer the dough to the prepared sheet pan. Spoon the cheese filling evenly in two curved lines along the top and bottom edges of the dough, leaving a border of 2 inches (5 centimeters) on the left and right sides. All along the top and bottom edges, roll the dough over the cheese mixture and seal it (a bit like a stuffed-crust pizza). Pinch together the dough on the left and right sides to form pointed tips, making a boat shape. Fill the center of the boat with the ratatouille mixture.

9. Lightly beat one of the eggs, then use a pastry brush to brush the exposed dough with the whisked egg. Bake the khachapuri for 15

(recipe continues)

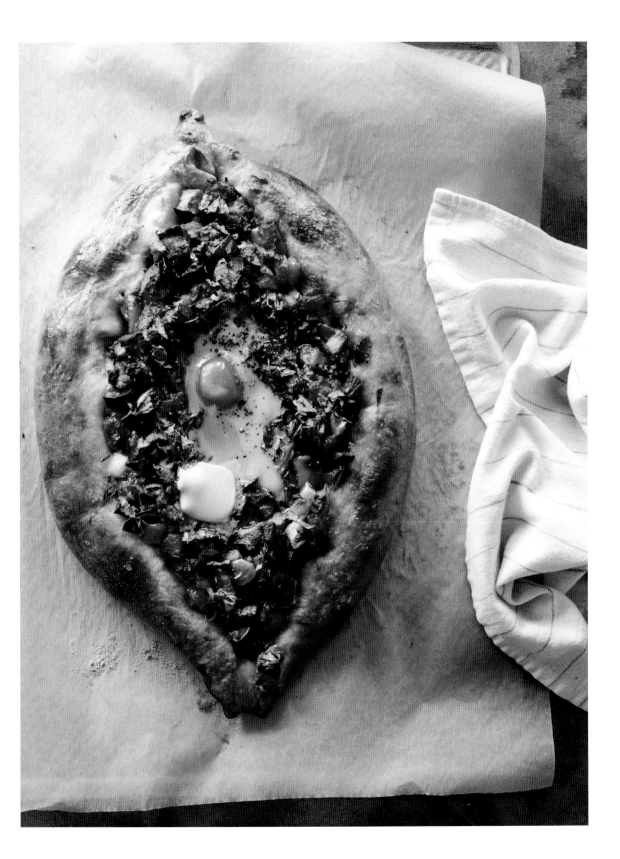

minutes, until the crust is golden. Carefully slide the remaining raw egg onto the center of the ratatouille filling, then return the bread to the oven for 2 to 3 minutes, until the egg white is cooked but the yolk is still runny. Remove from the oven.

10. Place the butter on the egg. Garnish with the basil and serve immediately. In Georgia, the filled crust is traditionally ripped off and dipped in the cheesy, eggy center of the boat. With this ratatouille-filled version, I suggest cutting the khachapuri into pieces like you would an oddly shaped pizza and eating them with your hands.

WASH YOUR HANDS WITH FLOUR

When I took the *métro* to the twentieth arrondissement, near the famous Père Lachaise cemetery, to buy some bread from Maxime Bussy, I arrived at five o'clock in the evening, moments before the bakery opened. *Weird hours*. This boulangerie was only open from five p.m. to eight p.m. There were a dozen Parisians standing on the sidewalk, queuing quietly, and they shot me annoyed glances when I took a photo of the line from across the street. (The twentieth arrondissement is a residential neighborhood; these people had no patience for tourists snapping shots of their local boulangerie ritual.)

I tucked my camera in my bag and shuffled into line as the front door swung open, ready for business. I wanted to meet this baker because I'd heard he cycles to a well outside Paris to collect water to use in his bread, then cycles back with jugs of well water rolling behind him. *Intense dude.* When I got to the front of the queue, just inside the door, I was faced with a counter piled bountifully with loaves of bread still radiating warmth from their time in the oven, and I inhaled deeply.

How cool that I get to come back here for my next apprenticeship.

FEELING SHOCKINGLY WELL RESTED FOR arriving at a boulangerie, I opened the door of Le Bricheton at nine in the morning, in time for the day's first big dough mix. I stepped in and saw Maxime, tall and slender and wearing all black like

Maxime Bussy of Le Bricheton

303

A Khorasan loaf just out of the oven at Le Bricheton bakery in Paris

Maxime Bussy works dough in the pétrin.

Maxime scores the loaves just before they enter the oven.

a ninja, standing in the corner. He waved me over—"Hello! Come, quickly."

He stood over a long rectangular wooden box, which looked like it was approximately the length of Maxime himself; like a raised garden bed he was about to plant, then take a nap in. That dough trough is called a *pétrin*, and he had just poured flour, sourdough starter, water, and salt into it. He began mixing by swirling the water in a circle and increasing the radius in which he moved, then eventually kneading the mass into a blubbery creature akin to a baby seal. Watching him work was enthralling. He put his entire body into the movements—including his breath, which was synchronized with his palms pressing into the pétrin. His face was expressive, and his focus was all-encompassing. It

was a meditation, and I was a hypnotized spectator. I had no idea watching him do the mixing would be such a visual feast; it was like when a movie opens with an action scene.

On average, Maxime made 230 kilos (500 pounds) of bread each day, and ten to twelve different kinds of bread (depending on the day). I watched him work the flour and water like he was practicing tai chi.

As soon as Maxime had given birth to the tabletop-size block of soft dough, he covered it with a cloth. "It took me a long time to learn to work with dough," he said, as he turned to me. "At the beginning, I touched it too much. But with repetition . . . do it, do it, do it . . . you know to touch less."

I recognized that rookie move in myself. "When do you feel like you learned

305

how to make great bread?" I asked.

"Never," he said, shaking his head. "I still try to do better each day."

Twelve years prior, Maxime had become a baker after attending the famous Parisian culinary school Ferrandi. The way he tells his story, he doesn't give culinary school any credit for launching his current career: "I had to reteach myself things"—hence his thirty-minute bicycle trip to pull water from a 700-meter-deep well rather than using water from the tap, and sourcing his flour from farmers with whom he's developed relationships, rather than a typical wholesaler.

"I have someone who cycles to the well to get it for me now," he said, as though it were somehow less astounding.

I asked the obvious question: "Why bother going to a well?"

"I only have two ingredients, so I get the best flour, and the best water." It was that simple for him. (He also adds salt, which he gets from the coast of France, "far from the pollution.")

When we began to work some dough he had mixed and proofed earlier, I experienced Maxime the teacher. He weighed a portion of dough, then swiftly shaped it into a boule, talking me through each step as he did it. He let me portion out and shape the rest of that pile of dough—weighing each chunk, then stretching it and forming it into its round shape, with a taut top skin. To create the top skin, I lightly cupped and pressed the bottom of the dough and dragged it toward myself. "Very good," he said, and went to begin another mix. After twenty

rounds, the pinky side of my palm was chapped from rubbing against the wooden table, but I was working proficiently.

Another of his helpers, a Polish woman named Marin who had lived in Paris for twenty years, walked into the bakery. "Are you a *stagiaire*, too?" I asked her.

She nodded. "Yes, I want to open a boulangerie like this in my neighborhood, and to make bread this way." She took classes at École International de Boulangerie in the South of France for four months, which is how she secured a long-term *stage* with Maxime. Marin stood along the worktable flouring the baskets for the boules and offering me tips as I needed them.

A timer went off, and Maxime went to the oven and removed loaves of rye

Talking with Marin during my stage

Maxime takes rye loaves out of the oven.

bread—inspecting them and knocking on the bottoms to make sure they were done. Meanwhile, I began mixing the measured portions of half einkorn flour and half Khorasan flour (both are ancient varieties of wheat) with water and starter. Once my hands were sufficiently sodden with the wet dough, Maxime glanced over and said, "Wash your hands with flour."

Wash my hands with flour? I thought we had a translation issue for a moment, but I did as he asked, grabbing a handful of flour from a nearby bag and rubbing my hands together with the flour. Sure enough, all the dough that had been acting like concrete on my skin fell off in dainty little balls. This would be sifted from the rest of the flour on the work surface; the powdery flour would be kept and used, and the chunks discarded, or rehydrated and used as a starter. I thought of all the pounds of dough I must have rinsed off

and flushed down the drain in the past—what a waste! Not anymore, now that I knew to wash my hands with flour.

(Please know that we also washed our hands thoroughly with soap and water before anything else, and throughout the day.)

With Maxime, everything seemed to be done by instinct. He followed ratios and measurements, but it was how the dough felt in his hands, how it rested on the bench that determined what he did with it. He and Marin were continuously cleaning up after themselves as they worked, so the bakery never appeared to be an unruly mess.

After the day with Maxime, I thanked him for opening his doors to me, and again inquired about a longer *stage*, to which he gave me the same response I'd already heard: there were legal obstacles. I continued to seek out other boulangeries.

GETTING CREATIVE

"I started baking at a boulangerie when I was a teenager—fourteen years old," Xavier Netry told me. "It was an obligation. My mom was sick and I lived in a rough neighborhood, so I had two options: to be out in the streets like other kids, or to work."

Xavier, who grew up in a suburb of Paris called Épinay-sur-Seine, will be the first to tell you that he lucked out with baking, because it turns out he had a knack for the craft and it's where his creativity found its outlet. He describes his style of bread as "original, atypical," and has been given carte blanche with his creations as "chef boulanger" at Boulangerie Utopie, a shop that won *La meilleure boulangerie de France* (a television competition) in 2016. It sits at the nexus of Parisian foodie culture: between the areas of Canal Saint-Martin, République, Oberkampf, and the Marais. It is the prime location for Xavier to experiment with his sourdough creations, because he bakes for a demographic happy to indulge his curiosity.

One of his staple creations is the Colombo—inspired by a dish from his mom's native Guadeloupe—which includes cumin, ginger, curry, and a West Indian pepper. And levain—he always bakes with sourdough starter as the leavener. That's one of the only constants, though, because Xavier is constantly experimenting—offering curious eaters and impressed

Baker Xavier Netry

Xavier carving la grigne onto his loaves at Boulangerie Utopie in Paris

bread-heads plenty to come back for. When I'm scrolling Instagram, I often see one of Xavier's new breads pop up on my feed, sourdough loaves with such imagination!—cranberries and vanilla, coffee and caramel, sun-dried tomatoes and onions, pear and feta (find @xvbaker to see for yourself).

"How do you come up with these ideas?" I asked him.

"Everywhere—from watching TV, or talking to friends . . . I see an ingredient and wonder if I can use it to make bread. If it works—*bingo*."

His ingenuity with bread isn't overly planned or precious. It's inspired and clearly something he finds enjoyment in—he's easy to smile, especially when he talks about bread. He found an ideal match for his imagination with the team at Boulangerie Utopie—the co-owners, Erwan Blanche and Sébastien Bruno, met in pastry school and proudly offer pastries that use sourdough as the base (their sourdough croissant is one of the most popular items). They trust Xavier to work his magic with the levain.

The steady rotation of various, innovative breads Xavier was churning out is what caught my attention. He, and other bakers like him, inspired me to shake up my sourdough loaf routine. Are you keen, but need some mix-in inspiration? If you want to boost your boule, there are endless combinations to keep your bread baking mojo feeling alive and nimble. Here are some favorites that have come out of my kitchen.

309

Bread Inspiration Well

These variations all use My Go-To Sourdough Bread (page 273) as a base and then incorporate additions in one of two forms: liquid or solid. In some cases, I suggest different flours, too.

The point at which the substituted or additional ingredient is added depends on whether it's liquid (which happens at step 2) or solid (at step 4). For the recipes in which I've suggested different kinds of flour, you will swap out the 50 grams whole wheat flour in step 2 for 50 grams of my substitution flour.

For any of these, a topping of oats or seeds (sunflower, sesame, poppy, pumpkin, etc.) is a fun addition. This step is done directly after shaping the dough, before it's placed in the banneton, cloth-lined bowl, or tin. Sprinkle the oats or seeds on a kitchen towel in a thin, even layer (sparse or dense, up to you), then, as soon as you've shaped your dough, roll the smooth top side of it in the oats or seeds on the towel; they should stick to the dough. Continue with the rest of the recipe as written.

SRIRACHA SOURDOUGH
Additional/substituted ingredients:

50 grams all-purpose flour
200 grams sriracha
200 grams warm water

PANE AL VINO
Additional/substituted ingredients:

50 grams all-purpose flour
200 grams red wine
200 grams water

Note: In the Pane al Vino pictured above right, you'll see slices from different loaves I baked in which I adjusted the ratio of wine to water. The recipe is my standard, because I find you get the hint of color without affecting the texture much. (Use different ratios of wine to water if you're keen to explore!)

HOW TO ADD THE VARIANT MATERIALS

LIQUIDS: For the Sriracha Sourdough and Pane al Vino loaves, adjust step 2, the autolyse step. Swap out the 50 grams whole wheat flour for 50 grams of all-purpose flour—a lighter canvas of dough makes these colors pop. Add the amount of liquid indicated and mix with the flour for autolyse. Follow the remaining directions of My Go-To Sourdough Bread to completion.

SOLIDS: For the Pain au Fromage, Walnut and Raisin Rye, Rosemary and Roasted Potato, Olive and Thyme Spelt, and Sultana Fennel loaves, when a flour substitution is called for, swap it out with the 50 grams of whole wheat flour in step 2 (autolyse).

For all the solid ingredients, make this addition, a little at a time, during step 4 (stretch-and-folds). Sprinkle a handful of the solid (grated cheese/nuts/herbs/dried fruit/veg) over the dough, then do your first stretch-and-fold. Sprinkle more solids on the dough, then do your next stretch-and-fold. Repeat with the remaining solid ingredients called for in whichever variation you're following as you complete the instructions of step 4. When you let the dough sit for bulk fermentation, the solids should be well incorporated throughout. Follow the remaining directions in My Go-To Sourdough Bread to completion.

PAIN AU FROMAGE
Additional ingredient:
150 grams Red Leicester or Colby cheese, grated

WALNUT AND RAISIN RYE LOAF
Additional/substituted ingredients:
50 grams rye flour
75 grams raisins, soaked in water for 1 hour, then drained
50 grams whole walnuts, toasted

Note: In the bread pictured above right, there are slices of an assortment of loaves; from bottom to top: rosemary and roasted potato loaf, walnut and raisin rye loaf, olive and thyme spelt loaf.

ROSEMARY AND ROASTED POTATO LOAF

Additional ingredients:

1 large Yukon Gold potato, cut into roughly ½-inch (1-centimeter) cubes, tossed with olive oil and salt, and roasted for 30 minutes at 375°F (190°C)
5 grams fresh rosemary, finely chopped

OLIVE AND THYME SPELT LOAF

Additional/substituted ingredients:

50 grams spelt flour
75 grams pitted kalamata olives, coarsely chopped
5 grams fresh thyme, finely chopped

SULTANA FENNEL LOAF

Additional ingredients:

75 grams sultanas (golden raisins), soaked in hot water for 30 minutes, then drained
10 grams fennel seeds (break them up with a mortar and pestle first if you don't want whole seeds in the loaf)

The Pain au Fromage sliced and ready to be enjoyed. Bon appétit!

BOUNCING AROUND BOULANGERIES

Back in London from Paris, I baked bread every day. I was constantly trying new recipes, too; it was a hyperactive curiosity that manifested as piles of loaves on the counter and in the freezer. I was more or less happy with the majority of them; Connor, on the other hand, was a highly discerning judge. I'd pull a fresh bake out of the oven, gushing like a mom at my creation, and Connor would respond as if I'd just presented him with a doorstop.

"Aren't loaves supposed to be round?" he'd ask. "Why isn't it puffier?"

"But it's not *dense*," I retorted. "You need to open your mind as to what a loaf needs to look like."

I'd cut it open and show him how soft and pocketed the crumb was. "Yes, and it tastes good," he'd cede, ". . . but I can't make a sandwich out of this."

I didn't want to admit he had a point.

That wasn't the only thing Connor and I were at an impasse about. We were looking at the final year before our visas expired, and we had no clue what was next. We didn't know if we'd stay in London, go to Italy, or move back to the States. We had a conversation that ended in a stalemate the evening before I was to return to Paris for another stint at a boulangerie. As I set off for the train station, I was in a gloomy mood.

Fittingly, when I stepped off the Eurostar in Paris, the city welcomed me with heavy rain and dense clouds. I had only a ten-minute walk in front of me, so

I darted out, taking short breaks under the awnings of brasseries and shops as I made my way to my friend's apartment. I stopped by the bakery Mamiche and picked up an assortment of carbs: a handful of *flûtes* (one with *fromage* and the other *aux olives*), miche sourdough, focaccia topped with pesto, and chocolate bread.

I couldn't show up empty-handed: my friend Rebekah Peppler was a consummate host, and I knew she'd have a cocktail mixed up for me in no time (she wrote a cookbook called *Apéritif*, and you better believe she lived what she glorified). The least I could do was bring the bread.

Some of the fondest memories I have from my culinary school days in Paris were of when Rebekah and I got together for

a drink and a meal of nibbles (bread and cheese, veg and dip, nuts and chips). We never used silverware. It's the beautiful thing about the apéritif ritual, and about bread: fingers suffice.

As soon as I stepped inside her flat, the clouds parted. As the sun came out, my sour mood dissipated, and she pulled out folding chairs on her long, narrow balcony. Perched high on the same hill Sacré-Coeur basilica rests on, we were above the rest of the city. I looked down over the rows of Haussmann apartment buildings, which mark the Paris aesthetic with their uniform, cream-colored stone walls and gray, four-sided roofs angled toward the sky. Being up there gave the impression of floating above everything.

"What are you doing tomorrow?" she asked after we washed the dishes.

"I'm going to Ten Belles Bread!" I was excited; I'd emailed them multiple times until they responded.

"Oh good! They're making the best bread in Paris right now."

"I THINK THERE'S A MASSIVE CRISIS IN France in terms of bread," Alice Quillet, cofounder of Ten Belles Bread, said pointedly when I met her in the morning. The bakery space was large and open, cheerful and well-lit, with floor-to-ceiling windows that faced the sidewalk. It was a busy kitchen, with the bread team on one side, the pastry team on another, and the sandwich and meal prep at the far end, but there was a welcoming feeling that extended beyond the literal openness of the space.

"It's changing slowly," she continued optimistically, "but it's odd: the French consumer has traditionally found out where their meat or fish or veg is from—which producer and region—but for some reason, with a bakery, the 'artisan' is sacrosanct, so no one goes into a bakery and asks where the wheat is from, and how the bread is made. It's full of improvers and additives! It's ready-made bags, just add water. Nothing is naturally fermented. It changed with the Industrial Revolution, and people post-war stopped expecting things from their baker. I think that's changing."

Alice was born in France, to a French father and an English mother. She's fully bilingual and has hired a diverse staff—French, Italian, American, Filipino, and Bulgarian—to make up her kitchen. I ventured to guess her French heritage gave the team some credibility among French bread consumers, and she acknowledged there was some truth to that. "But because [her cofounders] Anna is English and Anselme is Irish and French, we can also be rule-breakers, because there are no expectations." She grabbed the long wooden peel and removed oval-shaped dark brown loaves—*bâtards*—rather than a round boule.

Her bread was initially inspired by Chad Robertson's book *Tartine Bread*. It was an epiphany: she couldn't believe she hadn't been making bread that way forever. She ended up doing a weeklong *stage* at Chad's bakery and opened Ten Belles Bread inspired by his method. ("And Tartine bread is inspired by French bread, so it's gone full circle!" She chuckled.)

Anna Trattles, Alice's business partner and the Ten Belles pastry chef, walked into the kitchen and offered us Turkish delight. "From Turkey!" she said excitedly

Apéritif on Rebekah's balcony

Alice Quillet, co-owner of Ten Belles Bread

applaud. *I wonder if I'll ever be one of those women?* Alice and Anna said it wouldn't be possible without their husbands. "Ten Belles was *inspired* by having a family," Alice said. "We didn't want to be working in a restaurant nights and weekends anymore." I looked to Anna, who met my eyes and nodded.

I admired them both greatly, and not just for their work-life balance priorities. I was standing with two of the people who directly influenced and elevated the Paris coffee scene, with their Ten Belles café, and they were leading the charge of a similar shift in Parisian bread. "Do you see bread following a similar trajectory as coffee, in terms of more people caring about origin and quality? Growth in artisan production?"

"I do." Alice nodded. "With the gluten intolerances, people are asking questions and they're figuring out, in some cases, that it's not gluten they're intolerant of, it's just badly made stuff with wheat. People are understanding that fermentation is a good thing, for digestibility as well."

People are understanding fermentation is a good thing.

Alice handed me off to the head baker, Wing Mon Cheung, who's British. She approached me with a smile and an outstretched arm to shake my hand.

"I'm loving what a female powerhouse this is!" I gushed. "Not many bakeries have so many women, right?"

"In France, ninety-four percent of bakers are men," Alice confirmed, then absconded to fulfill her owner responsibilities.

as she pulled her apron over her head. She had bright eyes and was smiling from ear to ear, wearing her apron like the queen wears jewels. We savored the treats and Alice asked Anna about her kids—Anna had taken them to a doctor's appointment that morning and was late arriving at the bakery. I remarked how impressive it is that they are managing to raise children and be the hugely successful businesswomen in the food space that they are.

It's an unfortunate fact that businesswomen having children remains a topic of conversation—but it still *is* something of note, and when done well, to

As Wing Mon loaded and unloaded the steam-injected ovens—she baked around five hundred loaves a day—I shadowed her and took notes: *Load loaves in the oven, release steam; bake for twenty minutes; open the flute to release steam and turn the loaves; bake for another twenty minutes.* The bread would be sold in the shop and go to the best restaurants all around the city, about sixty in total.

Wing Mon used to work at an office job but left it to become a pastry chef— and discovered bread in the pastry course. "I had an amazing feeling as soon as I baked bread for the first time. It sounds corny, but it's true. I've never looked back." She had the energy that is uniquely associated with people who are doing a job they truly love; who are living their calling. She represented the bread community as I was coming to know it: passionate, incredibly hardworking, and generous. Sharing knowledge was important to her, and she happily gave me clarification on her steps ("Using a fridge helps with consistency"), gave credit to other bakers she admired (she enthusiastically expressed, "The most awesome, interesting loaf I've ever had was Richard Hart's miso rye bread"), and recognized her own evolution ("I used to be a sourdough purist, but I've mellowed out. Sourdough and added yeast each serve a purpose").

I don't know why it was such a shock that a bakery lauded for making some of

the best bread in Paris was so friendly and accommodating; I would have loved to have been a stagiaire with Ten Belles for a longer duration, but the reality was that, both there and elsewhere in France, if I wanted a long-term *stage*, I'd have to attend a specialized school. Although I briefly considered enrolling in the National Bread and Pastry Institute (INBP) in Rouen, I wouldn't get the experience I sought (it's not cheap, either). Rather than feel resigned, I changed course. I plotted to get out of Paris and see the bread scene beyond the capital.

As the day ended, I approached Alice and Anna to thank them for the opportunity.

"Here, take a loaf back to London." Alice snatched a loaf off the shelf and wrapped it for me.

"Thank you!" *You're welcome, Connor.* "Alice, I know this is an impossible question." I wanted to ask her about motherhood, about career pivots, but instead I asked, "What's the future of bread in France?"

Alice smirked like *who knows?*, but said, "A lot of young people are becoming paysans boulangers. They work with heritage blends, and they're growing their own wheat, making their bread with that. It's a trend; they call them the *néoruraux*, the new rurals. There's a guy, Nicolas Supiot, he's one of the first of the paysans boulangers; he's really respected."

It was the third time a baker had mentioned Nicolas Supiot to me; Maxime, too, said he'd trained with him. Third time's a charm: on my way out of Ten Belles, I Googled Supiot and found that he lived in the countryside of Brittany in northwest France. *I guess I'm going to Brittany . . .*

But first, Marseille and Toulouse.

LEFTOVER BREAD

When I returned to London after my Ten Belles experience, my suitcase had more loaves of bread in it than clothes, and not just from Ten Belles. I decided to do a taste test among all the places where I had been in the kitchen (Poilâne, Le Petit Grain, Le Bricheton, Ten Belles), in addition to others, like Du Pain et Des Idées, Mamiche, Circus Bakery, and Fermentation Générale. Every time I returned from Paris, I had loaves of bread (and usually some salted butter) in tow, but with this recent load, Connor was floored when I unpacked. "How are we going to consume all of this?" he asked. I brushed away his concern, saying I'd freeze the vast majority of them, and thaw them on a rolling basis, as we were ready to eat them.

Freezing is a great option to ensure no bread goes to waste. Before it starts to go stale, you should wrap the whole loaf (or pre-slice it, if that's how you know you'll be consuming it, toasting one piece at a time—although bread falls victim to freezer burn more easily if sliced) in aluminum foil, because that's how you'll

reheat it: in its foil in a 300°F (148°C) oven until warmed through.

If you forget to freeze the fresh bread, there are also countless uses for a stale loaf. The most common way I handle a gone-dry chunk is to turn it into croutons or bread crumbs, because I know they'll get used in no time: on pastas, soups, and salads. (I've been known to sprinkle bread crumbs on just about everything. Tip: excellent on hummus.)

For bread crumbs, trim off the crust and cut the loaf into large chunks—you'll throw those in your food processor and blitz them until they are your preferred size for bread crumbs (I like mine about half the size of a pencil eraser). From there, spread them on a rimmed sheet pan with a pinky-size amount of olive oil, stir, and bake at 375°F (190°C) for 10 to 12 minutes, stirring halfway through. As soon as they're out, add a sprinkle of salt and mix again, then let cool. Seal them in an airtight container and refrigerate for use within a few months or freeze for later use.

To make croutons, cut crustless bread into small cubes (whatever size you like

Leftover bread inspiration: An egg strata is the perfect brunch dish. This one has caramelized onion, Gruyère, and thyme.

your croutons). Put them onto a rimmed sheet pan, toss them with a restrained drizzle of olive oil, and bake at 370°F (190°C) for 15 minutes or so, making sure to move them around halfway through. As soon as they're out, add a sprinkle of salt and mix again. Let cool. To store, seal in an airtight container and keep in the fridge for a few months, or the freezer for longer.

If that all seems good but you just want to resurrect your stale loaf, there's a hack for that. Put the entirety of the (remaining) loaf under the faucet, briefly. Get it wet but don't soak it, then put it in the oven at 350°F (180°C) until it's toasted through and none of the inside is wet or gummy, 10 to 12 minutes (depending on the size of your loaf, if it's a baguette or a boule, and so on). I don't have a microwave anymore, but when I did, I'd wrap a stale baguette in a damp paper towel and microwave it on high for 10 seconds. It won't be as good as it was fresh, but it will get the job done.

IN ADDITION TO THE LOAVES I HAULED from France, I continued baking bread at home and adding it to the stockpile in our freezer; I could barely close the door for all the bread in there. Luckily for me, every culture where bread is a major source of sustenance has clever and delicious ways to use it up (invented long before freezers were a standard home appliance).

Of course, the French use leftover bread to soak up fondue (see page 19), Italians make *ribollita* soup, and a standard brunch dish for me is egg strata, which incorporates cubes of stale bread, whisked eggs, any vegetables about to go bad in my fridge, and ideally some cheese baked in a casserole dish (the one pictured opposite is a caramelized onion, Gruyère, and thyme egg strata).

There are endless ways to incorporate slightly stale bread, giving an imperfect loaf one heck of a makeover. Never let good bread go to waste.

MARSEILLE

Like London or New York City, Paris is not entirely representative of the rest of the country culturally or politically. Food systems—and in France, bread, especially—are a reflection of the cultural values and political priorities, so it was necessary I widen my scope outside of Paris.

"When you go to different parts of France, it's very different," baker Kamel Saci told me. Kamel was born in Bordeaux, has a bakery in Paris, and has launched bakeries all over the place—Greece, New York, Portugal, Spain. (He's an artisan and entrepreneur—a baker-preneur!)

He continued, "Paris is more open to make some change, when the rest of France is not there yet. But it will be, step by step." Kamel has baked with some big names in the culinary world: Éric Kayser, then Alain Ducasse; guys who have become famous and wealthy in the culinary industry, which is far rarer than seeing a shooting star. Before working in bread, Kamel was a professional athlete—a judo and jiujitsu champion on the French national team. When he injured his knee and had to take a break from the sport, he began a love affair with bread. In the end, he ditched the white *judogi* for baker's whites.

"There's a lot of similarity between martial arts and bread making," he said. "You have to be focused, and it's the same technique over and over again to become a master. Every day is different, with every person you fight, or every new shipment of flour. In both cases, you wake up and your body is a little different each day." I pictured him in the bakery using the bread paddle like a weapon, jiujitsu-style.

"Bread is the DNA of France," he continued. "Bread is the king of the table. I'd say you should go south. There are people doing good things with bread."

Go south. I could still taste the pistachio gelato from Sicily and remembered how I was encouraged to go south in Italy. I booked a ticket to Marseille, and from there to Toulouse.

THERE'S AN UNMISTAKABLE Mediterranean energy to Marseille— warm air, a lot of sun, and a lively spirit.

At the southern tip of France, it's one of the country's most significant port cities and has a history that tells a familiar tale of migration and trade. It's also known for seafood; case in point—bouillabaisse, the fish stew that historically featured the local catches of the day and ingredients like orange, saffron, and fennel—products of the trade routes.

Julia Child lived in Marseille for a period of time and cheekily noted in her book *My Life in France* the dogmatism of "*the only* right way" some French people thought dishes like bouillabaisse should be made—with tomatoes or without? Strain the broth, or not? "The disputes were endless, and people took great pleasure in hashing them out—one reason that *bouillabaisse* was a perfect reflection of Marseille itself," wrote Child.

Smithsonian magazine called the waves of immigration through Marseille its "ethnic *bouillabaisse*." The end of the 1800s and first part of the 1900s saw an influx of Italian immigrants (at one point the population of Marseille was 40 percent Italians), a lot of Germans during World War II, then Russians, Spanish, Vietnamese, and more recently Eastern Europeans, sub-Saharan Africans, and Northwest Africans from the Maghreb (the most delectable food I had while I was in Marseille was at a Tunisian restaurant).

The immigrant influence in France touches bread, too; the 2018 winner of an elite competition to determine the best baguette in Paris went to Mahmoud M'seddi, the son of a Tunisian immigrant. His father immigrated to France in the

1980s and brought with him a passion for bread—in Tunisia, like France, bread is a part of every meal. The champion bakery of this competition supplies the French president with the exceptional loaf for a year, and Mahmoud personally delivered the bread—a huge source of pride for him and his entire family.

I connected with a local Marseillais baker named Laurent Bocquet, whom Kamel introduced me to. He was a professional magician but found his true calling in bread: "There's something important about *creating the impossible*, which is a philosophy in magic that also applies to bread." Culinary influences around France are different, he said. "The north heavily uses butter, whereas the south is all about olive oil." (He uses olive oil to grease baking tins rather than butter.) The term *pain de campagne* means "country bread," but it's not just

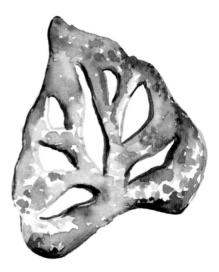

one kind of loaf—each region has its own specialty.

Sure, immigrant and Mediterranean culinary influences are more prominent in southern France, but bread is every bit a part of the region's pride and culture—contrary to what some Parisians might tell you. Bread is subject to snobbery, like wine (and anything else for that matter), but its global appeal has the ability to unite (religions, races, neighbors) better than almost any other foodstuff.

Still, opinions are rampant. Over breakfast at my B&B in Marseille, I made small talk with the owner, a friendly woman with heavy eyeliner and dark brown hair. She asked why I'd come to the city, and I told her I wanted to get to know the breads of southern France, like *fougasse*.

Fougasse is an oblong focaccia-esque flatbread, traditionally cut with lines, which create holes in the bread that make it resemble a leaf. The result is a bread that has the crunchy crust of a pizza woven throughout the center of the bread, too—a crust-lover's dream.

"It's not bread," she said abruptly in French. "When it's good, it's really good, but it's not bread."

Okay . . . "Why not?"

"Fougasse is more of a delicacy than a bread. For French people, bread is bread. There's a baguette and bread, and that's it."

I felt like I was in Lecce, Italy, with Michelle and Domenico. *Milk is milk. Pizza is pizza. Wine is wine.* In France, bread is bread.

The thought of pizza made me remember the *pissaladière*, a Provençal flatbread with caramelized onion, anchovies, and black olives. I asked my host about the regional specialty, and you can guess how she replied:

"Pissaladière is not quite bread, not quite pizza; it's something in between."

(Did you guess right?)

Most Americans would see it and think, *Pizza!* Then they would take a closer look at it and go, *Ooh, quirky pizza!* At least that's what I did. Here's how you can make your own pissaladière.

Sourdough Pissaladière
(Sourdough Pizza with Traditional French Toppings)

To make this dough takes some patience and forward thinking; start the recipe the day before you want to enjoy the pissaladière. Alternatively, you could make your pissaladière from store-bought pizza dough (or even store-bought puff pastry dough, if that's your thing). Both shortcuts will yield a yummy result, but nothing beats a homemade sourdough crust.

The traditional toppings are caramelized onions, black olives, and anchovies. As always when caramelizing those onions, keep going even after you think they're caramelized. Low heat, stirring, and time make for the sweetest umami bomb ever. I also top my pissaladière with sautéed kale because then I don't feel like I have to make a salad on the side. (Although this is lovely with a lightly dressed salad to munch on, too.)

You know what the French would say: It's like a pizza, but it's not pizza. It's a pissaladière.

My version leans toward pizza, though. Since I'm a sourdough pizza fanatic, I'm using this as my excuse to share my sourdough pizza crust recipe (I strongly suggest you try making good ol' pizza with it in addition to the pissaladière). A traditional rectangular pissaladière is cut into squares, but this one is shaped and cut like a pizza.

EQUIPMENT

Kitchen scale

Large mixing bowl

Cotton or linen kitchen towels (not terry cloth) to cover the dough in its bowl

Bench scraper

Large plastic zip-top bag (freezer storage bags work well)

Parchment paper

Pizza peel (or rimless baking sheet)

Pizza stone (or shallow Dutch oven, or baking sheet)

TO REFRESH YOUR STARTER

10 grams whole wheat flour

10 grams white bread flour

10 grams maintenance starter (see page 270)

15 grams room-temperature water

FOR THE DOUGH MIX

25 grams whole wheat flour

225 grams white bread flour

150 grams warm water (between 82° and 91°F/28° and 33°C)

5 grams fine sea salt

37 grams ripe sourdough starter (the refreshed starter will give you approximately this much, plus a little more, so measure it when you add it to the dough mix)

Bread flour or all-purpose flour, for dusting

Coarse cornmeal, for dusting

TOPPINGS

2 tablespoons extra-virgin olive oil

6 large yellow onions (about 2⅓ pounds/ 1.1 kilograms), thinly sliced

(recipe continues)

½ teaspoon fine sea salt

2 large kale leaves, stemmed and coarsely chopped (about 1-inch/2.5-centimeter pieces; optional)

3 tablespoons white wine (such as sauvignon blanc) or white wine vinegar

2 (80-gram) tins anchovies in olive oil

24 pitted black olives

1. **DAY 1, 7:30 A.M.** First, refresh your starter: Combine the whole wheat flour, white bread flour, maintenance starter, and water in a small bowl. Cover with a clean kitchen towel and let sit in a warm area of your kitchen for 6 hours, until it has doubled in size, is bubbly, and smells pleasantly acidic. Five hours after this step, complete the next step.

2. **12:30 P.M.–AUTOLYSE** Now make the dough mix: Combine the whole wheat flour, white bread flour, and water in a large bowl. Mix until there is no dry flour in the bowl. Cover with a clean kitchen towel and let the dough sit for an hour, until your starter is ready.

3. **1:30 P.M.** Pour the salt onto the dough and add the ripe dough mix starter. Wet your hands so they don't stick to the dough, then mix to incorporate the salt and starter into it. I do this by lifting the dough up and over itself, slapping it on the bowl, and pressing down with the heel of my palm, kneading it a bit, until all the ingredients are well combined. Cover with a clean kitchen towel and let sit for 30 minutes.

4. **2:00 P.M.** Start a series of stretch-and-folds. Grab a handful of dough and pull it up, stretching it but making sure not to stretch it so far that you tear it. Due to the low hydration of this dough, you will need to jiggle it and use your other hand to help it stretch (you're strengthening the gluten here). Stretch then fold it back over onto itself; do this four times total. Cover the bowl with a clean kitchen towel and let the dough rest for 30 minutes.

5. **2:30 P.M.** Repeat the stretch-and-fold process, cover the bowl with a clean kitchen towel, and let the dough rest for 30 minutes.

6. **3:00 P.M.** Repeat the stretch-and-fold process and cover the bowl with a clean kitchen towel. Let the dough sit on your counter (ideally in a warm spot) for 3 hours for bulk fermentation (see page 268). At the end of bulk fermentation, your dough should have grown in size but not doubled. If you press gently on the dough with your fingertip, it will slowly rebound, leaving a slight indentation.

7. **6:00 P.M.** Shape the dough: With this dough, you won't be flouring the work surface or your hands (at 61% hydration, you shouldn't have issues with it sticking to your fingers or the counter—though you will want to use a bench scraper to move it around). Tip the dough out onto a clean work surface, using a bench scraper to ease it from the bowl without knocking out much air. Using a bench scraper assisted by your free hand, form the blob of dough into a round by working the scraper around the outside of it, creating a circular shape. Now tighten the round by cupping the dough (on the counter) with a hand on either side of it and dragging it toward yourself while pressing down with your pinkies to ensure that the skin on top of the round is taut. Using the bench scraper, lift it from the counter into a large plastic zip-top bag. Make sure the bag is sealed around the dough and proof in the refrigerator overnight, until step 8 begins.

8. **THE NEXT DAY, 1:00 P.M.** Individual dough ball shaping and final proofing: Remove the dough from the refrigerator and transfer it from the bag to a clean (unfloured) work surface. Using the bench scraper, divide the

dough into two equal parts (215 grams each). Shape each portion into a tight ball with a taut top skin as you did in step 8. Place the shaped balls of dough on a 15.5 by 11-inch (40 by 28-centimeter) sheet pan with high sides, cover with plastic wrap and a clean kitchen towel (to minimize draft and maintain an even temperature), and let sit in a warm part of the kitchen for 4 to 6 hours, until noticeably larger but not doubled in size (this will take closer to 4 hours on a warm summer day, closer to 6 hours on a cold winter day).

9. **5:00 P.M.** (The rest of the steps will take about 3 hours total, but can vary.) While the dough undergoes its final proof, prepare the toppings: Heat the olive oil in a wide skillet over low heat. Add the onions and the salt (seasoning the onions early helps draw out their water) and cook, stirring frequently, for 30 to 45 minutes, until they just begin to turn from yellowish orange to auburn and are softened but not jammy. (You don't need to stand over the pan stirring continuously, but you should be attentive to the onions and stir often.) Add the kale and cook, stirring often, for 3 minutes. Add the wine and stir

to deglaze the pan, scraping up any browned bits from the bottom. Remove from the heat and let cool. (The onion-kale topping can be stored in an airtight container in the fridge for up to 1 day; remove it just before step 12. It will reheat in the oven as the dough cooks.)

10. **5:30 P.M.** Preheat the oven as hot as it will go (around 500°F/250°C). Insert the baking vessel you'll bake the pissaladière on for 30 to 60 minutes to preheat it before the dough bakes (the lower end of that if you're using a baking sheet, or longer if you're using a Dutch oven or pizza stone that will superheat).

11. **6:00 P.M.** Place a 12 by 16-inch (30 by 40-centimeter) sheet of parchment paper on the counter and sprinkle coarse cornmeal all over it. Lightly flour your work surface and your hands. Using a bench scraper, transfer one ball of proofed dough to the work surface and sprinkle another pinch of flour on top of it. Using your fingers, push the dough from the center toward the rim of the dough; you're gently pressing the air out of the center so the large bubbles form only at the rim. Stretch the dough into a round, 10 inches

(recipe continues)

Dragging the dough toward myself while pressing down with my pinkies to create a taut top of the round   **329**

(25 centimeters) in diameter. You can do this by keeping the dough on the countertop and slowly spinning the round (to ensure it doesn't stick to the counter) as you work it wider with your hands. (If you feel wet spots in the dough, you can add more flour.) Then pick it up, holding it in the air by the thicker crust portion of the dough (so the circle you've created is now perpendicular to the work surface). Moving quickly, rotate the circle of the dough, letting gravity pull down and distribute and stretch the dough. Place the shaped round on the cornmeal-dusted parchment and tweak the shape—the dough around the edges should be slightly thicker, and the round should be an even circle. (A traditional pissaladière is rectangular, but I like making mine round, like a pizza.) Spread half the onion-kale mixture evenly over the top, but not over the raised edges of the crust, then arrange the anchovies in diamond shapes (to make a lattice or crisscross pattern) on top of the onion-kale mixture. Place an olive in the center of each diamond. Repeat with the other dough ball if you have two pizza stones and intend to bake them at the same time. Alternatively, cover the other ball with a clean kitchen towel and refrigerate it while you finish the first pissaladière.

12. Slide a pizza peel (if you have one) or a rimless sheet pan under the parchment and transfer the dough (still on the parchment) to the pizza stone/Dutch oven/sheet pan. Bake for 8 to 15 minutes (a shorter time if using a pizza stone, a longer time if using a baking sheet—this will depend on your oven), until the crust is browned, with some darker splotches that got extra love from the oven.

13. Remove from the oven, slice, and serve as you would a pizza.

TOULOUSE—"BUT DOES IT HOLD THE COFFEE?"

From Marseille, I set out for a city to the west of the country's center line: Toulouse, the capital of southern France's Occitania region.

Toulouse is known as La Ville Rose—the Pink City—because of its terra-cotta brick buildings that paint the entire metropolis a warm bubblegum hue on a sunny day. The Garonne River meanders directly through its center, and the residents flow through the streets at an unhurried pace that matches that of the river. Toulouse has the youthful energy and cultural inquisitiveness of a university town (its university was founded in 1229—one of the oldest in Europe). In short, I knew within an hour of arriving that I loved it.

My mission in Toulouse was to further acquaint myself with bread in the South of France, so I put myself in the hands of the ever-capable Jessica Hammer, an American who moved to Toulouse and started a food tour business, Taste of Toulouse. She had her finger on the pulse of the people and places making great bread. She enlisted her French friend,

Mick, to come along and drive us around and help with translations.

The three of us set off to visit bakeries, and everywhere we stopped, we tasted. After half a dozen bites of exceptional bread, I started to pinpoint what I favored: a moist crumb; an almost creamy, tangy flavor; and a crackling, deeply caramelized crust. I was thinking about bread the same way I'd consider a glass of wine; it was a revelation.

The more I traveled around France, the more obvious the regional differences became—even the accent of the region reflected the general vibe of southern France: more relaxed. The sun shone brightly, and people spoke deliberately, making the Parisian accent I was familiar with seem rushed and harsh. One thing that tied the country together, though, was bread. At the end of our day of bread tasting (I deemed us the Three Breadsketeers), we ripped into our last loaf. "When you see the whole loaf, there's something so sensual," Mick said, in his French way. "The question is, how does it hold coffee?"

The Garonne River, Toulouse

Huh?

"Everyone in France dips their bread in coffee in the morning." (In the north, he declared, they put butter or cheese on the bread and then it's dipped in the coffee. I never witnessed this in Paris, but I didn't often have my coffee in a French person's home to corroborate.) It was a rhetorical question: *Does it hold the coffee?* was asked to determine its quality. I made a mental note to dip bread in coffee at my next opportunity.

THE NEXT DAY, AFTER I'D PARTED WAYS with the other two Breadsketeers, I met with an independent baker named Baptiste Chardin of Boulangerie Maurice. We convened at a brasserie for a chat—I wanted to hear about his internet-focused business model, through which he sold his sourdough bread wholesale.

I'd just sat down under the awning and ordered my espresso when a slight, sprightly man around my age came bounding toward the building. He wore a newsboy cap and sported a scruffy beard, and as soon as I saw him, I could tell he was a ball of energy.

He sat down at my table and we'd just introduced ourselves when he said, "People in France don't know anything about bread and wine."

Is this considered heresy? I set down my espresso cup and lifted my pen.

"They've been brainwashed by supermarkets," he continued. "They've forgotten."

What I had initially presumed would be a casual chat over an espresso quickly turned into a consuming deep dive into everything from the gluten structure of bread to the problems facing the French food system.

I'll be honest, for the first ten minutes I thought he might simply have been a brooding artist. It was after he explained, in depth, parts of bread and gluten structures and tied it to *why* he makes bread the way he does that I saw him as a man trying to do work he could believe in, within an endlessly entangled system of food production.

He talked about *gliadine* and *gluténine*—"I don't know how you say this in English," he said. Turns out they're cognates: gliadin and glutenin, the main components of gluten in wheat. They're proteins that are activated when wheat flour is mixed with water (or other liquid); they're necessary to help bread rise during baking and are associated with dough strength.

When dough is kneaded, gliadin and glutenin elongate and align to form gluten strands. The longer the dough is kneaded, or the farther it is stretched, the more the gluten network develops. Picture pasta dough being stretched thinner and thinner to create sheets of lasagna—that's thanks to the activated gluten in the flour. That same quality allows the dough to expand while baking, trapping the air inside rather than bursting. When the proteins cook and set, they create the air pockets we expect from a loaf of bread.

The way Baptiste explained it, modern flours have tinkered with these protein elements to work better with rapid kneading (i.e., machine kneading) and to facilitate the quicker rise you get from adding yeast. Basically, the flour of today has been transformed into a product that matches the speed of modern food production: fast. "That's *le nerf de la guerre*—the core of the matter," he said.

Baptiste uses only ancient varieties of wheat (much like Maxime Bussy of Le Bricheton) and swears by levain as the leavening best for eaters to get all the nutrition of bread without suffering symptoms of gluten sensitivity.

To double-check his assertions, I reached for my trusty fermentation bible, *The Art of Fermentation*, and found that Sandor Katz's words echoed Baptiste's: "The same dense, dry quality that makes grains stable for storage also makes them difficult to digest. To nourish us well, they *need* the pre-digestion of

Baptiste Chardin of Boulangerie Maurice

fermentation. Grains contain several types of anti-nutrients that inhibit their digestion, including a form of phosphorous called phytic acid. . . . Fermentation transforms phytic acid, as well as other toxic compounds found in grains, thereby neutralizing their harmful effects."

The lactic acid bacteria in sourdough enables an enzyme called phytase, which turns phytic acid into something our bodies can digest. (The phytase enzyme is also found in trace amounts in the small intestines, where it catches any indigestible bits of phytic acid that make it that far.)

Fermentation literally predigests foods for us, making it easier on our bodies when those foods find their way to our stomachs. In extreme cases, it can transform a toxic food into an edible food. Raw cassava, for example, contains cyanide, which fermentation renders benign—and thank goodness, because 800 million people globally rely on the root vegetable for sustenance. And many plants, including rhubarb leaves, contain a less deadly but still not entirely digestible antinutrient called oxalic acid, but this, too, is rendered benign through fermentation.

Baptiste took a long drag from his e-cigarette and exhaled the vapor to one side as he stared into the distance. "The word *artisan* should be a synonym for good quality, but so many artisan bakers are the arms of the industrial groups who produce flour with more gluten in it because it has to pass through all the machines. It's messed up, and it's interesting to notice how much people

don't know about what they consume. Even the French."

As I scribbled in my notepad that he uses *no refrigeration, no machines, just arms*, I realized the inconsistency of what he expounded and the fact that he vaped on and off throughout our entire conversation. Near the end of our time together, I couldn't help but point out this contradiction. He grinned at me and said, "Everyone has his paradox." *Touché.* Inconsistency in humans, inconsistency in fermentation: it's an inexplicable phenomenon that's only natural.

I meditated on this puzzle the next morning. I held a hunk of the bread I'd picked up with the other Breadskateers in my fingertips as I centered a mug of freshly brewed coffee on the table under my nose. I inhaled the coffee aromas, then plunged the bread into it, like a free diver going for the seafloor. I brought it up, let the air cool the full sponge of the crumb, then chomped down. *Oh yeah. This bread holds the coffee.*

PAYSAN BOULANGER

The word *culture* has been studied and considered among some of the greatest fermentation thinkers and doers of our time. Sandor Katz, the guardian angel of my ferments, wrote, "We use the same word—culture—to describe the community of bacteria that transform milk into yogurt, as well as the practice of subsistence itself, language, music, art, literature, science, spiritual practices, belief systems." David Zilber, coauthor (with René Redzepi) of *The Noma Guide to Fermentation*, observed how much these two seemingly disparate definitions have in common: "'Culture' and 'culture' mean different things to a biologist and

Nicolas Supiot, a "peasant baker" or paysan boulanger

Nicolas shows parts of the milled wheat grain.

an anthropologist, but in fermentation, they overlap completely," he said on the *Emergence Magazine* podcast.

I'll add to that and point out that it's more than an overhang on a Venn diagram: one affects and reflects the other, like imbricate tiles on a roof that rely on each other to stay in place.

I lived that culture overlap in Brittany, France's northwesternmost region, when I learned to bake with Nicolas Supiot, the highly regarded barefoot peasant farmer. I didn't anticipate living in a commune and peeing in an outhouse with the breeze brushing my butt cheeks, but that's exactly what came along with this *formation*

(training)—a weeklong apprenticeship that I hoped would answer the questions I still had about bread, even after all my home and boulangerie baking. I wanted to know more.

LEADING UP TO THE TRAINING, I HAD something like the first-day-of-school jitters that a foreign exchange student experiences: I'd be spending a week in rural France, in a house with ten French people—sharing a bedroom with the other women and using a composting toilet out back, baking with a French bread master, and speaking a language I could really only comfortably have casual conversations in. *What in the world did I sign up for?* I was so trepidatious, I considered backing out at the last minute, but Connor encouraged me: "You got this! You know you'll be glad you did it, like when you went to Sicily, right?" He was right.

The fact that Petra was the first person I met from my cohort was a godsend. We both flew into the Rennes airport on a Sunday evening—she came from Lyon and I came from London— and arranged to travel to Ecosite les Jardins de Siloé together. Petra was tall and lanky, much like I am, and she was a kindhearted, joyful creature. She'd lived in France for over thirty years— had a husband and three kids there—but having been born in the Netherlands, she could relate to my uncertain footing as a foreigner, so she was my language champion. She didn't speak English—aside from a few words—but if there was ever a concept I didn't grasp, she explained it to me again in French, deliberately and slowly. I felt shielded by her compassion.

When we arrived at the house where we'd be staying, it was eight in the evening, and two other stagiaires, Nathalie and Geoffrey, were already there, sitting around the fireplace, sipping a spirit, and nibbling on cheese and charcuterie.

A few more people arrived that evening and the following morning. We were an assorted crew. The youngest was Thomas, a rock-climbing instructor in his late twenties; the rest of the group were either farmers or bakers in their thirties, forties, fifties, and even sixties. Everyone lived in France, aside from me and Gabriele, an Italian who owned a farm near Bologna. (Thanks to Gabriele, I practiced my Italian that week, too— thoroughly exercising every lingual synapse of my brain.) We had all gathered in this rural farmhouse to learn from Nicolas Supiot.

IT WAS A CHILLY MORNING AS WE gathered around the large wooden table in the main room of our *gîte*, the house where we stayed, but the sun shone like it was a summer day, spilling into the house and reflecting off our coffee mugs.

Nicolas greeted me and each of us warmly—with a wide smile and firm handshake. As soon as he opened his mouth, a deep vocal resonance filled the room and gave us a glimpse at the fire inside him.

"Paysan boulanger is not a job, it's a lifestyle," he said in French. (You can assume all the conversations I quote here were in French; there was essentially no English spoken at all that week. A blessing and a challenge, of course.) To him, making bread was a natural extension of his holistic farm, one element of his entire farm operation.

"I left Paris twenty-seven years ago. I didn't know about farming or baking—I learned agriculture at the same time I learned to make bread," he said, looking each of us in the eye as he spoke. "In both farming and baking, the most important thing is to observe the rhythms of what you've done; the result and reality of it. This is the biggest difficulty in life: to be attentive."

He shifted in his seat and leaned his arms on the table. "We've lost the relationship between the farmer, the miller, and the baker."

The communication between these roles used to be the glue that held society together, but now the farmer follows industry procedures, so the wheat is determined to be stable and homogenous. In France, it's a package deal: the farmer buys the approved seed and is obligated to buy the nitrogen spray that comes with it. The miller buys the wheat from the farmer only if it checks those regulatory boxes. And the baker buys the flour but is divorced from the people and places that produced it. "This is what must be repaired," said Nicolas, and his life's work is a testimony to that.

We stood from the long table, and he walked us around his farm (the land surrounding the gîte) to demonstrate the immediacy of the agricultural element of making bread. We stopped to say hi to his cows before continuing to one of his fields of grain. He had harvested the cereals in July, but even in December, the soil was active and alive. He knelt to grab a fistful of it. "Grains bring the sun's energy down and into the soil in the form of carbons," he said, and I had déjà vu of Valentino (of L'Archetipo winery) proudly showing us his healthy soil in Puglia.

As if Nicolas had read my mind, he said, "While wheat takes carbon from the sun to make humus, grapevines do the opposite, bringing up nutrients from below. Bread and wine are complementary on the table *and in the field*!" Then, as an aside, he added, "With some cheese, perfect." (I nodded enthusiastically, of course.)

I imagined Nicolas standing in this same spot at the height of summer, just before harvesting the grains, the stalks reaching above his head. I'd seen photos of him that way, enveloped by the tall crop.

Nicolas said gravely, "Clones aren't adaptable. Technology isn't working." He looked down at the earth he held in his hand, as he crumbled it and let it fall.

Much of the wheat grown in the world is now cloned from a high-yielding hybrid version created in the 1950s; in contrast, Nicolas grows heritage grains, which are also called landrace grains, ancient grains, or population wheat; there are slight differences in their definitions, but all those terms are getting at the same thing: diversity in grain genetics.

The evolution of how grains are grown mimics the evolution of how cheese and wine are produced—they're influenced by decisions that were made in response to the current events and needs of the time (like how World War II impacted British farmhouse cheese—see page 88 for more on that), and those turning points have had lasting impacts.

The laws I mentioned earlier about farmers growing wheat to meet industry regulations were initially enacted to ensure a successful crop for the farmers and food security for their communities. These major moments of change in the system were not put into place malevolently. "But it has backfired," Nicolas said.

This feels like a mess, doesn't it? To understand how we got here, let's look at the single most significant grain invention and the Green Revolution. Both were kicked off by the same man: Norman Borlaug, an American agronomist whose work throughout the twentieth century changed wheat for the world. He won the Nobel Peace Prize

and the US Congressional Gold Medal and Presidential Medal of Freedom for his groundbreaking work, which led to improved food security around the world, an agricultural makeover dubbed the Green Revolution. Borlaug developed dwarfed, high-yield, disease-resistant varieties of wheat by crossing shorter varieties from Japan with taller, high-yielding varieties. Then, to ensure the success of production, he deployed modern agricultural techniques—such as spraying crops with nitrogen—to help increase the protein content in the grain and the crop yield. The fact that this hybrid variety had dwarfing genes meant the plant had shorter, stronger stems, making it less vulnerable to breaking with the high levels of nitrogen fertilizer Borlaug used, as well as preventing the stalks from collapsing under the increased weight of the abundant grain.

Borlaug's goal was to feed the world, and it worked; yields increased *dramatically*, and the world produced significantly more food. (From 1965 to 1970, Pakistan and India grew nearly twice as much wheat as they had before Borlaug's hybrid invention.) His miracle wheat delivered. That is an outstanding accomplishment; a success that belongs in a science-fiction novel that concludes with the creation of some kind of utopia. Except here on earth, there were downsides to the Green Revolution, and a big one was the loss of genetic diversity in wheat.

"If you don't grow it, you lose it," John Letts told me on a phone call after I returned to London from Brittany.

John is an archeobotanist; his PhD was on analyzing wheat, and after he left academia, he became a farmer and grew heritage grains in the UK.

"In diversity, there is strength," he asserted as his motivation for planting otherwise extinct varieties. He grew his grains from seeds that he accumulated from gene banks all around the world. He echoed Nicolas's assertion that cloned seeds are not a sustainable way to farm wheat, and diverse "population" wheat is the solution.

Like genetic differences among people—Joe has brown eyes and Sam has blue eyes—the levels of gluten in various kinds of wheat differ. Modern wheat, which is generally defined as wheat grown during the Green Revolution, is not only short-stemmed but also high in gluten (the added protein is a result of the nitrogen spraying), which is why eating bread made with modern wheat often triggers symptoms of gluten sensitivity, while breads made with other flours (like einkorn), which certainly still contain *some* gluten, don't trigger the same reaction. Gluten itself is not the issue.

John spoke bluntly about his goals: "I just want to change farming so it doesn't ruin the planet. What happened after the Green Revolution was that these pure, super-short grains planted everywhere were all clones of each other, and when farmers pumped nitrogen into them— guess what? Weeds like nitrogen, too. So now weeds are growing like crazy, and the farmer had to spray herbicides to handle the weeds. And if one problem started, the entire crop was at risk because they're clones, so the farmer had to keep spraying more chemicals to prevent any threat to the crop. Modern varieties completely rely on sprays."

Spraying becomes a vicious cycle, and it ends up weakening the entire system in the long run. "We're destroying the planet with conventional farming," John said, his voice urgent.

He reminded me of Mimi Casteel, the other farmer-scientist I talked with, who lives in Oregon and makes wine. Their academia-meets-real-world conclusions mirrored each other.

WE FOLLOWED NICOLAS BACK INSIDE AND found seats around the hearth. He and a few others wrapped tobacco in rolling paper and sat closest to the fire, blowing their smoke in the direction of the chimney. He asked us what we hoped to learn that week, why we had made the journey. Geoffrey said he wanted a change in his life, he wanted to work with his hands, and, *en fait*, he'd chosen the first

day of this experience as his moment to quit smoking after twenty years.

Nicolas nodded at Geoffrey's desire to redirect his path, and connected it to his own: "I'm from Paris, from an intellectual family. I should have grown up to be a banker, or some job like that, but I chose a path of revolt. I have no regrets." As the fire crackled behind him, he went on to talk about the food system and how its consequences were unsustainable. "There's an urgency to what I've chosen to do. My role—the peasant's role—is to transmit the life of the earth in a way that helps humans to thrive in a sustainable way."

He talked about being influenced by thinkers like Rudolf Steiner and his biodynamic principles, and Masanobu Fukuoka's "do-nothing farming"—people and philosophies I had learned about on my journey in the wine world; he talked about the significance of the good microbes in *lait cru*, raw milk, touching on takeaways from my time making cheese. My past several years of research were coalescing around this baker's fireplace: bread, cheese, and wine were all in attendance.

I had signed up for this apprenticeship—and others had, too—to learn to bake bread from Nicolas. It was the third day there, so . . . *Why haven't our hands touched dough yet?* I remember wondering, perhaps with a bit of agitation. I was missing the point. For Nicolas, bread wasn't just bread. It was the result of the baker's behavior—*why* he did things, which led to *how* he did things.

It started with the grain, the grain

that would become the flour. "The wheat genome is more complex than the human genome," he said. "It adapted and diversified as it traveled east. Same genome, incredible diversity." He brought out an easel with a flip-chart pad on it and mapped out the evolution of grain, introducing me to timeworn Latin names for the oldest wheats that have been labeled "trendy" as of late (Khorasan, einkorn, and so on).

The grains he grew were a local population of diverse seeds, which he called *blé de pays*, known as landrace grains in English. The reason Nicolas preferred the term *landrace grains* rather than "ancient grains" was that grains continue to adapt: no grain still in use today is truly ancient, he argued—it has evolved into its current version.

I saw him for the intellectual he was—an intellectual in peasant's clothes, baking loaves of bread rather than writing dissertations.

THE NEXT MORNING OVER BREAKFAST, there was a steady buzz among us stagiaires around the table. Nicolas wasn't there yet, but the conversation from the day before barreled forward at full steam. In fact, it never stopped. Nicolas had stayed at our gîte into the evening, sharing the bottles of wines we opened as the discussion about seeds, agriculture, French laws, society, and flour continued, morphed, and circled back around. I was the first to go to bed at one o'clock in the morning. Seven hours later, we were all gathered round again, merely picking up

where the last night's topics left off. The earnest interest, even obsession, among my fellow apprentices was unlike any group dynamic I'd experienced before.

It wasn't all so serious, though, as Thomas played pop songs on the guitar and Nathalie taught me cheeky French phrases like *"J'ai la tête dans le cul"*—"I have my head up my ass." We trainees spent every moment together, rallied by a collective aspiration.

Halfway through the week, we stagiaires woke early on a cold, overcast morning to go to the nearby outdoor farmers' market to refresh our larder at the gîte.

As I strolled past stalls, I walked toward a woman from our group, Valentine. Valentine grew wheat grass at her farm in Paris (yes, Paris has farms!), La Ferme de Montaquoy. At the market, Valentine was gleefully eating something that, from afar, looked like a burrito or possibly a rolled-up crêpe. When her gaze met mine, she lifted what she was eating in the air and said, "Katie! Have you ever had a galette?"

"Yeah . . . ," I said, perplexed, because what she was waving over her head did not look like the galettes I'd made and eaten before. *Galette* is a term that applies to almost any free-form crusty pastry, but a Breton galette is in its own category. Brittany is famous for the buckwheat galette (*galette de sarrasin* or *galette de blé noir*), a thin pancake made with buckwheat flour. You can get Breton galettes with various things folded in, like honey and butter or egg and ham.

Valentine had hers with just thick smears of salted butter, which melted into a pool at the bottom of her paper holder.

"You cannot visit Bretagne and leave without trying this. Follow me." She led me to a stall where a cantankerous Frenchman poured buckwheat batter on circular griddles. She ordered for me, giggled at the man's grouchiness, and said, "My treat," as she dropped coins in the vendor's cupped palm.

I bit into the warm, folded dough and my lips caught the butter dripping from the galette's soft, thin pleats. Just like that, I was a die-hard fan of buckwheat (which is ironically gluten-free. I do *not* recommend substituting a wheat flour for buckwheat flour in any of the recipes in this book; the dough will behave entirely differently!).

Another woman from our group, Dominique, was exploring the market separately from the rest of us, because she was fending for herself that week in terms of meals due to her various dietary restrictions, including an intolerance to gluten. *Why is she doing training on how to make bread, then?* She was a passionate baker and had discovered that she could eat bread made with einkorn without a problem. Although einkorn doesn't have less protein than other wheats, its gluten structure is different. So Dominique wanted to learn the basics of bread baking from Nicolas, and then use einkorn to make her loaves.

Einkorn is gaining popularity, so you might find it at your local grocery store (it's stocked in the shops in my London neighborhood), but depending on where you live, it might be difficult to source. Most Whole Foods and health food stores carry it, and ordering online directly from a producer (such as Jovial Foods or Young Living) is an option, too.

Einkorn absorbs water and fats more slowly, and therefore, "Bread dough that contains oils, eggs, and fats rise slower when made with einkorn flour," author Carla Bartolucci says in her book, *Einkorn*. For this reason, you'll notice slightly longer bulk fermentation in the following recipe (which includes olive oil in the dough), which is why I have you mixing your dough mix starter the evening prior.

This loaf, adapted from a formula on the blog The Perfect Loaf, is one I always have in my bread box. The olive oil and honey make it exceptionally moist, with just a hint of sweetness, and the shape is ideal for making sandwiches.

Honey and Olive Oil Loaf with Einkorn

MAKES 1 (2-POUND) LOAF

EQUIPMENT

Kitchen scale

Cotton or linen kitchen towels (not terry cloth) to cover the dough in its bowl

Reusable plastic bag to cover the dough in its pan as it proofs

Large bowl

Bench scraper to help maneuver the dough and to clean your work surface

9 x 4 x 4-inch (22 x 10 x 10 centimeter) loaf pan

Large cake pan to hold boiling water to create steam

TO REFRESH YOUR STARTER

25 grams einkorn flour

25 grams white bread flour

25 grams maintenance starter (see page 270)

45 grams warm water (between 82° and 91°F/28° and 33°C)

FOR THE DOUGH MIX

230 grams einkorn flour

230 grams white bread flour

340 grams warm water (between 82° and 91°F/28° and 33°C)

80 grams active dough starter (from the refreshed starter above)

15 grams honey

15 grams olive oil, plus more for greasing the pan

8 grams sea salt

1. **DAY 1, 9:00 P.M.** The evening before doing the dough mix, make your dough starter by combining 25 grams einkorn flour, 25 grams bread flour, 25 grams maintenance starter, and 45 grams warm water. Stir vigorously and cover with a small plate. Let sit at room temperature until the following morning.

2. **DAY 2, 7:00 A.M—AUTOLYSE** In a large bowl, combine the 230 grams einkorn flour, 230 grams white bread flour, and 340 grams warm water. I mix the ingredients together with one hand, which I've wet with water to keep the dough from sticking, and I hold the bowl onto the counter with my dry hand. Your mixing hand will still have clumpy dough on it at the end of this process, so wet your non-dough hand and squeegee the dough off it. Let sit, covered with a clean kitchen towel, for 3 hours.

3. **10:00 A.M.** Three hours after the autolyse is mixed, add the dough starter (which you fed the prior evening), honey, olive oil, and salt to the autolyse and mix well. To mix, hold the bowl with one hand, and with your other hand—get it wet so it doesn't stick to the dough—lift the autolyse up and over the other ingredients, working your way around the bowl. Continue mixing by pressing your palm into the dough until the ingredients are well incorporated.

4. **10:15 A.M.** Start a series of stretch-and-folds in the bowl. Wet your hands, which helps prevent the dough from sticking to your fingers. Grab a handful of dough on its north side and pull it up, stretching it but making sure not to stretch it so far you tear it, then fold it back over on itself (toward the south side). Now rotate the bowl a quarter turn and do this again; stretch and fold the dough four times total (north, east, south, west). Wet your hands again whenever the dough starts to stick to them. Cover the bowl with a clean kitchen towel. Let the dough rest for 15 minutes.

(recipe continues)

5. Repeat once every 15 minutes two more times (10:30 a.m., and 10:45 a.m.), then once every 30 minutes two more times (11:15 a.m., 11:45 a.m.), covering with a clean kitchen towel between each set of stretch-and-folds.

6. **11:45 A.M.** After the last set of stretch-and-folds, cover the dough with a clean kitchen towel and let rest for 4 hours of bulk fermentation. Over this time, you should see your dough bulk up (but not double in size).

7. **3:45 P.M.** Grease the loaf pan with olive oil. Now you'll preshape the dough using a "wet shaping" technique, in which you *don't* dust your work surface with flour or get your hands floury. Rub some water on the work surface and wet your hands. Place a small bowl of water on the counter to dip your hands in if they start to stick to the dough. Tip the bowl with the fermented dough onto the wet work surface, using a bench scraper to help guide the dough out, and try not to knock out much air. Using your bench scraper and one wet hand, rotate the dough into a taut round.

8. Shape the dough with wet hands: Stretch the left side of the dough up and over to the right, folding it at about halfway. Next, stretch the right side of the dough up and over to the left, placing it on top of the folded dough flap you just placed. Now take a handful of the top (north) portion of the dough and stretch it up, then over and toward you (south), folding over the flaps you just placed and creating a ball-like shape. With your fingers and palms cupping the dough, gently roll it back and forth to ease it into a more elongated shape (you're lengthening it to fit in the tin). To create a taut top surface of dough, push your pinkies (which are wrapped around the back side of the dough) down against the work surface as you pull your arms in, dragging the dough toward you.

9. Place the dough in the greased pan. Cover the pan with a reusable plastic bag and let sit in a warm part of your kitchen for 1 to 2 hours (closer to 1 hour in the summer, closer to 2 hours in the winter). It's ready when the dough has relaxed and expanded into its pan, and when you press a floured finger firmly on the dough, it slowly springs back.

10. **BETWEEN 4:45 AND 5:45 P.M.** One hour before you'll bake, position one rack in the center of the oven and a second rack in the bottom. Set a large empty cake pan in the center of the bottom rack. Preheat the oven to 485°F (250°C).

11. A couple of minutes before baking, reduce the oven temperature to 430°F (220°C). Bring 2 cups (500 milliliters) water to a boil (you'll use it to create steam as soon as you put the dough in the oven). Place the loaf pan on the center rack. Taking care not to burn yourself with steam (stand to the side of the oven as you do this), pour the boiling water into the hot empty pan on the lower rack and close the oven door as quickly (and safely) as possible to trap the steam inside. (I talk more about the importance of steam in the next chapter—it is naturally contained within a lidded Dutch oven, but we have to create some steam here.)

12. Bake for 20 minutes, then remove the empty pan from the bottom rack, rotate the loaf pan, and bake for 20 to 25 minutes more, placing a sheet of aluminum foil over the top for the last 10 to 15 minutes if it's getting dark brown (this will depend on your oven). You want it richly browned, but not almost black. It's ready when a thermometer inserted into the center of the loaf registers around 205°F (96°C).

13. Carefully remove the pan from the oven and set it on a wire rack. When the loaf is

cool enough to handle, turn it out onto the rack and let cool completely before slicing. Cut slices from the loaf as you're ready to eat them. Store your bread wrapped in a cotton cloth or in a cotton bread bag or a paper bag. This bread can also be frozen (whole or sliced); thaw it and warm it in the oven when ready to eat.

HANDS IN THE DOUGH

There was animated chatter as the group of us walked past Nicolas's enormous wood-fired oven to the door of the fournil, his bread-baking room. We'd been waiting all week for this!

Nicolas showing his freshly milled flour

We first had to take off our shoes (remember his reputation as the barefoot baker?), and as our socks pitter-pattered across the floor, he let us loose like a Montessori teacher. *"Touchez, goutez, sentez,"* he instructed us. *Touch, taste, smell.*

The space itself was noticeably tranquil, like a temple (complete with a painting of the Hindu deity Ganesh hanging in the corner). The room was made of raw materials like stone and wood, casting their natural color palette from cream to burnt orange to coffee bean brown.

"How do you feel?" he asked me as I admired his woven bannetons—the wicker baskets the dough would be placed in after shaping. I paused. "I feel calm" was all I could think to respond, and it was true. *Je me sens calme.*

Turns out, he had set up the fournil to evoke exactly that feeling. "Baking bread is a discipline, like all other disciplines, and you need to leave your ego behind when you change into your baker's outfit. It's important to center yourself before

Bannetons in Nicolas's fournil

you start mixing the dough. Get in the headspace to feel." He then performed a brief pre-baking ritual (a short chant followed by a brief meditation) before he dug his hands into the flour.

He asked us to choose among his bags of flour to begin. He mills the flour himself from the grains grown in his fields, using a mill in the room just behind the fournil. I began mixing dough, and I needed help tilting the water from a demijohn into my measuring jug. He poured and pulled back when the water hit the line at one liter exactly. Just as with my

mom measuring salt for her bread, it was muscle memory.

We paid attention to the temperatures of each ingredient, and how the heat and humidity of the December day would affect them. The aim was to have a dough between 26° and 28°C (78.8° and 82.4°F), which is called the "final dough temperature." This helped determine how warm our added water should be (warmer on cool days and cooler on hot days).

When mixing the warm, salted water and flour with the levain, Nicolas kept a watchful eye to see that we weren't too

347

aggressive in our mixing; the gluten in his wheats wasn't as robust as the gluten in the flours we were accustomed to baking with. "Pull it up from under and let it fall. Don't push it over," he said as we did the initial mixing of the ingredients, which reminded me of cheesemaking, and Debbie's gentle reminders to slow down when I hastily sloshed the curds from the whey.

Nicolas mixed his dough in a large wooden trough, like Maxime Bussy at Le Bricheton. (Or rather, *Maxime* did it like Nicolas—Maxime had done this same

training with Nicolas before he launched Le Bricheton.) We stagiaires, on the other hand, mixed in big plastic bowls.

After I stretched and pulled the dough over itself a few times (that's all the *pétrissage*, or kneading, it needed— "Modern wheat is made to be beaten with a machine; this flour is not like that," Nicolas said), I touched the dough mound with the palm of my hand like a proud mom rubbing her baby's belly. I finished with an affectionate *pat-pat* before letting it rest for a few hours, the step known as bulk fermentation.

Nicolas preshapes dough in his pétrin.

He dismantles the stone-ground flour mill to explain how it works.

This seems like a good time to discuss final dough temperature, which is the temperature reading of the dough when all the ingredients are first mixed together. We know by now how important temperature is to fermentation, right? And there are only so many elements that you, the baker, can control. The temperature of the water you add is perhaps the easiest factor to adjust. Having a target final dough temperature helps you calculate how warm your added water should be, and therefore puts your fermentation on the path to success.

Some bakers absolutely swear by this calculation as the key to a consistently great loaf; other bakers don't even own a thermometer and choose to adjust more intuitively. I'm somewhere in the middle. If any of you lean toward the former stance, here's a calculation you can use:

water temperature = (final dough temperature x 4) – (ambient room temperature + dough starter temperature + flour temperature)

The ideal final dough temperature can vary based on the type of dough, but for the purpose of making the sourdough loaves in this book, it's safe to have 78°F (25.5°C) as your target final dough temperature. The reason you multiple it by 4 is to account for the four inputs, which include the temperatures of the room, starter, and flour, and something called the "friction factor," which is only a consideration for doughs being mixed or kneaded more heavily than we'll be doing with our sourdough. Your friction factor is zero, but its variable existence is why we still account for it in this formula.

Let's try an example (in °F—it works the same in °C). If your target final dough temperature is 78°F, the room temperature is 73°F, the flour temperature is 70°F, and the dough starter temperature is 73°F . . .

water temperature = (78 x 4) – (73 + 70 + 73)
water temperature = 312 – 216
water temperature = 96°F

"Lactofermentation is of the utmost importance," Nicolas said, referring to the wait time between steps necessary for the lactic acid bacteria to transform the composition of the dough by neutralizing the phytic acid of the grains and breaking down the gluten and carbohydrates, making the resulting bread easier to digest and allowing our bodies to absorb them. By placing such importance on lactofermentation (also called lactic acid fermentation), he was advising us, his overeager trainees, to be patient.

We live in a society that is inhospitable to patience. Scientists have invented workarounds to speed up the bread-making process so we don't have to be patient when we bake, but it's with our patience that the microbes in bread reach their full transformative potential.

WHEN WE RETURNED TO THE DOUGH WE'D mixed three hours prior, it showed signs of fermentation—subtle growth and air pockets barely emerging from the heap. The next step, shaping, was again brief and delicate. We weighed out portions of the dough, pulled the four corners of it up and over itself, then twirled the dough between our palms into a ball or sometimes an oblong shape. Into the cloth-lined bannetons the dough balls went! Covered with another cloth, our loaves would complete their final rise in these little homes, kept sheltered and warm.

There was a sense of something alive in each banneton. The magic of making bread filled the fournil, and time was the last ingredient. In these final hours we waited for a bit more expansion before putting the loaves into the inferno of an oven.

MIX · REST · SHAPE · PROOF · BAKE · EAT

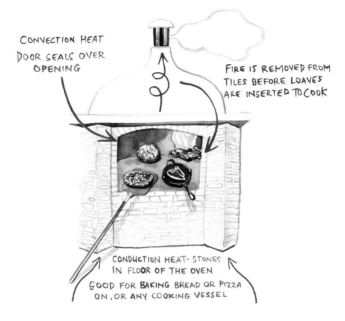

CONVECTION HEAT
DOOR SEALS OVER OPENING

FIRE IS REMOVED FROM TILES BEFORE LOAVES ARE INSERTED TO COOK

CONDUCTION HEAT- STONES IN FLOOR OF THE OVEN
GOOD FOR BAKING BREAD OR PIZZA ON, OR ANY COOKING VESSEL

STEAM IN THE OVEN HELPS DEVELOP A good crust on the bread, and every bakery I'd worked in had a steam-injected oven—except for Nicolas's. What he did before the loaves were inserted (and between batches) was to push a wet towel at the end of a wooden stick around the inside of the oven, which both cleaned the oven floor of any remaining ash (left over from heating the oven with burning wood) and created residual steam for the bread.

Steam is an important ingredient in baking bread and allows for ultimate "oven spring"—the last burst of rising just after the dough goes into the oven, before the crust forms. In his tome *Bread*, Jeffrey Hamelman explains, "In a steamed oven, the surface of the dough remains moist longer, enabling greater oven spring to occur before the formation of a surface crust, and the result is bread with superior volume."

The other reason steam is important to form a superior crust is the Maillard reaction, the sequence of chemical reactions that occur when amino acids and sugars are transformed by high heat.

Bread is baked at a very high temperature. At home, I bake my bread at the absolute hottest my oven will go, because this bakes the outside of the bread into a crunchy crust while maintaining a light crumb inside.

Humans built ovens long before we were literate; ovens came about as soon as it was discovered that fire cooked food. In the book *Catching Fire: How Cooking Made Us Human*, Richard Wrangham writes that ovens probably began as earth ovens—a big hole dug in the ground—but evolved into masonry ovens made of stone, clay, or brick, which likely coincided with the appearance of grain agriculture.

Nicolas built his own wood-fired brick oven, with a diameter that could fit 60 kilograms (132 pounds) of dough (baking thirty huge 2-kilo loaves at a time) and a domed roof that directed heat onto the tops of the loaves. When he first built it in the space outside his fournil, it was outdoors. Over the years he's added a roof and created a simple den, complete with wooden picnic tables joined together, where feasting would commence at the end of a long day of baking.

To heat the oven, he inserts pieces of wood—either oak or fruitwood, both of which impart their aroma to the bread— and lights them, adding more wood until he deems the bricks hot enough. The style of wood-fired brick oven he uses is known as a "black oven" (versus a "white oven") because the logs are placed right on the bricks themselves and the ash is later swept out.

The oven room also acted as a shelter for Nicolas's family dog, a gentle old black Lab mix who lay as close to the oven as she could without being in the way, and his family cat, who had recently given birth to a curious little kitten who rolled around the space like a tumbleweed.

It was in this den of mammals that we gathered to watch our loaves go into the oven. Working expeditiously, Nicolas uncovered each banneton, turned it upside down on his wooden peel, swiftly marked the loaf with the grigne, or baker's stamp, and inserted it into the oven.

The wood-fired oven built by Nicolas at his home in Brittany

When all the loaves were in, he placed a heavy metal door over the opening and sealed it shut with excess dough—he reused the floury bits that were shed when we "washed our hands" with flour, rehydrating them into a paste that he then used like a glue to secure the oven door.

Then we waited for the final transformation: dough to bread.

Am I right that one of the most tempting things in the world is to break into a freshly baked loaf of bread? Yet here, again, patience is key. After the loaves are removed from the oven, their centers continue to bake even as they cool, so Nicolas insisted we resist that aroma and wait until the loaves were fully cooled.

To help us avoid the temptation to jump the gun, there was always a loaf from yesterday's bake on the table near the oven. After we'd cleaned our stations in the fournil and while we waited for the loaves to bake, we'd enjoy slices from the ready-to-eat loaf to satisfy us until Nicolas removed the richly browned loaves from the oven. It was at this constantly replenished bread station that I learned the best way to cut a loaf of crusty country bread: from the side.

Rather than pushing down on the loaf, from top to bottom, which compresses those bubbles of air you worked so hard to promote, prop it on its side and cut down toward the cutting board from that angle. The resistance of the crust there is sturdy

enough to keep its shape as you press down on it.

The other matter is which knife to use. One of my favorite food writers, Laurie Colwin, poo-pooed the serrated bread knife as highly overrated (and even unnecessary) in her book *Home Cooking*. It would appear that Nicolas concurred. In Brittany, we only ever used a big chef's knife to cut into his loaves, rather than a long, serrated bread knife. Colwin was right; the chef's knife worked just as well. (Though I still typically use my bread knife at home.)

The only obstacle to cutting the bread chez Nicolas was the playful kitten, who pounced up on the table to distract us. As I swatted away the frisky kitty, I realized this bread didn't *need* butter . . . but with a smear of salted butter on a slice, it was perfect. I poured a mug of coffee to dip it in, then removed my shoes and reentered the fournil to shape the next batch.

GETTING IT RIGHT

Connor and I had met at work in New York City, both in our mid-twenties and career-focused. I was seated at my desk when I saw him walk into the office for an interview. "Who's that?" I GChatted a coworker; the attraction was immediate. He got the job and was assigned the seat across from me. We fancied each other from the get-go, and the draw intensified as we became friends. We were colleagues, however, and didn't dare cross boundaries—*let's keep things within the lines.*

I've always preferred to color outside the lines, though. He asked me to dinner one evening, then afterward insisted on walking (rather, cycling) me home through Prospect Park, and when we stood awkwardly on my Brooklyn doorstep, he asked, "Is it okay if I kiss you?" When our lips met, I felt as if a hawk had swooped down and lifted me from the sidewalk.

AS LOAVES RISE, TIME PASSES. YEARS drift by, new questions form, and we live with the trepidation of uncertainty. Bread is used as the ultimate metaphor for a reason: from grain to transcendence, it is the rare food that is simple yet indulgent, historic yet trendy, and utterly life sustaining.

It's my bread and butter.
It's the bread basket of the country.
Show me some dough!
She's the breadwinner.
Let's break bread.

"'Man does not live by bread alone,'" Connor said as he cut into the fennel and golden raisin sourdough loaf I had baked that morning, about a month after I returned from Brittany. "Isn't that how the saying goes? You're definitely testing that one!" He slathered butter on the slice and ate it standing at the countertop.

Looking down at my hands, my fingers began to fidget. "I was thinking about how this book might end. What if . . . it ends with me having *a bun in the oven*?" I said with a rising inflection. *Pause.*

"Nah, too predictable." He said as he took another bite.

It had been almost exactly three years since we moved to London, and it was unreal to consider the speed at which my world had evolved. I couldn't help but wonder if this fascination with life's most ancient and essential foods—the triptych of cheese, wine, and bread—somehow provoked thoughts of starting a family.

I WAS IN AWE OF MY STARTER'S ABILITY TO reflect my mental state. It took the shape of my absence when I was neglectful; it sprang to life when I was attentive. This correlation hooked my interest as I began baking more, although I had a persistent question about my new hobby: *Why are there so many tools for this?* I was miffed by the cool-kid gear involved in sourdough baking—the special bakeware and bespoke baskets.

When I began, I didn't have any of that—and you don't need it to make bread. You can use a sheet pan instead of a spun-iron baking cloche; you just won't get an indestructibly thick crust, which needs the conductivity of something like cast iron or a Dutch oven. You don't *need* to calculate the final dough temperature with a thermometer, it just helps nudge the fermentation in the right direction if you're armed with that knowledge. The kit is not necessary, but it is helpful. Over the course of the two years it took to write this book, I collected the bannetons, the thermometers (ambient air and probe), a special glass jar for my starter so I could track its rising and falling, and a razor (called the lame) to score the grigne.

Even with the kit, my bakes weren't always consistent. It didn't bother me much; I am the person who labels any imperfect dish I make "rustic" and moves on without fretting. I care about what it's like in my mouth, but Connor's all about the aesthetics. We're a good team. Thanks to his prodding, I got organized: I made the same loaf every day for a week, and once I felt like I could make it well consistently, I'd adjust a single aspect of the formula each day and keep track of it all in a notebook I left open on the kitchen table.

There are endless tweakable things in a bread formula, even with so few ingredients and generally predictable steps. To change only one element each time went against everything in my personality. Five grams more salt one day. Ten grams less starter the next. I wanted to make all the changes at once, but I wouldn't learn anything that way. Many bakers I talked to reinforced this, and I knew they were right. With every ounce of self-restraint at play, I experimented with my bread as scientifically as I could, inspired by people like the "cheese nun" Mother Noella and Eros's precise note-taking in the cellar at the Comelli Winery.

After a solid year of dabbling in sourdough, it was in this concentrated stretch of several weeks that things clicked. My experiments were useful; I wasn't just flailing around the kitchen *feeling* productive. (Which is a shame, because I am good at flailing around.) I learned the more rye, the flatter the loaf, and how to gingerly shape a high-

hydration dough. When I baked with whole wheat flour, I found it particularly helpful to do the additional autolyze step, which you've seen in my sourdough bread recipe (page 273).

I enjoyed experimenting with a pre-dough-mix step known as pregelatinization. It's common practice in cultures around the world—like in Japan (where it's called *tangzhong*, and popularly used in milk bread) and Germany (where it's known as *mehlkochstück*)—to soften the interior crumb and prevent it from drying out after a couple of days. (It's also a popular technique in gluten-free baking.) The step involves cooking a small portion of flour and water in a pot on the stove until it thickens and reaches 150°F (65°C), then adding it to the final dough mix. You typically let it cool first, but if it's a cold winter day, I add it while it's still warm to increase the final dough temperature to boost fermentation.

Once you understand temperature regulation and get yourself some good-quality flour and sea salt and a filter for your water, you have all the elements you need to upgrade your next loaf.

REMEMBER SON-MAT, THE KOREAN concept of "hand taste" I mentioned when I visited the washed-rind cheesemaker? You'd think the same would be true with baking bread, right? In a study of the microbial interaction between bakers and sourdough, though, the conclusion was the opposite. "The microbes on the hands of the bakers mirrored the microbes within their starters. The bakers had become their bread," reported the *New York Times* in a 2020 article. One of the biologists researching this noted, "The bakers' hands reflect the life they have lived, a life with their fingers and thumbs in dough."

I had my hands in dough constantly, and Connor was my willing taste-tester.

"A bread loaf a day keeps the doctor at bay!" he chirped as he helped himself to a slice.

"I don't think that's how the idiom goes." I slathered Bungay butter from Fen Farm Dairy on a slice of my newly birthed sourdough and topped it with a forkful of the egg-jalapeño-cheddar-cilantro scramble Connor had just thrown together for us.

I'm not sure how I got too preoccupied to notice that my husband had become an awesome cook. Maybe it was all the time I left him alone to noodle in the kitchen while I was in Italy or France, but since my fermentation journey began, he'd become an exceptionally able home cook. Somewhere along the way, he had evolved from the bachelor who preferred eating a bowl of cereal in order to avoid dirtying dishes.

"This flavor combination is on point," I told him as I caught a stray dribble of hot sauce sliding down my finger with my tongue. (His own creation, made of blitzed fermented hot chiles and on par with the awesomeness of sriracha.)

"Glad you like it, but *this bread*! It's a home run." We sat at the kitchen table and chewed, licked, and crunched at Sunday morning's breakfast. With the morning's light hitting the kitchen, we were encapsulated in our own bubble. We were in our early thirties, without a clue what the future held for us, but hopeful for it all the same.

If fermentation is the preservation of food, those same principles of change and transformation must apply to us as humans. We bring a bit of our past selves (whether it be trailing spouse or wine voyager) with us, and a hope for the future. When a new obstacle, opportunity, or question arises—as one always does—all we need to do is take a deep breath and let things ferment.

Don't overthink it. Just let it ferment.

The celebratory meal after the grape harvest at Comelli Winery

ACKNOWLEDGMENTS

I always love flipping to the gratitude pages of my favorite books. It's like peeking behind the curtain of a play. Here's what it looks like behind the scenes of this book.

Thanks to: Tamar Adler, whose book *An Everlasting Meal* I reread at the perfect moment to inspire the idea of the entire journey you find in these pages. Her work, and the work of women like Patience Gray, Julia Child, and M. F. K. Fisher, gave me the confidence to pursue this project.

The team at William Morrow/ HarperCollins for recognizing my vision, believing in it, and helping me bring this to life: Cassie Jones, my enthusiastic editor, as well as Jill Zimmerman, Liate Stehlik, Ben Steinberg, Alison Coolidge, Kayleigh George, Rachel Meyers, Renata De Oliveira, Mumtaz Mustafa, Owen Corrigan, and Anna Brower.

My agent, Alison Fargis. You were as excited about this idea as I was when it was just a spark. Thank you for believing in it, and in me.

A massive *merci* to Jessie Kanelos Weiner, who illustrated the book and made it something I dreamed of having on a bookshelf one day!

To the incredible photographers I worked with across the continent who have made this experience a gorgeous one for you all to witness: Charlotte Hu (who also edited all my photos), Izy Hossack, Joann Pai, Roberto Pastrovicchio, Jacob Harrell, and Connor Boals. I couldn't have done it on my own.

To my dad, Tom Quinn, for reading through every word of a few drafts of this manuscript early in the process, and again late in the process, just before it went to the printer. Your eyes on this were indispensable. Thank you, too, to Alice Peck—your editorial guidance helped shape this book, and I so enjoyed that process with you.

The recipes, which hopefully have brought these pages to your table, dear reader, were tested by a team of people. Thanks to my recipe tester Izy Hossack. Huge gratitude to my mom, Susan Quinn, for diving into sourdough with me and testing a handful of recipes; thanks to her (and my dad) for being accommodating when I'd randomly call asking for information on what's available in American grocery stores and the nuances of American cup measurements, and to my brother, Brian Quinn, and Kizer Shelton for foolproofing the sourdough explanations. Thanks to these generous testers: Kristen Miglore, Claire Matern, Henrietta Inman, Cat Banks, Carey Jones, Sam Stamler, Annie Brooking, Sarah Long, Clare Boals, and Molly McElheny.

From my first murmurs, there were people who offered support and advice: Melissa Hemsley, Maggie Hoffman, Nick Fauchald, Yasmin Khan, Rebekah Peppler. My cohort at the Business of Food workshop—especially Joyce Hostyn and Maureen Timmons—helped offer larger context. Each little conversation and piece of advice made this book come together.

Lindsey Tramuta—your early encouragement included words I held close throughout this process, and I'm so appreciative of your generous sharing of contacts and knowledge in/around Paris.

Michael Harlan Turkell and Megan Krigbaum—you two have been steadfast cheerleaders and pivotal sources of expertise and knowledge in bread and wine (respectively) and in the publishing world in general. Thank you. Gil is a lucky one.

Bronwen Percival, my dairy godmother—thank you for opening so many doors for me, and for reading over an early draft to make it worthy of sharing. Thanks to Francis Percival, too, and the team at Neal's Yard Dairy: David Lockwood, Jason Hinds, Estelle Reynolds, Jennifer Kast, and my cheesemonger crew—Miranda, Gareth, Fiona, Amy, Phil, Sebastian, Olga, Beth, and all the other passionate cheese lovers I worked with over these years. Thanks to Jean-Louis Carbonnier for sharing your passion for great cheese and making introductions. The Sleight Farm team—thank you for welcoming me to Somerset and teaching me the goat cheese ropes!

Others in the cheese world who were friendly and generous with their time and knowledge: Joe Schneider, Jonny Crickmore, Martin Gott, Jamie Montgomery, Tom Calver, Mary Quicke, Ashley Morton, Ned Palmer, Nathalie Quatrehomme, Rory Stamp, and the team behind the World Cheese Awards.

For welcoming me into the wine fold, I have massive gratitude for Nicola Comelli, Daniela and Pigi Comelli, and others in their sphere: Eros, Nonna Anilla, Felicia and Christian, and Michele. Of course, none of this would have been possible without Lara Mancinelli, my sister from another Susan, and Maria Mancinelli.

During my Italy travels, I couldn't have done it without the help and kindness of Michelle Fix (and Domenico!) and Danilo Marcucci and the wineries he took me to: Conestabile della Staffa, Il Signor Kurtz, Tiberi, Piccolo Podere il Ceppaiolo, and Vini di Giovanni (special thanks to Giovanni and Cosetta!). I'm grateful to Mina and Natalino Del Prete, Valentino at L'Archetipo wines, Gea Cali (and Jennifer Cole, for connecting us), Arianna Occhipinti and Gian Marco Iannello, and Biagio Distefano at COS. Others include Brittany Carlisi, Giuseppe and Valeria at Vino Scrito, Rosario at Alice Bonaccorsi winery, Valentina Passalacqua, Paolo Cantele, and Benjamin Spencer. *Grazie a tutti.*

The world of wine would have been much more intimidating without talking with these smart, friendly humans: Mimi Casteel, Sam and Oli of Natural Born Wine, Carla Capalbo, Elizabeth Minchilli, Doug Wregg, Katie Parla, Lindsay Gabbard, Hande Leimer, Rachel Roddy (thanks for the intro, Hester Cant!), Adam Centamore, Simon Levine, Wayne Young, Mitja Sirk, Chas Boynton, Jonathan Rodwell, Cha McCoy, Helen Johannesen, Tanisha Townsend, Kristina Gill, and Elena Pantaleoni and Nico Sciackitano. Oh, and thanks to Jess and Rami for drinking wine with me in Rome; it's a tough life we have.

The bread world was chock-full of really intelligent people who were outstandingly open and excited to talk with me about bread, notably Sarah Owens, Ian Lowe, Kimberley Bell, Kamel Saci, and Xavier Netry.

Thanks to the bakers who welcomed me into their bakeries: Apollonia Poilâne, Edward Delling-Williams and his team (Marie, Ulyccio, Diana), Maxime Bussy, Alice Quillet, Anna Trattles, and Wing Mon Cheung. Thanks to Jessica Hammer (and Mikael) for taking me to Benjamin of Grignote and the Cadenet brothers.

And thanks to the other bakers and journalists I spoke with about bread: Ben Mackinnon, Sarah Lohman, Jane Sigal (and Gina Bergman for connecting us), Pamela Yung, David Miller of Breid Bakery, Sam Wren-Lewis, John Letts, Michael Hanson, Jane Bertch, and Baptiste Chardin.

Merci beaucoup, Nicolas Supiot and my Triticum Folium crew (Petra, Geoffrey, Nathalie, Gabriele, Jean Luc, Thomas, Nicolas and Dominique, and Valentine Franc, for connecting me with John Letts).

Thanks to QKatie fans—those of you who have stuck with me through all the iterations of my career—you've seen how far I've come, and I so appreciate your support. Don't forget to keep it quirky.

And Connor—for believing in me, always.

PHOTOGRAPHY CREDITS

Photography by Katie Quinn unless stated below:

CHARLOTTE HU: pages ii, 140, 157, 180, 183, 191, 192, 193, 202, 216, 232, 244, 245, 265, 274, 285, 288, 301, 302, 310, 311, 312, 320, 327, 345, 355, 358, 359, 364, 366

ROBERTO PASTROVICCHIO: pages iv, v, 122, 128, 146, 149, 153, 154

CONNOR BOALS: pages 37, 50, 69, 71, 73, 75, 135, 136, 269, 277, 329, 374

JOANN PAI: pages viii, x, 248, 251, 262, 275, 279, 303, 304, 305, 306, 307, 308, 309, 314, 317

JACOB HARRELL: pages 8, 28

IZY HOSSACK: pages 20, 34, 49, 60, 85, w86, 91, 104, 110, 118, 119

MARIA MANCINELLI: page 175

I can't get enough of Spaghetti all'Ubriaco (recipe on page 156).

RECIPES IN THIS BOOK

to assieme ai cuccioli e abbaia fino a stordirsi.
olini sonnacchiosi si lamentano con la madre.
sa c'è? che cosa c'è? che cosa c'è? La madre
a: «Come, che cosa c'è? che cosa c'è?» La madre
d uno ad uno anche gli altri cani sono messi in
eone, cane da pastore, sveglia quelli che sono
del mulino, i cani dei depositi del genio
i delle stalle dei carrettieri. Càlvaro, col
cani delle villette che sono sulle colline
one sempre gli scoli odore

FURTHER READING

Here are some of the works I've referred to in the course of writing this book, with a special shout-out to the book I referenced throughout my research on cheese, wine, and bread: Sandor Katz's *The Art of Fermentation*, 2012.

CHEESE

Asher, David, *The Art of Natural Cheesemaking*, 2015

Donnelly, Catherine, editor, *Cheese and Microbes*, 2011

Donnelly, Catherine, editor, *The Oxford Companion to Cheese*, 2016

Hinds, Jason, *A History of British Cheese*, 2013

Kindstedt, Paul, *Cheese and Culture*, 2012

Le Jaouen, Jean-Claude, *The Fabrication of Farmstead Goat Cheese*, 1990

López-Alt, J. Kenji, *The Food Lab*, 2015

Neal's Yard Dairy employee handbook, 2017

Percival, Bronwen, and Francis Percival, *Reinventing the Wheel: Milk, Microbes and the Fight for Real Cheese*, 2017

Rance, Patrick, *The Great British Cheese Book*, 2nd edition, 1988

Tulloh, Jojo, *The Modern Peasant*, 2013

WINE

Anderson, Burton, *The Wine Atlas of Italy and the Traveller's Guide to the Vineyards*, 1990

Camuto, Robert V., *Palmento: A Sicilian Wine Odyssey*, 2010

Feiring, Alice, *For the Love of Wine*, 2016

Fukuoka, Masanobu, *The One-Straw Revolution: An Introduction to Natural Farming*, 1978

Goulding, Matt, *Pasta, Pane, Vino*, 2018

Robinson, Jancis, *The Oxford Companion to Wine*, 4th edition, 2015

Smith, Clark, *Postmodern Winemaking*, 2014

Wilson, Jason, *Godforsaken Grapes*, 2018

BREAD

Adler, Tamar, *An Everlasting Meal*, 2012

Brown, Edward Espe, *The Tassajara Bread Book*, 1971

Fromartz, Samuel, *In Search of the Perfect Loaf*, 2015

Hamelman, Jeffrey, *Bread*, 2nd edition, 2013

Jago, William, *A Text-Book of the Science and Art of Bread-Making: Including the Chemistry and Analytic and Practical Testing of Wheat, Flour, and Other Materials Employed in Baking*, 1895

Kaplan, Steven Laurence, *The Bakers of Paris and the Bread Question, 1700–1775*, 1996

Robertson, Chad, *Tartine Bread*, 2010

Solway, Andrew, *The Science in a Loaf of Bread*, 2008

Wells, Patricia, *The Food Lover's Guide to Paris*, 3rd edition, 1994

Whitley, Andrew, *Bread Matters*, 2009

Wrangham, Richard W., *Catching Fire: How Cooking Made Us Human*, 2009

INDEX

FOR A LIST OF RECIPES, SEE PAGE 365.

FIRST EDITION

Designed by Renata De Oliveira

Illustrations by Jessie Kanelos Weiner

Library of Congress Cataloging-in-Publication Data

Names: Quinn, Katie, author.

Title: Cheese, wine, and bread : discovering the magic of fermentation in England, Italy, and France / Katie Quinn.

Description: First edition. | New York : William Morrow, [2021] | Includes bibliographical references and index. | Summary: "In this delightful, beautifully photographed tour of France, England, and Italy, YouTube star Katie Quinn shares the stories and science behind everyone's fermented faves—bread, cheese, and wine—along with classic recipes"—Provided by publisher.

Identifiers: LCCN 2020047860 | ISBN 9780062984531 | ISBN 9780062984548 (print) | ISBN 9780062984549 (digital edition)

Subjects: LCSH: Cooking (Cheese)—Europe. | Wine and wine making—Europe. | Cooking (Bread)—Europe. | Cheese—Varieties—Europe. | LCGFT: Cookbooks.

Classification: LCC TX759.5.C48 Q56 2021 | DDC 641.6/73—dc23

LC record available at https://lccn.loc.gov/2020047860

ISBN 978-0-06-298453-1

21 22 23 24 25 TC 10 9 8 7 6 5 4 3 2 1

"An engaging food-and-drink odyssey written with irresistible enthusiasm by Katie Quinn. Openhearted and buoyant, the book weaves together her hands-on experiences in Europe and introduces us to a rich cast of people who make, sell, and care about cheese, wine, and bread. Underlying the lively stories and appealing recipes is a solid foundation of food knowledge. A book about the transformative wonders of fermentation, underpinned by personal journey."

—JENNY LINFORD, author of The Missing Ingredient

"Katie's honest curiosity about food and the many ways it intersects with a culture's identity is infectious. She is a dynamic and compelling storyteller who will surely inspire readers to go on their own culinary adventures. This is a fantastic new addition for food-driven travelers!"

—LINDSEY TRAMUTA, author of The New Parisienne